Lecture Notes in Computer Science 10744

Commenced Publication in 1973
Founding and Former Series Editors:
Gerhard Goos, Juris Hartmanis, and Jan van Leeuwen

Editorial Board

More information about this series at http://www.springer.com/series/7410

Peng Liu · Sjouke Mauw
Ketil Stølen (Eds.)

Graphical Models for Security

4th International Workshop, GraMSec 2017
Santa Barbara, CA, USA, August 21, 2017
Revised Selected Papers

 Springer

Editors
Peng Liu
Pennsylvania State University
University Park, PA
USA

Sjouke Mauw
University of Luxembourg
Esch-sur-Alzette
Luxembourg

Ketil Stølen
SINTEF ICT Blindern
Oslo
Norway

ISSN 0302-9743   ISSN 1611-3349   (electronic)
Lecture Notes in Computer Science
ISBN 978-3-319-74859-7   ISBN 978-3-319-74860-3   (eBook)
https://doi.org/10.1007/978-3-319-74860-3

Library of Congress Control Number: 2018930744

LNCS Sublibrary: SL4 – Security and Cryptology

Printed on acid-free paper

This Springer imprint is published by Springer Nature
The registered company is Springer International Publishing AG
The registered company address is: Gewerbestrasse 11, 6330 Cham, Switzerland

Preface

Welcome to the proceedings of GraMSec 2017, the 4th International Workshop on Graphical Models for Security. This workshop seeks to bring together researchers from academia, government, and industry to report on the latest research and development results on graphical models for security, and to have productive discussion and constructive debate on this topic. The workshop was a single day event co-located with the 30th IEEE Computer Security Foundations Symposium (CSF 2017). Out of a total of 19 submissions from Europe and North America, we accepted five regular papers and four short papers.

These proceedings also contain the abstract of an invited talk by Anoop Singhal (U.S. National Institute of Standards and Technology) on "Security Metrics and Risk Analysis for Enterprise Systems." This valuable and insightful talk gave us a better understanding of the topic. In addition, these proceedings include an invited paper by members of the WISER project, entitled "Employing Graphical Risk Models to Facilitate Cyber-Risk Monitoring – the WISER Approach." We expect that the results and experiences from this project will help the reader to explore the WISER approach to graphical modeling for security.

Putting together GraMSec 2017 was a team effort. We thank all authors who submitted papers. We thank the Program Committee members and additional reviewers for their great effort toward a thought-provoking program. We are also very grateful to the invited speaker for his presentation and the financial support received from the Fonds National de la Recherche Luxembourg (FNR-CORE grant ADT2P). Finally, we thank the IEEE CSF organizers, particularly the general chair, Pedro Adão, for his support and help.

December 2017

Peng Liu
Sjouke Mauw
Ketil Stølen

Organization

Program Committee

Mathieu Acher	University Rennes 1/Inria, France
Massimiliano Albanese	George Mason University, USA
Ludovic Apvrille	Télécom ParisTech, CNRS LTCI, France
Thomas Bauereiß	University of Cambridge, UK
Kristian Beckers	Technical University of Munich, Germany
Giampaolo Bella	Università di Catania, Italy
Stefano Bistarelli	Università di Perugia, Italy
Marc Bouissou	EDF and Ecole Centrale Paris, France
Binbin Chen	Advanced Digital Sciences Center, Singapore
Frédéric Cuppens	Télécom Bretagne, France
Nora Cuppens-Boulahia	Télécom Bretagne, France
Hervé Debar	Télécom SudParis, France
Harley Eades Iii	Augusta University, USA
Mathias Ekstedt	KTH Royal Institute of Technology, Sweden
Ulrik Franke	Swedish Institute of Computer Science, Sweden
Frank Fransen	TNO, The Netherlands
Olga Gadyatskaya	University of Luxembourg, Luxembourg
Paolo Giorgini	University of Trento, Italy
Dieter Gollmann	Hamburg University of Technology, Germany
Joshua Guttman	Worcester Polytechnic Institute, USA
René Rydhof Hansen	Aalborg University, Denmark
Maritta Heisel	University of Duisburg-Essen, Germany
Hannes Holm	Swedish Defence Research Agency, Sweden
Siv Hilde Houmb	Secure-NOK AS, Norway
Sushil Jajodia	George Mason University, USA
Ravi Jhawar	University of Luxembourg, Luxembourg
Henk Jonkers	BiZZdesign, The Netherlands
Florian Kammueller	Middlesex University London, UK and TU Berlin, Germany
Nima Khakzad	Delft University of Technology, The Netherlands
Dong Seong Kim	University of Canterbury, New Zealand
Barbara Kordy	INSA Rennes, IRISA, France
Pascal Lafourcade	Université Clermont Auvergne, France
Jean-Louis Lanet	Inria, France
Peng Liu	Pennsylvania State University, USA
Sjouke Mauw	University of Luxembourg, Luxembourg

Per Håkon Meland	SINTEF, Norway
Jogesh Muppala	Hong Kong University of Science and Technology, SAR China
Simin Nadjm-Tehrani	Linköping university, Sweden
Andreas L. Opdahl	University of Bergen, Norway
Xinming Ou	University of South Florida, USA
Stéphane Paul	Thales Research and Technology, France
Wolter Pieters	Delft University of Technology, The Netherlands
Sophie Pinchinat	University Rennes 1, IRISA, France
Vincenzo Piuri	University of Milan, Italy
Ludovic Piètre-Cambacédès	EDF, France
Marc Pouly	Lucerne University of Applied Sciences and Arts, Switzerland
Nicolas Prigent	Supélec, France
Cristian Prisacariu	University of Oslo, Norway
Christian W. Probst	Technical University of Denmark, Denmark
David Pym	University College London
Saša Radomirović	University of Dundee, UK
Indrajit Ray	Colorado State University, USA
Arend Rensink	University of Twente, The Netherlands
Yves Roudier	Université Côte d'Azur, CNRS, I3S, UNS, France
Guttorm Sindre	Norwegian University of Science and Technology, Norway
Mariëlle Stoelinga	University of Twente, The Netherlands
Ketil Stølen	SINTEF, Norway
Xiaoyan Sun	California State University, USA
Axel Tanner	IBM Research - Zurich, Switzerland
Alexandre Vernotte	KTH Royal Institute of Technology, Sweden
Luca Viganò	King's College London, UK
Lingyu Wang	Concordia University, Canada
Jan Willemson	Cybernetica, Estonia

Additional Reviewers

Audinot, Maxime
Puys, Maxime
Venkatesan, Sridhar

Security Metrics and Risk Analysis for Enterprise Systems (Abstract of Invited Talk)

Anoop Singhal

Computer Security Division, National Institute of Standards
and Technology (NIST), Gaithersburg, MD 20899, USA
psinghal@nist.gov

Abstract. Protection of enterprise systems from cyber attacks is a challenge. Vulnerabilities are regularly discovered in software systems that are exploited to launch cyber attacks. Security analysts need objective metrics to manage the security risk of an enterprise systems. In this talk, we give an overview of our research on *security metrics* and *challenges* for security risk analysis of enterprise systems. A standard model for security metrics will enable us to answer questions such as "are we more secure than yesterday" or "how does the security of one system compare with another?" We present a methodology for security risk analysis that is based on the model of attack graphs and the common vulnerability scoring system (CVSS).

Contents

Graphical Modeling of Security Arguments: Current State and Future Directions

Dan Ionita[1]([✉]), Margaret Ford[2], Alexandr Vasenev[1], and Roel Wieringa[1]

[1] Services, Cybersecurity and Safety group, University of Twente,
Drienerlolaan 5, 7522 NB Enschede, The Netherlands
{d.ionita,r.j.wieringa}@utwente.nl
[2] Consult Hyperion, 10-12 The Mount, Guildford GU2 4HN, UK
margaret.ford@chyp.com

Abstract. Identifying threats and risks to complex systems often requires some form of brainstorming. In addition, eliciting security requirements involves making traceable decisions about which risks to mitigate and how. The complexity and dynamics of modern socio-technical systems mean that their security cannot be formally proven. Instead, some researchers have turned to modeling the claims underpinning a risk assessment and the arguments which support security decisions. As a result, several argumentation-based risk analysis and security requirements elicitation frameworks have been proposed. These draw upon existing research in decision making and requirements engineering. Some provide tools to graphically model the underlying argumentation structures, with varying degrees of granularity and formalism. In this paper, we compare these approaches, discuss their applicability and suggest avenues for future research. We find that the core of existing security argumentation frameworks are the links between threats, risks, mitigations and system components. Graphs - a natural representation for these links - are used by many graphical security argumentation tools. But, in order to be human-readable, the graphical models of these graphs need to be both scalable and easy to understand. Therefore, in order to facilitate adoption, both the creation and exploration of these graphs need to be streamlined.

Keywords: Risk assessment · Security requirements
Argumentation · Graphical modeling

1 Introduction

Complete security is impossible and security decisions have to be selective: some risks can be mitigated in several ways while others will have to be accepted. Thus, security decision making involves an opportunity cost - the loss of the value that would have been realized by making an alternative decision.

The ability to trace back previous decisions is important if they have to be defended or revised, or if new security decisions have to taken. Firstly, the decision maker may have to justify mitigation decisions made earlier, for instance

P. Liu et al. (eds.): GraMSec 2017, LNCS 10744, pp. 1–16, 2018.
https://doi.org/10.1007/978-3-319-74860-3_1

in the case of a successful attack [16] or to satisfy the "reasonable security" requirements of regulators [4]. Second, the ever changing security landscape and forces decision makers to frequently revisit security decisions. In fact, the new European GDPR (General Data Protection directive) explicitly requires data controllers and processors to ensure "ongoing" confidentiality, integrity, availability and resilience of processing systems and services [12, art 32(1)(b)]. Third, related systems may face related but not identical risks and therefore, reusing (parts of) the arguments made for similar systems facilitates decision making for given systems [13]. By recording the argumentation behind security decisions, risk assessments can be re-visited when an attack takes place, extended when new risks surface, and re-used in related products or contexts. Altogether, this highlights a need to document security decisions and the rationale behind them.

With respect to previous research, security arguments can be compared to safety cases [1,9,25], in that they summarize the reasons why, and the extent to which, a system is thought to be acceptably secure (or safe). Several techniques for modeling security arguments exist, some inspired from legal argumentation (Toulmin-like argumentation structures [19,22]), others from formal methods (deontic logic [15], defeasible logic [35]). The various approaches differ in their scope and applicability. However, security argumentation schemas have only been applied to toy examples so far and have not yet been adopted (or even evaluated) in practice, raising questions with regard to their practical *usability, utility and scalability.*

A characteristic feature of security risk assessments is that stakeholders with varying backgrounds must contribute to or check the assessment, and that these stakeholders have no time to first learn a specialized language for argumentation. Therefore, we argue difficulties in understanding the notation used to represent security arguments are major threats to the *usability* of any security argumentation methodology and that some form of graphical model is needed in order to enhance understanding. However, a graphical representation with low expressiveness may have reduced *utility* while one which is too granular may face *scalability* issues. This paper looks at argumentation models have evolved over time and cross-examines graphical security argumentation frameworks in order to support researchers in advancing the graphical modeling of security arguments, as well as inform specialists involved in the security requirements elicitation or risk assessment about existing security argumentation frameworks and tools.

We start in Sect. 2 with reviewing argumentation theory and its application in the security domain. In Sect. 3 we review the graphical representation of security arguments provided by graphical argumentation tools available at the time of writing. In Sect. 4 we cross-compare the various representations employed by each of the tools and draw conclusions with regard to their expressiveness and applicability. In Sect. 5 we draw conclusions from the comparison and indicate some topics for future work in the direction of making security argumentation graphs more practically usable.

2 Background

Structured argumentation has its roots in legal reasoning, with examples of diagrams being used to capture the justifications of judges or juries dating back to as early as 1913 [17]. With the advent of computers, attempts to capture reasoning first behind design decisions and later behind decisions in general also proliferated [8,14,26]. Significant effort was invested into developing complex tools and even more complex approaches for automated decision support [27,33]. However, it quickly became apparent that capturing arguments is most useful when no formal proof is possible but defensibility of the decision is required [30]. This is of course the case for legal reasoning, but a similar situation exits in the fields of safety and security. Indeed, safety arguments (in the form of safety cases) were quickly adopted by the industry as a standard way of claiming their systems are safe [7]. With laws such as the European DPD (Data Protection Directive) and, in the US, Sect. 5 of the Federal Trade Comission (FTC) act requiring companies to show that they took reasonable steps in protecting their customer's data, argumentation-based approaches started finding their way into the field of information security. The remainder of this section explores the evolution of argumentation structures from the court of law to their more recent incarnations in security requirements engineering and in risk assessment. We leave the discussion of the graphical representations of these arguments for the next sections.

2.1 Argumentation Modeling

Stephen Toulmin laid the foundations for modeling arguments in his 1958 book The Uses of Argument [41]. He proposed subdividing each argument into six components (as shown in Fig. 1): a central *claim*, some *grounds* to support that claim, a *warrant* connecting the claim to the evidence, a factual *backing* for the warrant, a *qualifier* which restricts the scope of the claim and finally a *rebuttal* to the claim. He later identified applications of his framework in legal reasoning [40].

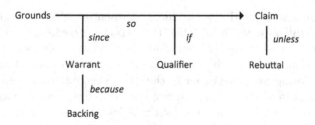

Fig. 1. The Toulmin argument structure

In the late 1980's and early 90's, argumentation models started being used to support design decisions. Specifically, the emerging field of design rationale began investigating ways to capture how one arrives at a specific decision, which alternate decisions were or should have been considered, and the facts and assumptions that went into the decision making [26]. In 1989 MacLean et al. [28] introduced an approach to represent design rationale which uses a graphical argumentation scheme called QOC (for Questions, Options and Criteria) - depicted in Fig. 2. Buckingham Shum et al. [38] later showed how the QOC notation can be used as a representative formalism for computer-supported visualization of arguments, with applications in collaborative environments. Mylopoulos et al. [31] introduced Telo, a language for representing knowledge about an information system intended to assist in its development. Similarly, Fischer et al. [14] claim that making argumentation explicit can benefit the design process itself.

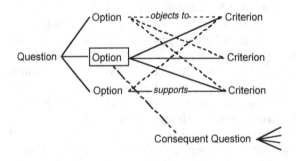

Fig. 2. The Questions, Options and Criteria (QOC) graphical argumentation scheme

Soon, modeling of arguments found even wider applications in decision making - especially when related to critical systems - where they started being used to make expert judgment explicit, usually by means of so-called 'cases' [8]. Safety cases, for instance, are structured arguments, supported by evidence, intended to justify that a system is acceptably safe for a specific application in a specific operating environment [9]. These arguments should be clear, comprehensive and defensible [25]. Two established approaches to safety cases are the CAE (Claims Arguments Evidence) notation [10] and the GSN (Goal Structuring Notation) [24].

Both approaches prescribe a graphical representation of the argumentation structure but differ in terms of what this structure contains. The CAE was developed by Adelard, a consultancy, and views safety cases as a set of *claims* supported by *arguments*, which in turn rely on *evidence*. Although these concepts are expressed using natural language, the cases themselves are represented as graphs and most implementations suggest their own graphical symbols. Figure 4 shows the CAE representation used by the Adelard's own ASCE tool [1]. The GSN (Fig. 3) was developed by the University of York and provides a more granular decomposition of safety arguments into *goals, context, assumptions, strategy, justifications* and *solutions* [24]. The arguments are also represented as a graph, with one of two types of links possible between each pair of nodes: (1) a decompositonal *is solved by* between a goal and one or more strategies or between a strategy and one or more goals, as well as (2) a contextual *in context of*

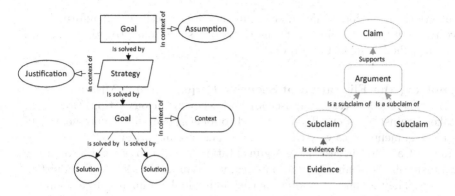

Fig. 3. The Goal Structuring Notation (GSN)   **Fig. 4.** The Claims Arguments Evidence (CAE) notation

between a goal, strategy or solution and an assumption, justification or context. The notation comes with a well defined graphical language which - according to its creator - attempts to strike a balance between power of expressiveness and usability [25].

Other, more general representations such as concept maps [29], mindmaps [2] or generic diagrams can of course also be used to represent and share knowledge, including arguments [11]. These representations have no (formal or informal) argumentation semantics and we ignore them in the rest of the paper.

2.2   Argumentation in Security

The success of safety cases has inspired other similar approaches, such as trust cases [18], conformity cases [8] and, in the field of security, assurance cases [3,32] used to show satisfaction of requirements and misuse cases [39] used to elicit security requirements. Similarly, argumentation schemes for design rationale have been adapted to provide support for security decisions. Recently, argumentation modes have been used to encode the entire risk assessment process, from risk identification to countermeasure selection. This subsection provides an overview of these applications.

Arguing Satisfaction of Security Requirements. Assurance cases are an argumentation-based approach similar to the safety cases described in Sect. 2.1. They use structured argumentation (for instance using the GSN or CAE notations) to model the arguments of experts that a system will work as expected. However, while safety cases only make claims pertaining to the safe operation of a system, assurance cases are also concerned with other important system functions, in particular security and dependability [37].

Haley et al. [21] laid the groundwork for an argumentation framework aimed specifically at validating security requirements. It distinguishes between *inner* and *outer* arguments. Inner arguments are formal and consist mostly of claims about system behavior, while outer arguments are structured but informal and serve to justify those claims in terms of trust assumptions. Together, the two form a so-called "satisfaction argument".

Supporting the Elicitation of Security Requirements. Misuse cases - a combination of safety cases and use cases - describe malicious actions that could be taken against a system. They are used to identify security requirements and provide arguments as to why these requirements are important [39].

Rowe et al. [36] suggest using argumentation logic to go beyond formalizing domain-specific reasoning and automatically reason about security administration tasks. They propose decomposing each individual argument into a Toulmin-like structure and then representing defeasability links between the arguments as a graph. This would allow both encoding unstructured knowledge and applying automated reasoning, for example by using theorem provers. They suggest two applications: attack diagnosis, where experts argue about the root-cause of an attack, and policy recommendation, where security requirements are elicited.

Haley et al. [20] built their conceptual framework for modeling and validating security requirements described in [21] into a security requirements elicitation process, which can help distill security requirements from business goals. The same authors later integrated their work on modeling and elicitation of security requirements into a unified framework for security requirements engineering [19]. The framework considers the context, functional requirements and security goals before identifying security requirements and constructing satisfaction arguments for them. However, it does not consider the risks the system may or may not be facing when not all security requirements are satisfied, or when not all security goals are achieved.

Argumentation-Based Risk Assessment. Franqueira et al. [15] were among the first to propose using argumentation structures to reason about both risks and countermeasures in a holistic fashion. OpenArgue (discussed in Sect. 3.1) supports the construction of argumentation models. Their proposed method, RISA (RIsk assessment in Security Argumentation) links to public catalogs such as CAPEC (Common Attack Pattern Enumeration and Classification) and the CWE (Common Weakness Enumeration) to provide support for security arguments using simple propositional logic. The method does not consider the possibility that a security threat may not be totally eliminated. Later, Yu et al. [43] integrated the RISA method and Franqueira's argumentation schema into a unified argumentation meta-model and implemented it as part of tool - Open-RISA - which partly automates the validation process. This tool is discussed in Sect. 3.1.

Prakken et al. [35] proposed a logic-based method that could support the modeling and analysis of security arguments. The approach viewed the risk assessment as an argumentation game, where experts elicit arguments and counter-arguments about possible attacks and countermeasures. Arguments derive conclusions from a knowledge base using strict or defeasible inference rules. The method is based on the ASPIC+ framework [34] and uses defeasible logic. This restricts its usability in practice.

Prakken's solution inspired a simplified approach, which used spreadsheets to encode and analyze the arguments [22]. Each argument was decomposed into only a *claim* and one or more supporting *assumptions* or *facts*. Similar to Prakken's approach, any argument could counter any other argument(s) and formulas (this time built-into the spreadsheets) were used to automatically compute which arguments were defeated and which were not. Argumentation spreadsheets are discussed in detail in Sect. 3.2.

Later, a dedicated tool was developed which employed the same simplified argument structure but without differentiating between assumptions and facts. However, most arguments were found to refer to attacks, while most counter-arguments proposed countermeasures to attacks. To simplify this, and further improve usability, an online version was developed which also flattened the inter-argument structure by only allowing counter-arguments to refer to countermeasures. These tools are part of the ArgueSecure family, discussed in Sect. 3.3.

3   Graphical Security Argumentation Tools and Techniques

Both (formal) first order logic and (informal) structured argumentation provide methods for analyzing the interaction between arguments. However, structured argumentation also provides a foundation for presenting arguments for or against a position to a user [36]. Of the argumentation notations reviewed above, we now zoom in on those having a graphical representation, and discuss this representation in more detail by applying them to the same sample scenario. Graphical security argumentation modeling tools mainly differ in the amount of detail they use to describe the structure of, and links between, arguments. Therefore, we evaluate each tool on its expressiveness in terms of intra-argument granularity E1 (i.e. the number of components an argument has to be decomposed into), inter-argument granularity E2 (i.e. how many types of rebuttals are possible). Tools also provide secondary functionality, usually aimed at improving usability and scalability. We therefore also identify relevant features provided by each tool (labelled F1–F6) and summarize everything in a cross-comparison table (Table 1), to be discussed in Sect. 4.

3.1   OpenArgue/OpenRISA

OpenArgue is an argumentation modeling tool featuring both a syntax editor and a graphical editor, which comes with the ability to derive an argumentation diagram from a textual specification [42]. OpenArgue assumes security requirements are known at the time of analysis and focuses on identifying ways by which these requirements could be invalidated. This means all arguments are linked to a specific security requirement (F1). It benefits from syntax highlighting as well as a built-in model checker which can identify formal inconsistencies in the

8   D. Ionita et al.

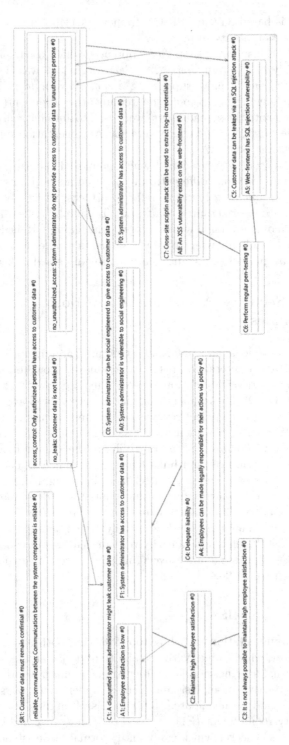

Fig. 5. OpenArgue - sample assessment

argumentation diagram. OpenArgue has a simplified Toulmin intra-argument structure consisting of a central *claim*, supported by *grounds*, the relevance of which is supported by *warrants* (E1 = 3). However, OpenArgue allows specifying rather complex inter-argument relationships: arguments can rebut or mitigate one or more other arguments (F3, F4) by challenging either their grounds or their warrants (E1= 4). This can lead to inter-twined graphical representations of the argumentation model that are hard to understand. This effect is amplified by the fact that the tool does not come with a custom editor but rather uses a generic Eclipse UML editor and thereby poses significant usability and scalability issues. Figure 5 shows a sample assessment built using OpenArgue.

OpenRISA is an extension of OpenArgue which can, in addition, check the argumentation model against online knowledge bases and verify that the risks identified are valid rebuttals.

3.2 Argumentation Spreadsheets

Tables have long served as a convenient means of storing and communicating structured data [6]. The argumentation spreadsheets attempt to decompose arguments into three elements: a claim, one or more assumptions and one or more facts [22] (E1 = 3). Each row encodes one argument divided across several columns. A screenshot of a sample assessment using argumentation spreadsheets is shown in Fig. 6.

ARGUMENTS											TAGS	
Claim		Assumptions		Facts		Re-	Asset(s)	Status	Notes			Assets
#	txt	#	txt	#	txt	buts	ID(s)	IN / OUT	Transf./ Red.		ID	NAME
C0	System administrator can be social engineered to give access to customer data	A0	System administrator is vulnerable to social engineering	F0	System administrator has access to customer data			IN				
											T1	policy
C1	A disgruntled system administrator might leak customer data	A1	Employee satisfaction is low	F1	System administrator has access to customer data			OUT				
											T2	web-frontend
C2	Maintain high employee satisfaction	A2	-	F2	-	A1		IN				
C3	It is not always possible to maintain high employee satisfaction	A3	-	F3	-	C2		OUT				
C4	Delegate liability	A4	Employees can be made legally responsible for their actions via policy	F4	-	C3	T1,	IN	Transf.			
C5	Customer data can be leaked via an SQL injection attack	A5	web-frontend has SQL injection vulnerability	F5	-		T2,	OUT				
C6	Perform regular pen-testing of the web-frontend	A6	-	F6	-	A5	T2,	IN	Red.			
C7	Cross-site scripting attack can be used to extract log-in credentials	A8	An XSS vulnerablity exists on the web-frontend	F8	-		T2,	OUT				
C8	Perform regular pen-testing of the web-frontend	A9	-	F9	-	A8	T2,	IN	Red.			

Fig. 6. Argumentation spreadsheets - sample assessment

An argument describes either a risk or a risk mitigation and can rebut one argument of an opposite type. This leads to a linear, attacker versus defender game-like process of filling in the table: first, a risk is described; then, either the risk is accepted or a counterargument describing a mitigation is added; this back-and-forth rhetoric can continue until the risk is completely eliminated or the residual risk is accepted. The tool keeps track of each argument's state (IN for arguments without rebuttals or arguments whose rebuttal was defeated and OUT for arguments with an IN rebuttal), as well as automatically tagging arguments which mention one of the assets in the asset column (F2). Finally, the user can tag risk mitigation arguments with either a "Red." or a "Transf." tag signifying that the suggested countermeasure only partially mitigates the risk, or that it transfers the risk to a third-party (F5). Since this means a rebuttal can be full or partial, the spreadsheets score a 2 on the inter-argument granularity.

In total therefore, four types of risk response exist: (1) ignore (undefeated attacker argument), (2) eliminate (defeated attacker argument), (3) mitigate (partially defeated attacker argument) and (4) transfer.

3.3   ArgueSecure

ArgueSecure is an umbrella terms for a pair of tools - one online and one offline - derived from the spreadsheets described in the previous section.

The *offline* version is designed to streamline the manual process of filling in the argumentation spreadsheets. Therefore, ArgueSecure-online maintains the risk assessment game philosophy, where attacker arguments make claims with regard to risks and defender arguments rebut them by describing mitigations. However, it drops the concept of "facts" and does not support linking arguments to assets [23] ($E1 = 2$), and it also does not differentiate between partial or full mitigation ($E2 = 1$). In addition to the other tools reviewed so far, it provides keyboard shortcuts, various report generation functionality (F9) and differentiates between implemented and planned countermeasures (F7). It represents the risk assessment as an indented, collapsible list, with color-coded argument statuses (see screenshot in Fig. 7).

The *online* version makes the risk assessment process a collaborative one: participants no longer have to be in the same room; they can contribute remotely and asynchronously thereby transforming the argumentation model into a living document which keeps track of risks as they are discovered and countermeasures as they are proposed and implemented (F6). ArgueSecure-online also comes with a simplified interface (see Fig. 8 for a screenshot) aimed at non-experts and similar report generation functionality as its offline counterpart (F9), as well as differentiating risk transfers from other types of mitigations (F5). However, it also introduces new functionality, namely the ability to define many-to-many relationships between risks and attacks (F3) and between attacks and defenses (F4) and re-introduces the ability to relate arguments to assets (F2). This turns the argumentation model into a graph, but in order to avoid inter-twined links, the tool represents it as a tree by duplicating nodes with multiple incoming links.

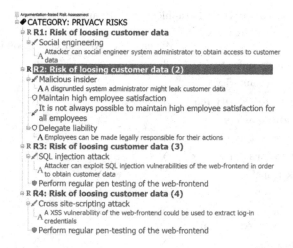

Fig. 7. Arguesecure-offline - sample risk assessment

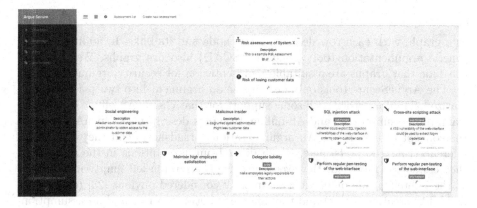

Fig. 8. Arguesecure-online - sample risk assessment

4   Comparison and Discussion

Table 1 compares the features provided by the graphical security argumentation modeling tools described in the previous section.

In OpenRISA (and its predecessor, OpenArgue) a risk, by definition violates a known security requirement. ArgueSecure does not have such a restriction, allowing more flexibility and creativity but for this reason it also cannot support linking countermeasures back to security requirements. Therefore the two have slightly different application scenarios: OpenRISA assumes Security Requirements are known and they need to be implemented, while ArgueSecure can help identify them.

OpenRISA and both of the ArgueSecure tools use a graph to encode the argumentation model. The argumentation spreadsheet could also be represented

Table 1. Feature comparison of graphical security argumentation modeling tools

	OpenArgue	Arg. sheets	AS-offline	AS-online
E1: intra-argument granularity	3	3	2	2
E2: inter-argument granularity	4	2	1	1
F1: ability to relate to security req.	Y	N	N	N
F2: ability to relate to assets	N	Y	N	Y
F3: multiple attack vectors per risk	Y	N	N	Y
F4: multiple mitigations per attack	Y	N	N	Y
F5: supports risk transfer	N	Y	Y	Y
F6: collaborative	N	N	N	Y
F7: differentiates between implemented and planned mitigations	N	N	Y	N
F8: search and filtering	N	N	N	Y
F9: export and reports	N	N	Y	Y

as a graph, with each row describing one node and its links. In addition, most generic argumentation tools (such as ASCAD) also use graphs. We therefore conclude that graphs are a suitable representation for security arguments (O1).

The ArgueSecure tools only decompose an argument into two parts: a summarized claim, together with some support for that claim (AS-offline calls them claim plus assumptions, and AS-online, title plus description). OpenArgue adds the concept of a warrant. An argumentation spreadsheets call the warrant an inference rule and adds facts, which differ from assumptions in the sense that they cannot be rebutted. However, these fields are often left empty in practice, as the inference rule or backing are mostly considered obvious [23] (e.g. a vulnerability creating a risk) and the difference between a fact and an assumption is many times only philosophical (e.g. facts can change with the specification). This leads us to our second observation: in order to describe a security argument, one needs to be able to specify at least the vulnerability or vulnerabilities involved, the risk they create and which mitigations are relevant (O2).

ArgueSecure only shows which argument attacks which other argument, but in the argumentation spreadsheets it is possible to specify which component of the argument is being attacked and in OpenRISA even how. Because OpenRISA allows to model rebuttal relationships in more detail, the resulting diagrams are more complex and inter-twined (see Fig. 5 vs. Fig. 8). The argumentation spreadsheets also model rebuttals in similar detail, but due to the tabular representation, the result is more compact and readable (see Fig. 6). ArgueSecure, which only supports binary rebuttal relationships between attacks and countermeasures and therefore manages to achieve similar scalability as the argumentation spreadsheets (see Figs. 8 and 7). Our tentative observation is that while rebuttals are necessary for relating security arguments, anything other than binary rebuttals can pose a significant scalability challenge (O3).

With regard to usability, the two ArgueSecure tools are the only ones which use icons. In addition, they also attempt to manage scalability by collapsing and expanding any part of the argumentation graph. The online version even supports filtering nodes by tags. In our toy examples scalability was not much of an issue. But realistic assessments can have hundreds of nodes, and therefore features to help navigate the argumentation graph are critical to making it human-writable and human-readable (O4).

5   Conclusions and Outlook

Perfect security is invisible, and also impossible. Security arguments can show that a system is secure to some extent by providing structured, but human-readable explanations as to which risks were considered and how they were mitigated. This is important for a variety of reasons, ranging from certification to compliance, and from awareness to assurance.

Unsurprisingly, most argumentation modeling tools employ a simplified version of Toulmin's argument structure for conceptualizing security arguments but vary in terms of either the granularity by which they decompose the argument or in the way they represent inter-argument structures. However, very few tools exist which address the specifics of security argumentation, and their audience is mostly academic.

Indeed, confronting the tools of Sect. 3 with practical security arguments shows that in order to be usable, security argumentation techniques need to be simple and reduce themselves to the essential information that needs to be present in order to argue about (in-)security of a system or software: the links between mitigations, risks and system components or modules. As these links can be of type "many-to-many", graphs are a natural fit for representing these links.

In the words of Buckingham-Shum [5], diagramming tools differ not only in the type of information they are able to represent, but especially in regard to the trade-off they make between expressiveness and usability. This is true also for argumentation graphs, which can explode in size when all known risks and relevant mitigations pertaining to a real system are added. Therefore, ensuring scalability is critical to maintaining reasonable usability. Only some of the tools available provide ways of navigating the graph, for example by searching, filtering or collapsing parts of the argumentation structure. We believe this topic has to be better investigated before security argumentation modeling becomes usable in practice. To further enhance scalability, automation and re-usability are also relevant topics not only in security argumentation, but security in general. Future work could look therefore into ways by which the argumentation graph can be filled in semi-automatically, for instance by recognizing patterns, linking to knowledge bases or parsing the output of vulnerability scanners. This might require (re-)introducing some level of formalism into the argumentation structure.

References

1. Adelard Safety Case Development (ASCAD) Manual, London, UK (2010)
2. Beel, J., Langer, S.: An exploratory analysis of mind maps. In: Proceedings of the 11th ACM Symposium on Document Engineering, pp. 81–84. ACM (2011)
3. Bloomfield, R.E., Guerra, S., Miller, A., Masera, M., Weinstock, C.B.: International working group on assurance cases (for security). IEEE Secur. Priv. 4(3), 66–68 (2006)
4. Breaux, T.D., Baumer, D.L.: Legally "reasonable" security requirements: a 10-year FTC retrospective. Comput. Secur. 30(4), 178–193 (2011)
5. Buckingham Shum, S.: The Roots of Computer Supported Argument Visualization, pp. 3–24. Springer, London (2003)
6. Campbell-Kelly, M.: The History of Mathematical Tables: From Sumer to Spreadsheets. Oxford University Press, Oxford (2003)
7. Cleland, G.M., Habli, I., Medhurst, J.: Evidence: Using Safety Cases in Industry and Healthcare. The Health Foundation, London (2012)
8. Cyra, L., Górski, J.: Support for argument structures review and assessment. Reliab. Eng. Syst. Saf. 96(1), 26–37 (2011). Special Issue on Safecomp 2008
9. Defence standard 00-56 issue 4 (part 1): Safety management requirements for defence systems, July 2007
10. Emmet, L.: Using claims, arguments and evidence: a pragmatic view-and tool support in ASCE. www.adelard.com
11. Eppler, M.J.: A comparison between concept maps, mind maps, conceptual diagrams, and visual metaphors as complementary tools for knowledge construction and sharing. Inf. Vis. 5(3), 202–210 (2006)
12. Regulation (EU) 2016/679 of the European Parliament and of the Council of 27 April 2016 on the protection of natural persons with regard to the processing of personal data and on the free movement of such data, and repealing Directive 95/46/EC (General Data Protection Regulation). Off. J. Eur. Union L119/59, 1–88, May 2016. http://eur-lex.europa.eu/legal-content/EN/TXT/?uri=OJ:L:2016:119:TOC
13. Firesmith, D.G.: Analyzing and specifying reusable security requirements. Technical report DTIC Document (2003)
14. Fischer, G., Lemke, A.C., McCall, R., Morch, A.I.: Making argumentation serve design. Hum.-Comput. Interact. 6(3), 393–419 (1991)
15. Franqueira, V.N.L., Tun, T.T., Yu, Y., Wieringa, R., Nuseibeh, B.: Risk and argument: a risk-based argumentation method for practical security. In: RE, pp. 239–248. IEEE (2011)
16. Gold, J.: Data breaches and computer hacking: liability & insurance issues. American Bar Association's Government Law Committee Newsletter Fall (2011)
17. Goodwin, J., Fisher, A.: Wigmore's chart method. Inf. Logic 20(3), 223–243 (2000)
18. Górski, J., Jarzbowicz, A., Leszczyna, R., Miler, J., Olszewski, M.: Trust case justifying trust in an it solution. Reliab. Eng. Syst. Saf. 89(1), 33–47 (2005)
19. Haley, C., Laney, R., Moffett, J., Nuseibeh, B.: Security requirements engineering: a framework for representation and analysis. IEEE Trans. Soft. Eng. 34(1), 133–153 (2008)
20. Haley, C.B., Laney, R., Moffett, J.D., Nuseibeh, B.: Arguing satisfaction of security requirements. In: Integrating Security and Software Engineering: Advances and Future Visions, pp. 16–43 (2006)

21. Haley, C.B., Moffett, J.D., Laney, R., Nuseibeh, B.: Arguing security: validating security requirements using structured argumentation. In: Proceedings of Third Symposium on Requirements Engineering for Information Security (SREIS 2005) held in conjunction with the 13th International Requirements Engineering Conference (RE 2005) (2005)
22. Ionita, D., Bullee, J.W., Wieringa, R.J.: Argumentation-based security requirements elicitation: the next round. In: 2014 IEEE 1st Workshop on Evolving Security and Privacy Requirements Engineering (ESPRE), pp. 7–12. Springer, Heidelberg, August 2014
23. Ionita, D., Kegel, R., Baltuta, A., Wieringa, R.: Arguesecure: out-of-the-box security risk assessment. In: 2016 IEEE 24th International Requirements Engineering Conference Workshops (REW), pp. 74–79, September 2016
24. Kelly, T., Weaver, R.: The goal structuring notation - a safety argument notation. In: Proceedings of Dependable Systems and Networks 2004 Workshop on Assurance Cases (2004)
25. Kelly, T.P.: Arguing Safety: A Systematic Approach to Managing Safety Cases. University of York, York (1999)
26. Lee, J., Lai, K.Y.: What's in design rationale? Hum.-Comput. Interact. **6**(3–4), 251–280 (1991)
27. Liao, S.H.: Expert system methodologies and applications - a decade review from 1995 to 2004. Exp. Syst, Appl. **28**(1), 93–103 (2005)
28. Maclean, A., Young, R.M., Moran, T.P.: Design rationale: the argument behind the artefact. In: Proceedings of the Computer Human Interaction conference (CHI) (1989)
29. Markham, K.M., Mintzes, J.J., Jones, M.G.: The concept map as a research and evaluation tool: further evidence of validity. J. Res. Sci. Teach. **31**(1), 91–101 (1994)
30. Mosier, K.L.: Myths of expert decision making and automated decision aids. In: Naturalistic Decision Making, pp. 319–330 (1997)
31. Mylopoulos, J., Borgida, A., Jarke, M., Koubarakis, M.: Telos: representing knowledge about information systems. ACM Trans. Inf. Syst. (TOIS) **8**(4), 325–362 (1990)
32. Park, J.S., Montrose, B., Froscher, J.N.: Tools for information security assurance arguments. In: Proceedings of the DARPA Information Survivability Conference, DISCEX 2001, vol. 1, pp. 287–296 (2001)
33. Polikar, R.: Ensemble based systems in decision making. IEEE Circ. Syst. Mag. **6**(3), 21–45 (2006)
34. Prakken, H.: An abstract framework for argumentation with structured arguments. Argument Comput. **1**, 93–124 (2010)
35. Prakken, H., Ionita, D., Wieringa, R.: Risk assessment as an argumentation game. In: Leite, J., Son, T.C., Torroni, P., van der Torre, L., Woltran, S. (eds.) CLIMA 2013. LNCS (LNAI), vol. 8143, pp. 357–373. Springer, Heidelberg (2013). https://doi.org/10.1007/978-3-642-40624-9_22
36. Rowe, J., Levitt, K., Parsons, S., Sklar, E., Applebaum, A., Jalal, S.: Argumentation logic to assist in security administration. In: Proceedings of the 2012 New Security Paradigms Workshop, NSPW 2012, pp. 43–52. ACM, New York (2012)
37. Rushby, J.: The interpretation and evaluation of assurance cases. SRI International, Menlo Park, CA, USA (2015)
38. Shum, S.J.B., MacLean, A., Bellotti, V.M.E., Hammond, N.V.: Graphical argumentation and design cognition. Hum.-Comput. Interact. **12**(3), 267–300 (1997)
39. Sindre, G., Opdahl, A.L.: Eliciting security requirements with misuse cases. Requirements Eng. **10**(1), 34–44 (2005)

40. Toulmin, S., Rieke, R., Janik, A.: An Introduction to Reasoning. Macmillan, Basingstoke (1979)
41. Toulmin, S.E.: The Uses of Argument. Cambridge University Press, Cambridge (1958)
42. Yu, Y., Tun, T.T., Tedeschi, A., Franqueira, V.N.L., Nuseibeh, B.: Openargue: supporting argumentation to evolve secure software systems. In: 2011 IEEE 19th International Requirements Engineering Conference, pp. 351–352, August 2011
43. Yu, Y., Franqueira, V.N.L., Tun, T.T., Wieringa, R., Nuseibeh, B.: Automated analysis of security requirements through risk-based argumentation. J. Syst. Soft. **106**, 102–116 (2015)

Evil Twins: Handling Repetitions in Attack–Defense Trees
A Survival Guide

Angèle Bossuat[1,3] and Barbara Kordy[2,3(✉)]

[1] University Rennes 1, Rennes, France
[2] INSA Rennes, Rennes, France
[3] IRISA, Rennes, France
{angele.bossuat,barbara.kordy}@irisa.fr

Abstract. Attack–defense trees are a simple but potent and efficient way to represent and evaluate security scenarios involving a malicious attacker and a defender – their adversary. The nodes of attack–defense trees are labeled with goals of the two actors, and actions that they need to execute to achieve these goals. The objective of this paper is to provide formal guidelines on how to deal with attack–defense trees where several nodes have the same label. After discussing typical issues related to such trees, we define the notion of well-formed attack–defense trees and adapt existing semantics to correctly capture the presence of repeated labels.

1 Into the Wild: Introduction

Security analysis and risk assessment are essential to any system facing potential threats. Attack–defense trees allow the security experts to represent and assess the system's security, by illustrating different ways in which it can be attacked and how such attacks could be countered. Formally speaking, attack–defense trees are simple AND-OR trees, but their strength and expressive power relies on intuitive labels that decorate their nodes. These labels describe what the attacker and the defender need to do to achieve their goals, i.e., to attack and defend the system, respectively.

To provide accurate evaluation results, an attack–defense tree must be as precise and versatile as possible. Yet, no hard rules exist on how to label their nodes. To be able to exploit the graphical aspects of attack–defense trees, experts tend to prefer laconic labels which are often too short to fully express the desired meaning. Furthermore, attack–defense trees are frequently reused from one system to another, they may be borrowed from generic libraries of standard attack patterns, and are usually constructed by merging subtrees devised by several experts, not necessarily communicating with each other. Due to all these reasons, it is not rare to find identical labels on separate nodes in an attack–defense tree.

The aim of this work is to formalize attack–defense trees with repeated labels and develop guidelines to handle them properly. We distinguish between simple mislabeling, and cases where the nodes should indeed have the same label. For

P. Liu et al. (eds.): GraMSec 2017, LNCS 10744, pp. 17–37, 2018.
https://doi.org/10.1007/978-3-319-74860-3_2

the latter, we bring out some important differences, and propose solutions more elaborate and less problematic than simply modifying the labels to make them all unique in a given tree. Our specific contributions are as follows

1. *Repeated labels:* we classify repeated labels according to their meaning and propose a new labeling format to properly handle trees with repetitions.
2. *Well-formedness:* we study frequently observed problems related to mislabeling and introduce a notion of well-formed trees to address them.
3. *Formal basis:* we adapt existing formal semantics for attack–defense trees to make sure they are in line with the new labeling scheme that we propose.
4. *Quantification:* we finally show how to preform quantitative analysis using well-formed attack–defense trees.

Related Work. The attack–defense tree's origins lie in attack trees, introduced in 1999 by Schneier to represent attack scenarios in the form of AND-OR trees [15]. Nowadays, there exist numerous variants of attack trees [9], some of which are popular and widely used in the industry to support real-life risk assessment processes [5,13]. Attack–defense trees extend the classical attack trees by complementing them with the defensive point of view [7]. They aim to represent interaction between the attacker and the defender, to give a more precise image of reality.

Although, in practice, attack tree-based models often possess multiple nodes with the same labels, not much fundamental research exists on the topic. From the formal perspective, a semantics based on multisets has been used in [7,12] to interpret an attack tree and respectively an attack–defense tree with a set of multisets representing potential ways of attacking a system. This approach supposes that every node with the same label is a separate action to be executed. On the contrary, other works formalize attack tree-based models with propositional formulæ where, due to the use of the logical conjunction and disjunction which are idempotent, all repetitions are ignored [10,16].

Repeated labels might have an impact on quantitative analysis of attack trees. The standard, bottom-up algorithm for quantification, recalled in Sect. 2.3, treats all repeated nodes as separate events [8]. Since quantifying trees with repeated nodes may increase the complexity of the underlying algorithms, some authors, e.g., Aslanyan et al. in [1] restrain their considerations to linear trees, i.e., trees with no label repetition, to gain efficiency. The authors of [14] go even further, and provide two variants of an algorithm for the probability computation on attack-countermeasure trees[1] with and without repeated nodes. Finally, most of the works do not consider repetitions explicitly but rather assume that all nodes (including those with the same labels) represent independent events [2,11].

We believe that both approaches – treating all nodes as independent or ignoring repetitions – are too restrictive. The objective of the formalization proposed in this work is to accommodate both of these cases and thus allow for a more faithful modeling of the reality.

---

[1] Attack-countermeasure trees are yet another security model based on attack trees.

Finally, studying the problem of labels' repetition led us to propose the notion of well-formedness for such trees. Previously, well-formedness of attack(–defense) trees has been addressed in various ways. In [1], attack–defense trees are formalized as typed terms over actions of the attacker and the defender, and well-formed trees are simply identified with the well-typed ones. In [3], Audinot et al. analyze the problem of well-formedness (that they call correctness) of an attack tree with respect to the modeled system. They focus on the well-formedness of the tree refinements by introducing four correctness properties which allow them to express how well an AND/OR combination of the child nodes represents the goal of the parent node. The objective of the well-formedness developed in our work, and defined in Definition 5, is to capture the intuitive construction of a security scenario represented as an attack–defense tree, in a formal way.

2   Know the Flora: Attack–Defense Trees

We start by briefly introducing the attack–defense tree model and summarizing the state of the art on its existing formal foundations. We especially focus the attention on aspects that may influence the meaning and the treatment of trees with repeated labels. For more detailed information on attack–defense trees, their semantics, and their quantitative analysis, we refer the reader to [7].

2.1   The Model

An *attack–defense tree* (ADTree) is a rooted tree with labeled nodes, aiming to describe and evaluate security scenarios involving two (sets of) competing actors: the attacker trying to attack a particular system[2] and the defender trying to protect it against the potential attacks. Labels of the nodes represent the goals that the actors must achieve. Each node has one of two types – *attack* (red circle) or *defense* (green rectangle) – depending on which actor's goal it illustrates. The nodes of an ADTree can have any number of children of the same type. These children represent the *refinement* of the parent's goal into subgoals. The refinement can be *disjunctive* (OR node) or *conjunctive* (AND node). To achieve the goal represented by an OR node, it is necessary and sufficient to achieve at least one of the subgoals represented by its children. To achieve the goal represented by an AND node, it is necessary and sufficient to achieve all of the subgoals represented by its children. To graphically distinguish OR from AND nodes, we use an arc to connect the children of the AND nodes. The nodes that do not have any children of the same type are called *non-refined nodes*. Their labels represent the so called *basic actions*, i.e., the actual actions that the actors need to execute to achieve their (sub)goals. Finally, each node of an ADTree can also have at most one child of the opposite type, which represents a *countermeasure*, i.e., a goal of the other actor, the achievement of which disables the goal of the node. Graphically, countermeasures are connected to the nodes they counter by dotted edges. A countermeasure can, in turn, be refined and/or countered.

---

[2] The system can be an infrastructure, a computer program, an organization, etc.

Remark 1. Note that the root node of an ADTree can be of the attack or the defense type. The actor whose goal is represented by the label of the root node is called the *proponent*, and the other one is called the *opponent*. In practice, the proponent is the attacker, in most cases.

Example 1. Figure 1 shows a simple example of an ADTree. In this scenario, the attacker (proponent) is a student who wants to pass a multiple choice test examination. To be sure that she will answer all questions correctly, she needs to learn the exam questions and get the solutions in advance, in order to memorize the correct answers. She can get a copy of the exam by accessing the teacher's computer, finding the file containing the questions, and storing it either by printing it or by saving it on a USB stick. She can proceed in a similar way to get a copy of the file with the solutions, which is located on the same computer. However, to better protect his exam, the teacher (opponent) could archive and encrypt the solutions' file using PKZIP [6]. The student would then need to break the encryption, for example using the CrackIt tool [17], to be able to access the solutions.

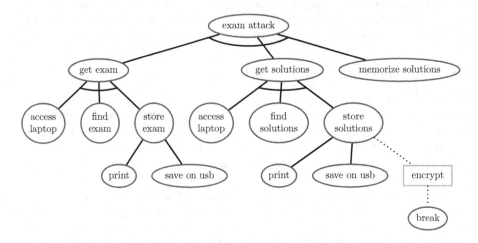

Fig. 1. An ADTree for passing the examination

Since, in ADTrees for real-life scenarios, the number of nodes tends to grow drastically, the graphical representation, as used in Fig. 1, is often not the most appropriate one. To formally describe and manipulate ADTrees, we therefore introduce an alternative, term-based notation.

Let $\mathbb{B}$ be the set of all basic actions. We assume that the elements of $\mathbb{B}$ are typed, i.e., that $\mathbb{B}$ is partitioned into the basic actions of the proponent $\mathbb{B}^{\mathrm{P}}$ and those of the opponent $\mathbb{B}^{\mathrm{o}}$. The ADTrees are generated by the following grammar

$$T^{\mathrm{s}}:\quad \mathsf{b}^{\mathrm{s}}\ \mid\ \mathtt{OR}^{\mathrm{s}}(T^{\mathrm{s}},\ldots,T^{\mathrm{s}})\ \mid\ \mathtt{AND}^{\mathrm{s}}(T^{\mathrm{s}},\ldots,T^{\mathrm{s}})\ \mid\ \mathtt{C}^{\mathrm{s}}(T^{\mathrm{s}},T^{\bar{\mathrm{s}}}), \qquad (1)$$

where $s \in \{p, o\}$, $\bar{p} = o$, $\bar{o} = p$, and $b^s \in \mathbb{B}^s$. Whenever the type s of a basic action b^s is clear from the context, we omit the superscript s to simplify the presentation. Note that, as explained in [7], a term of the form $C^s(T_1^s, T_2^{\bar{s}})$ represents the ADTree obtained from attaching (using a dotted edge) the tree $T_2^{\bar{s}}$ to the root of the tree T_1^s.

According to Remark 1, terms of the form T^p represent ADTrees, since the label of the root node always illustrates the proponent's goal. In the rest of this paper, we identify an ADTree with its corresponding term. The set of all ADTrees is denoted by $\mathbb{T}$.

Example 2. The term representation of the ADTree from Fig. 1 is the following

$$\text{AND}^P\Big(\text{AND}^P\big(\text{lapt}, \text{ex}, \text{OR}^P(\text{pr}, \text{usb})\big),$$

$$\text{AND}^P\big(\text{lapt}, \text{sol}, C^P(\text{OR}^P(\text{pr}, \text{usb}), C^o(\text{enc}, \text{break}))\big), \text{memo}\Big).$$

2.2 Existing Semantics for ADTrees

It is well-known that two security experts may produce two visually different ADTrees to represent the same security scenario. The simplest (but far from the sole) example of this situation are the two trees $T = \text{AND}^P(\text{card}, \text{pin})$ and $T' = \text{AND}^P(\text{pin}, \text{card})$. Here, the objective of the proponent is to get the necessary credentials to withdraw money from a victim's account. The order in which the proponent obtains the card and the corresponding pin is not relevant – the only thing that matters is that eventually, he gets both: the card and the pin.

To formally capture the notion of equivalent ADTrees, formal semantics for ADTrees have been introduced. Different semantics focus on different aspects (e.g., order of actions, their multiple occurrences, or cause-consequence relationships) and allow to partition the set $\mathbb{T}$ into equivalence classes according to these aspects. This is achieved by assigning mathematical objects to ADTrees, for instance propositional formulæ or multisets of basic actions, in such a way that trees representing the same scenario are interpreted with the same object. It is important to note that two trees may represent the same situation with respect to some aspects, i.e., be equivalent in one semantics, but differ substantially when other aspects are taken into account. Formal semantics also facilitate the reasoning about ADTrees, because they reduce it to the analysis of the corresponding mathematical objects. In general, any equivalence relation on $\mathbb{T}$ can be seen as a semantics for ADTrees.

Definitions 1 and 2 recall two major semantics for ADTrees – the propositional and the multiset semantics. Full details can be found in [7].

Definition 1. *The propositional semantics for ADTrees is a function $\mathcal{P}$ that assigns to each ADTree a propositional formula, in a recursive way, as follows*

$$\mathcal{P}(b) = x_b, \qquad \mathcal{P}(\text{OR}^s(T_1^s, \dots, T_k^s)) = \mathcal{P}(T_1^s) \vee \cdots \vee \mathcal{P}(T_k^s),$$
$$\mathcal{P}(C^s(T_1^s, T_2^{\bar{s}})) = \mathcal{P}(T_1^s) \wedge \neg \mathcal{P}(T_2^{\bar{s}}), \quad \mathcal{P}(\text{AND}^s(T_1^s, \dots, T_k^s)) = \mathcal{P}(T_1^s) \wedge \cdots \wedge \mathcal{P}(T_k^s).$$

where x_b, for $b \in \mathbb{B}$, is a propositional variable. Two ADTrees are equivalent wrt $\mathcal{P}$ if their interpretations are equivalent propositional formulæ.

The recursive construction from Definition 1 starts by assigning a propositional variable to each basic action $b \in \mathbb{B}$. This means that if a tree contains two nodes having the same label, these nodes will be interpreted with the same propositional variable. In addition, the logical disjunction ($\vee$) and conjunction ($\wedge$) used to interpret the refined nodes are idempotent. This implies that the propositional semantics $\mathcal{P}$ is unable to take the multiplicity of actions into account, as illustrated in Example 3.

Example 3. Consider the student/teacher scenario from Example 1. In order to access the teacher's laptop, the student would need to access the teacher's office. To do so, she needs to access the building – either by breaking-in through the window or by picking the lock – and then access the office by picking its lock, as illustrated in Fig. 2. When the propositional semantics is used, this tree is equivalent to its simplified form composed of a single node `lock-picking`. This is due to the absorption law which implies that $f_1 = (\text{window} \vee \text{pick}) \wedge \text{pick}$ and $f_2 = \text{pick}$ are equivalent formulæ. We discuss the link between the two trees in more detail in Remark 2.

Example 3 shows how the propositional semantics models that the execution of one of the repeated actions in the tree activates all other occurrences of this action in the considered scenario. In contrast, the multiset semantics, that we denote with $\mathcal{M}$ and briefly present below, treats each repeated action as a separate event. The multiset semantics has first been introduced in [12] to formalize attack trees and has then been extended to ADTrees in [7]. This semantics interprets

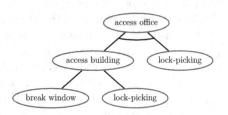

Fig. 2. ADTree for accessing office

an ADTree with a set of pairs of the form (P, O) of *multisets*[3] describing how the proponent can reach the goal represented by the tree: the first multiset P consists of basic actions from $\mathbb{B}^p$ that the proponent has to do, and the second multiset O contains basic actions from $\mathbb{B}^o$ that the proponent must stop the opponent from performing. The construction of $\mathcal{M}$ uses the distributive product $\otimes$ defined for two sets of pairs[4] as:

$$S \otimes Z = \{(P_S \uplus P_Z, O_S \uplus O_Z) | (P_S, O_S) \in S, (P_Z, O_Z) \in Z\},$$

where $\uplus$ is the multiset union. Definition 2 formalizes the construction of $\mathcal{M}$.

---

[3] A multiset is a collection that allows multiple occurrences of an element.

[4] $\otimes$ can be generalized on any finite number of set of pairs, in a natural way.

Definition 2. *The multiset semantics for ADTrees is a function* $\mathcal{M}$ *that assigns to each ADTree a set of pairs of multisets, as follows*

$$\mathcal{M}(\mathsf{b}^{\mathrm{p}}) = \{(\{\!|\mathsf{b}|\!\}, \emptyset)\}, \qquad\qquad \mathcal{M}(\mathsf{b}^{\mathrm{o}}) = \{(\emptyset, \{\!|\mathsf{b}|\!\})\},$$

$$\mathcal{M}\left(\mathsf{OR}^{\mathrm{p}}(T_1^{\mathrm{p}}, \ldots, T_k^{\mathrm{p}})\right) = \bigcup_{i=1}^{k} \mathcal{M}(T_i^{\mathrm{p}}), \quad \mathcal{M}\left(\mathsf{OR}^{\mathrm{o}}(T_1^{\mathrm{o}}, \ldots, T_k^{\mathrm{o}})\right) = \bigotimes_{i=1}^{k} \mathcal{M}(T_i^{\mathrm{o}}),$$

$$\mathcal{M}\left(\mathsf{AND}^{\mathrm{p}}(T_1^{\mathrm{p}}, \ldots, T_k^{\mathrm{p}})\right) = \bigotimes_{i=1}^{k} \mathcal{M}(T_i^{\mathrm{p}}), \quad \mathcal{M}\left(\mathsf{AND}^{\mathrm{o}}(T_1^{\mathrm{o}}, \ldots, T_k^{\mathrm{o}})\right) = \bigcup_{i=1}^{k} \mathcal{M}(T_i^{\mathrm{o}}),$$

$$\mathcal{M}\left(\mathsf{C}^{\mathrm{p}}(T_1^{\mathrm{p}}, T_2^{\mathrm{o}})\right) = \mathcal{M}(T_1^{\mathrm{p}}) \otimes \mathcal{M}(T_2^{\mathrm{o}}), \quad \mathcal{M}\left(\mathsf{C}^{\mathrm{o}}(T_1^{\mathrm{o}}, T_2^{\mathrm{p}})\right) = \mathcal{M}(T_1^{\mathrm{o}}) \cup \mathcal{M}(T_2^{\mathrm{p}}).$$

Two ADTrees are equivalent wrt $\mathcal{M}$ *if they are interpreted with the same set of pairs of multisets.*

Due to the use of multisets, the multiset semantics models that the execution of one of the repeated actions has no effect on other occurrences of this action in the considered scenario. In particular, the two trees considered in Example 3 are not equivalent when the multiset semantics is used. Indeed, the tree from Fig. 2 is interpreted with the set $\{(\{\!|\mathtt{window}, \mathtt{pick}|\!\}, \emptyset), (\{\!|\mathtt{pick}, \mathtt{pick}|\!\}, \emptyset)\}$ and the tree composed of a single node `lock-picking` with the set $\{(\{\!|\mathtt{pick}|\!\}, \emptyset)\}$.

Remark 2. The scenario considered in Example 3 shows that both semantics — $\mathcal{P}$ and $\mathcal{M}$ — are useful. When the modeler is interested only in what skills are necessary to perform the access office attack, then the propositional semantics is sufficient. Here, we assume that the attacker who has lock-picking skills will be able to use them at any time. However, if the goal of the security expert is to enumerate and analyze the actual ways of attacking, then the multiset semantics is the correct one to be used.

2.3 Quantitative Evaluation of ADTrees

To complete the overview of formal foundations for ADTrees, we briefly recall the bottom-up procedure for their quantitative evaluation. The simple tree structure of ADTrees can be exploited to easily quantify security scenarios. The security expert's objective might be to find out which way of attacking is the cheapest or the fastest one, whether the proponent's goal can be reached even in the presence of some countermeasures deployed by the opponent, to estimate the probability that the root goal will be achieved, etc. The idea is to assign values to the non-refined nodes and then propagate them all the way up to the root, using functions that depend on the refinement and the type of the node. This process is called *bottom-up attribute's evaluation*, and it is formalized in Definition 3. We refer the reader to [8] for a detailed classification of existing attributes, and to [4] for practical guidelines regarding the attributes' evaluation on ADTrees.

Definition 3. *Let D_α be a set of values. An attribute α is composed of*

- *a basic assignment $\beta_\alpha : \mathbb{B} \to D_\alpha$ which assigns a value from D_α to every basic action, and*
- *an attribute domain $A_\alpha = (D_\alpha, \mathrm{OR}^\mathrm{p}_\alpha, \mathrm{AND}^\mathrm{p}_\alpha, \mathrm{OR}^\mathrm{o}_\alpha, \mathrm{AND}^\mathrm{o}_\alpha, \mathrm{C}^\mathrm{p}_\alpha, \mathrm{C}^\mathrm{o}_\alpha)$, where for $\mathrm{OP}^\mathrm{s} \in \{\mathrm{OR}^\mathrm{s}, \mathrm{AND}^\mathrm{s}, \mathrm{C}^\mathrm{s}\}$, $\mathrm{OP}^\mathrm{s}_\alpha : D^k_\alpha \to D_\alpha$ is an internal operation on D_α of the same arity as OP^s.*

The bottom-up algorithm for α assigns values from D_α to ADTrees as follows

$$\alpha(\mathbf{b}) = \beta_\alpha(\mathbf{b}), \qquad \alpha\big(\mathrm{OP}^\mathrm{s}(T^\mathrm{s}_1, \ldots, T^\mathrm{s}_k)\big) = \mathrm{OP}^\mathrm{s}_\alpha\big(\alpha(T^\mathrm{s}_1), \ldots, \alpha(T^\mathrm{s}_k)\big).$$

Example 4 illustrates the evaluation of the minimal time attribute on the ADTree from Fig. 1.

Example 4. Here, we are interested in the minimal time required for the student to perform the exam attack illustrated in Fig. 1. First, we build the basic assignment function β_α which assigns a value (in minutes) to each basic action, as illustrated in Table 1.

Table 1. Basic assignment for the minimal time attribute in the student attack (The $+\infty$ value assigned to the basic actions of the defender signifies that the attacker cannot successfully perform these actions, see [8] for a detailed explanation.)

goal	β_α	goal	β_α	goal	β_α	goal	β_α
access laptop	45	print	6	find solutions	5	break	18
find exam	5	save on usb	1	memorize	90	encrypt	$+\infty$

To propagate the values of minimal attack time up to the root node, the following attribute domain is used $A_{\text{time}} = (\mathbb{N} \cup \{+\infty\}, \min, +, +, \min, +, \min)$. The corresponding bottom-up computation is given in Fig. 3, and shows that the student's attack will take at least 210 min.

3   The Root of the Problem: Common Issues

Although constructing an ADTree seems to be a simple and intuitive task, this process may suffer from several issues. They are related to the completeness or correctness of the models. One of the important sources of modeling problems is a presence of multiple nodes having the same label. In this section, we illustrate the most common mistakes made while creating ADTrees and provide hints to avoid them. This is the first step towards the notion of well-formed ADTrees formalized in Sect. 5.

3.1   Incomplete Refinement

As we have explained in Sect. 2, the children of a refined node represent subgoals that need to be achieved so that the goal of the node is achieved. Figure 4a shows an example of a tree where in order to access the teacher's computer, the student needs to get their username and password. This example presents a problem of incomplete refinement, as getting the username and the password is not sufficient to access the computer – the action of actually accessing the machine is also necessary. The corrected tree is given in Fig. 4b.

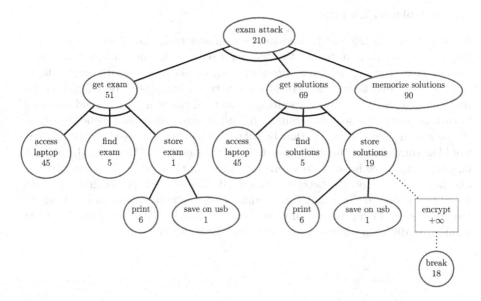

Fig. 3. Minimal time for the student to perform the exam attack

The aim of this example is to illustrate that the label of a refined node cannot represent any additional action to be executed along those already represented by its children. This label is just a short description *replacing but not complementing* the refinement of the node. Note that this is due to the way in which the formal semantics for ADTrees work: the meaning of a refined node is fully expressed as the combination of its children. Similarly, in the case of the bottom-up quantification of ADTrees, the value of a refined node is computed as the combination of the values of its children.

Hint 1: One can easily check whether all nodes of an ADTree are fully refined by hiding the labels of the refined nodes and judging whether the corresponding goal is achieved, or if additional children nodes need to be added.

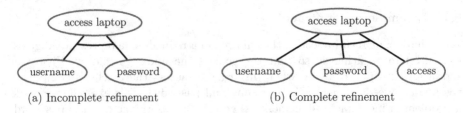

(a) Incomplete refinement   (b) Complete refinement

Fig. 4. Well-formedness and refinements

3.2 Misplaced Counter

A second frequent mistake is to misplace a counter node. Consider the tree from Fig. 5a, where in order to get the teacher's password, the student can find a post-it where the password has been written, or perform a brute force attack. In order to prevent the first attack, a security training could be offered to the teachers to advise them against writing down their passwords. The student could in turn overcome the security training by social engineering the teacher to reveal the password. Note, however, that by social engineering the teacher, the student would already achieve the `get password` goal. In the case of this tree, the `social engineering` node is not a counterattack to security training. It is actually yet another option to get the teacher's password. The correct tree should therefore look like the one in Fig. 5b. A simple analysis of the two trees from Fig. 5 shows that they are not equivalent in any semantics. Similarly, the bottom-up algorithm would give different quantitative results on these two trees.

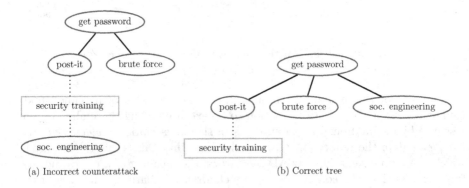

(a) Incorrect counterattack   (b) Correct tree

Fig. 5. Well-formedness and counter placement

Hint 2: A countermeasure node of type s is correctly placed if its achievement disables the goal of the node of type s̄ it is supposed to counter.

3.3   Repeated Labels

Due to the fact that ADTrees are often reused to model similar situations and that libraries of standard attacks might be used to ease the creation of an ADTree, it is not rare to see trees that contain several nodes having the same label. In this case, the modeler needs to ensure that the same labels really represent the same goals to be achieved. As a consequence, subtrees rooted in the nodes having the same label need to have the same refining subtrees. More precisely, the subtrees rooted in these nodes, and obtained by removing all nodes of the other type, should be equivalent with respect to the semantics that is used.

Hint 3: If two nodes in an ADTree have the same labels but their refining subtrees are not equivalent with respect to the considered semantics, then

- If the subgoals represented by the refinement of each of these nodes actually apply to the other one as well, then the refining nodes present in only one of the subtrees should be added to the other one and the labels of the two nodes stay unchanged.
- If at least one subgoal does not apply to both nodes, the corresponding goals are not identical, and at least one of the labels should be modified. Note that it does not, however, mean that these goals cannot have common subgoals.

3.4   Repeated Basic Actions

Finally, we need to ensure that nodes labeled with the same basic action represent the same actions to be executed. This implies that, if two non-refined nodes have the same label, then there must not exist any attribute for which they have a different value. If there is at least one attribute that differentiates them, then the basic actions they represent are not identical, and should therefore be modeled with different labels. For instance, if we assume that the exam considered in the tree from Fig. 1 is a multiple choice test composed of five pages of questions, the two `print` nodes should not have the same label, because printing the exam would take more time than printing just the solutions that fit on one page.

Hint 4: To decide whether the non-refined nodes are correctly labeled, the modeler should ensure that, for every attribute α that will be considered, all nodes with the same label are indeed getting the same value by the assignment β_α.

4   Poisonous or Edible: ADTrees with Repeated Labels

As we have seen in Sect. 3, ADTrees may contain several nodes with identical labels. In this section, we propose a methodology to handle such trees properly. We first discuss different origins of repeated labels, and then propose solutions to avoid an incorrect labeling that could lead to miscalculations.

4.1   Meaning of Repeated Labels

While analyzing ADTrees for real-life scenarios, one can observe that there are two kinds of nodes with repeated labels. We call them *cloned* nodes and *twin* nodes. We explain the difference between them below. To clarify the explanation, we say that the node has been *activated* if the goal represented by its label is achieved by the corresponding actor. When the goal of a node has been countered by the other actor, we say that the node has been *deactivated*.

> *Cloned nodes* – when activating one node means activating another one having the same label, we say that the two nodes are cloned. This means that cloned nodes represent exactly the same instance of an action, so deactivating one of the cloned nodes deactivates all its clones.
>
> *Twin nodes* – when activating one node does not activate another one having the same label, we say that the two nodes are twins. This means that each individual twin node represents a separated instance of the same action, thus all twin nodes having the same label need to be deactivated separately.

Example 5. Consider the scenario from Example 1 illustrated in Fig. 1. The two `access laptop` nodes are cloned: since the exam and the solution files are stored on the same laptop, accessing the laptop needs to be done only once. In contrast, the two `save on usb` nodes are twins: obviously, saving the exam file on a usb stick does not result in saving the solution file, and vice versa. Note that one could dispute the fact that the two `save on usb` nodes have the same label, but according to *Hint 4*, this is correct. Even though the solution and the exam are two different files, they have roughly the same size and will therefore take the same time to be copied to the usb stick. Every other attribute gives unquestionably the same value.

Existing semantics for ADTree have a rather restrictive view on ADTrees with repeated labels. The propositional semantics acts as if all nodes having the same labels were cloned: the labels of non-refined nodes are interpreted as propositional variables and idempotent logical operators $(\lor, \land)$ are used to interpret the refinements. In contrast, the multiset semantics assumes that all nodes with repeated labels are twins: due to the use of the multisets, where the multiplicity of elements in the collection is relevant, each node is viewed as representing a separate instance of an action. In practice, however, the same scenario may contain both cloned and twin nodes, as illustrated in Example 5. To overcome this issue and accommodate cloned and twin nodes, we propose a more precise labeling scheme, that we present in Sect. 4.2.

4.2   Extended Labeling for ADTrees with Repetitions

A naive solution would be to relabel all twin nodes to remove repetitions. This would make the use of the propositional semantics possible, but this solution is not preferred due to the following issues

- It would prohibit the re-use of models created for similar scenarios, and make the use of libraries of standard attacks more complex.
- Since the number of possible labels, i.e., the size of $\mathbb{B}$, would increase, the effort of defining β_α would be (unnecessary but inevitably) greater. E.g., instead of providing one single value to quantify the complexity of brute forcing a 15 char password, one would need to define two values: for `brute force a 15 char pwd for a laptop` and for `brute force a 15 char pwd for a smartphone`. However, these two values would obviously be the same.
- Relabeling could result in peculiar, non-intuitive labels, which could have a disadvantageous influence on the tree analysis, especially regarding the estimation of the values for basic actions, i.e., definition of β_α.
- Finally, the cloned nodes would still be considered multiple times when the multiset semantics would be used.

To bypass the above issues, we propose a solution which relies on labels being pairs in $\mathbb{G} \times \Gamma$, where $\mathbb{G}$ is a typed set of goals containing $\mathbb{B}$ and Γ is a finite set of indices. Instead of label g, a pair (g, γ) is used. Its first component $g \in \mathbb{G}$ describes the goal to be achieved and the second component $\gamma \in \Gamma$ is an index which allows us to distinguish between cloned and twin nodes.

Definition 4. *Let T be an ADTree whose nodes are labeled with the elements of $\mathbb{G} \times \Gamma$, and consider two nodes having the same goal g, i.e., labeled with (g, ι) and (g, γ), respectively. If $\iota = \gamma$, then we say that the two nodes are cloned; if $\iota \neq \gamma$, then we say that the two nodes are twins (or twin nodes).*

From now on, the word *label* stands for the pair of the form (g, γ) and g is called its *goal*. Note that, since goals are typed, the set $\mathbb{G}$ is partitioned into goals of the proponent's type ($\mathbb{G}^P$) and those of the opponent's type ($\mathbb{G}^O$). However, if this does not lead to confusion, we omit the superscript denoting the goal's type.

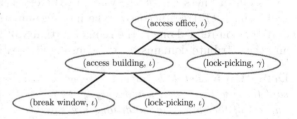

Fig. 6. Extended labeling of ADTree nodes

Example 6. While using the extended labeling based on pairs, the tree from Fig. 2 is relabeled as shown in Fig. 6. It is now clear that (`lock-picking`, ι) and (`lock-picking`, γ) represent two separate instances of picking a lock, as $\iota \neq \gamma$.

5   Survival Kit: Well-Formed ADTrees

The purpose of ADTrees is to represent and analyze the security scenarios in a rigorous way. In order to obtain meaningful analysis results, an ADTree must model the reality in the most faithful way possible. To achieve this, we have developed a set of rules that guide the security expert in creating well-formed trees.

This is feasible thanks to the new labeling introduced in Sect. 4, which undoubtedly increases the expressive power of ADTrees. In this section, we formalize the notion of well-formed ADTrees that overcome the typical problems illustrated in Sect. 3. Then, we explain how to use them correctly, by adapting previously seen formal semantics and the quantification algorithm to our pair-based labeling.

5.1   Definition of Well-Formed ADTrees

To be able to address the issues presented in Sect. 3, we first extend the grammar (1) so that the generated terms capture the labels of the refined nodes:

$$T^s : (b^s, \gamma) \mid OR^s[(g,\gamma)](T^s, \dots, T^s) \mid AND^s[(g,\gamma)](T^s, \dots, T^s) \mid C^s(T^s, T^{\bar{s}}), \quad (2)$$

where $s, \bar{s} \in \{p, o\}$, $b^s \in \mathbb{B}$, and $g \in \mathbb{G}$ are goals of refined nodes. The term starting with C does not mention any label, since the goal of the root node expressed by the term $C^s(T_1^s, T_2^{\bar{s}})$ is contained in the label of the root node of T_1^s.

The presence of extended labels in the terms generated by grammar (2) allows us to explain the meaning of refinement and counter, formalize the hints from Sects. 3.1–3.3, and differentiate between the cloned and the twin nodes. This is captured by the notion of well-formed ADTrees that we introduce in Definition 5. Note that, identifying well-formed ADTrees with the well-typed ones, as in [1], is not sufficient for our work, in particular because it does not capture the problems described in Sect. 3. Indeed, all trees considered in that section are well-typed, but we have shown that they suffer from multiple construction drawbacks that could hinder the security analysis. We therefore believe that the definition of well-formed ADTrees needs to take into account the labels of every node (not only the non-refined ones), the semantics that will be used for the tree analysis, and the attribute domains for the considered attributes.

Definition 5. *Let T be an ADTree generated by grammar (2). ADTree T is said to be well-formed if and only if the type of its root node is p (proponent) and all of the following conditions are satisfied for all of its subtrees Y, where g_i denotes the goal of the root node of Y_i.*

1. ***The meaning of* OR**
   Let $Y = OR^s[(g,\gamma)](Y_1^s, \dots, Y_k^s)$. The goal g is achieved if and only if at least one of the subgoals g_i is achieved.
2. ***The meaning of* AND**
   Let $Y = AND^s[(g,\gamma)](Y_1^s, \dots, Y_k^s)$. The goal g is achieved if and only if all of the subgoals g_i are achieved.
3. ***The meaning of* C**
   Let $Y = C^s(Y_1^s, Y_2^{\bar{s}})$. If g_2 is achieved then g_1 cannot be achieved.
4. ***Cloned and twin nodes***
   Let $\mathcal{I}$ be a semantics that will be used for the analysis of T and assume that T contains two subtrees of the form $Y_i = OP_i^s[(g_i, \gamma_i)](Y_{i_1}, \dots, Y_{i_k})$, where $OP_i^s \in \{OR^s, AND^s\}$, for $i \in \{1, 2\}$. Let $Y_{i|s}$ denote the term obtained from Y_i

by recursively replacing all of its subterms of the form $C^s(U_{i_1}, U_{i_2})$ by U_{i_1}.[5] If $g_1 = g_2$, then $\mathcal{I}(Y_{1|s}) = \mathcal{I}(Y_{2|s})$, i.e., the subtrees refining g_1 and g_2 are equivalent wrt $\mathcal{I}$. Moreover, if $(g_1, \gamma_1) = (g_2, \gamma_2)$, i.e., the corresponding nodes are cloned, then $\mathcal{I}(Y_1) = \mathcal{I}(Y_2)$.

5. *Correct labeling*

Let α be an attribute that will be used for the analysis of T and assume that T contains two subtrees of the form $Y_i = OP_i^s[(g_i, \gamma_i)](Y_{i_1}, \dots, Y_{i_k})$, where $OP_i^s \in \{OR^s, AND^s\}$, for $i \in \{1, 2\}$. Additionally, let $Y_{i|s}$ be as in the previous item. If $g_1 = g_2$, then $\alpha(Y_{1|s}) = \alpha(Y_{2|s})$. Moreover, if $(g_1, \gamma_1) = (g_2, \gamma_2)$, i.e., the corresponding nodes are cloned, then $\alpha(Y_1) = \alpha(Y_2)$.

Rules 1 and 2 guarantee the correctness and completeness of refinements. They implement *Hint 1* from Sect. 3. For instance, the tree from Fig. 4a is not well-formed, because it does not satisfy Rule 2. Rule 3 is related to *Hint 2*. The tree from Fig. 5a does not satisfy Rule 3 because a successful social engineering attack does not counter the security training. Rule 4 formalizes *Hint 3*. It makes sure that nodes with the same goals (in particular the twin nodes) have equivalent refining subtrees and nodes with the same labels (goals and indices), i.e., the cloned nodes, have equivalent subtrees (including countermeasures). In particular, Rule 4 forbids two cloned nodes from being placed on the same path to the root node. Rule 5 corresponds to *Hint 4*. It ensures that nodes with the same labels and non-countered nodes with the same goals always get the same value when the bottom-up quantitative analysis is performed.

In Example 7, we modify the tree from Fig. 1 by extending its labels with the second component, and renaming some of the goals to ensure the well-formedness of the tree. We remark that the unique purpose of the index from Γ is to allow the distinction between the cloned and the twin nodes having the same goal. If two nodes have different goals, the fact that they have the same index does not model any additional relationship between them.

Example 7. As already discussed in Example 5, the two `access laptop` nodes are cloned. They therefore get the same index ι. Since printing the exam will be substantially longer than printing the solutions, the two `print` nodes cannot have the same goal. We therefore rename them to `print exam` and `print sol`. The exam and the solutions differ in terms of the number of pages, nevertheless the size of the corresponding pdf files is practically the same. Therefore, the two `save on usb` nodes may keep the same goal, but their indices must be different, as these nodes are twins. The updated well-formed ADTree is given in Fig. 7.

5.2 Formal Semantics for Well-Formed ADTrees

We now discuss the formal semantics for well-formed ADTrees labeled with pairs from $\mathbb{G} \times \Gamma$.

---

[5] In other words, $Y_{i|s}$ is the tree Y_i in which all countermeasures have been disregarded.

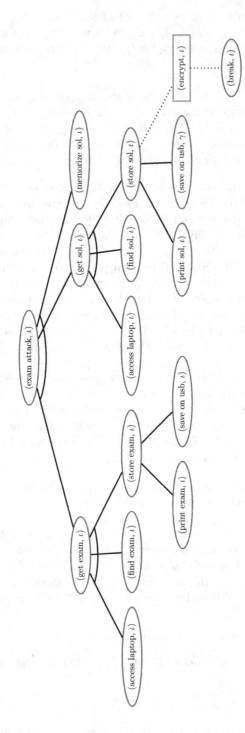

Fig. 7. Well-formed ADTree for passing the examination

Propositional semantics. We require that the propositional variables are associated with labels (i.e., pairs) and not only with goals. We therefore have $\mathcal{P}((\mathsf{b}, \gamma)) = x_{(\mathsf{b}, \gamma)}$, and the rest of Definition 1 stays unchanged. If the pair-based labeling is adopted, then cloned nodes are represented with the same variable and are only counted once in the semantics; twin nodes, in turn, correspond to different variables, say $x_{(\mathsf{b}, \gamma)}$ and $x_{(\mathsf{b}, \gamma')}$, and will thus be treated as separated actions to be performed. The propositional semantics of a well-formed ADTree T can be expressed as a formula in a minimized disjunctive normal form.

$$\mathcal{P}(T) = \bigvee_{i=1}^{l} \left(\left(\bigwedge_{j=1}^{n_i} x_{(\mathsf{p}_{ij}, \gamma_{ij})} \right) \wedge \left(\bigwedge_{j=1}^{m_i} \neg x_{(\mathsf{o}_{ij}, \gamma_{ij})} \right) \right), \tag{3}$$

where $\mathsf{p}_{ij} \in \mathbb{B}^{\mathsf{P}}, \mathsf{o}_{ij} \in \mathbb{B}^{\mathsf{o}}$, and $\forall i, \forall j$, if $j \neq j'$, then $(\mathsf{p}_{ij}, \gamma_{ij}) \neq (\mathsf{p}_{ij'}, \gamma_{ij'})$ and $(\mathsf{o}_{ij}, \gamma_{ij}) \neq (\mathsf{o}_{ij'}, \gamma_{ij'})$.

Set semantics. The objective of using multisets in the semantics introduced in Definition 2 was to be able to recall the multiplicity of the same goal. When the labeling from $\mathbb{G} \times \Gamma$ is used, the indices already take care of storing information about which actions need to be repeated several times (twin nodes get different indices) and which ones are only executed once (cloned nodes get the same index). We therefore replace the multisets from Definition 2 with regular sets. The corresponding semantics is formally defined in Definition 6, where

$$S \odot Z = \{(P_S \cup P_Z, O_S \cup O_Z) | (P_S, O_S) \in S, \ (P_Z, O_Z) \in Z\},$$

for $S, Z \subseteq \mathbb{B}^{\mathsf{P}} \times \mathbb{B}^{\mathsf{o}}$.

Definition 6. *The set semantics for ADTrees labeled with pairs from $\mathbb{G} \times \Gamma$ is a function $\mathcal{S} \colon \mathbb{T} \to \mathcal{P}\big(\mathcal{P}(\mathbb{B}^{\mathsf{P}} \times \Gamma) \times \mathcal{P}(\mathbb{B}^{\mathsf{o}} \times \Gamma)\big)$ that assigns to each ADTree a set of pairs of sets of labels, as follows*

$$\mathcal{S}\big((\mathsf{b}^{\mathsf{P}}, \gamma)\big) = \big\{ \big(\{(\mathsf{b}^{\mathsf{P}}, \gamma)\}, \emptyset \big) \big\}, \qquad \mathcal{S}\big((\mathsf{b}^{\mathsf{o}}, \gamma)\big) = \big\{ \big(\emptyset, \{(\mathsf{b}^{\mathsf{o}}, \gamma)\} \big) \big\}$$

$$\mathcal{S}\big(\mathsf{OR}^{\mathsf{P}}(T_1^{\mathsf{P}}, \dots, T_k^{\mathsf{P}})\big) = \bigcup_{i=1}^{k} \mathcal{S}(T_i^{\mathsf{P}}), \qquad \mathcal{S}\big(\mathsf{OR}^{\mathsf{o}}(T_1^{\mathsf{o}}, \dots, T_k^{\mathsf{o}})\big) = \bigodot_{i=1}^{k} \mathcal{S}(T_i^{\mathsf{o}})$$

$$\mathcal{S}\big(\mathsf{AND}^{\mathsf{P}}(T_1^{\mathsf{P}}, \dots, T_k^{\mathsf{P}})\big) = \bigodot_{i=1}^{k} \mathcal{S}(T_i^{\mathsf{P}}), \qquad \mathcal{S}\big(\mathsf{AND}^{\mathsf{o}}(T_1^{\mathsf{o}}, \dots, T_k^{\mathsf{o}})\big) = \bigcup_{i=1}^{k} \mathcal{S}(T_i^{\mathsf{o}})$$

$$\mathcal{S}\big(\mathsf{C}^{\mathsf{P}}(T_1^{\mathsf{P}}, T_2^{\mathsf{o}})\big) = \mathcal{S}(T_1^{\mathsf{P}}) \odot \mathcal{S}(T_2^{\mathsf{o}}), \qquad \mathcal{S}\big(\mathsf{C}^{\mathsf{o}}(T_1^{\mathsf{o}}, T_2^{\mathsf{P}})\big) = \mathcal{S}(T_1^{\mathsf{o}}) \cup \mathcal{S}(T_2^{\mathsf{P}}).$$

The set semantics of a well-formed ADTree T can be expressed as follows

$$\mathcal{S}(T) = \bigcup_{i=1}^{l} \left\{ \left(\bigcup_{j=1}^{n_i} \{(\mathsf{p}_{ij}, \gamma_{ij})\}, \bigcup_{j=1}^{m_i} \{(\mathsf{o}_{ij}, \gamma_{ij})\} \right) \right\}. \tag{4}$$

Note that expressions (3) and (4) correspond to the canonical form of an ADTree in the respective semantics, i.e., the form that explicitly enumerates possible ways to achieve the tree's root goal, giving the minimum amount of information necessary to reconstruct an equivalent ADTree. Example 8 illustrates the use of the set semantics on a well-formed ADTree.

Example 8. While interpreting the tree from Fig. 7 with the set semantics, we obtain the following eight ways of performing the student attack:

$$\{(\{(\texttt{lapt}, \iota), (\texttt{ex}, \iota), (\texttt{sol}, \iota), (\texttt{memo}, \iota), (\texttt{break}, \iota), (\texttt{pr ex}, \iota), (\texttt{pr sol}, \iota)\}, \emptyset),$$
$$(\{(\texttt{lapt}, \iota), (\texttt{ex}, \iota), (\texttt{sol}, \iota), (\texttt{memo}, \iota), (\texttt{break}, \iota), (\texttt{pr ex}, \iota), (\texttt{usb}, \gamma)\}, \emptyset),$$
$$(\{(\texttt{lapt}, \iota), (\texttt{ex}, \iota), (\texttt{sol}, \iota), (\texttt{memo}, \iota), (\texttt{break}, \iota), (\texttt{usb}, \iota), (\texttt{pr sol}, \iota)\}, \emptyset),$$
$$(\{(\texttt{lapt}, \iota), (\texttt{ex}, \iota), (\texttt{sol}, \iota), (\texttt{memo}, \iota), (\texttt{break}, \iota), (\texttt{usb}, \iota), (\texttt{usb}, \gamma)\}, \emptyset),$$
$$(\{(\texttt{lapt}, \iota), (\texttt{ex}, \iota), (\texttt{sol}, \iota), (\texttt{memo}, \iota), (\texttt{pr ex}, \iota), (\texttt{pr sol}, \iota)\}, \{\texttt{enc}\}),$$
$$(\{(\texttt{lapt}, \iota), (\texttt{ex}, \iota), (\texttt{sol}, \iota), (\texttt{memo}, \iota), (\texttt{pr ex}, \iota), (\texttt{usb}, \gamma)\}, \{\texttt{enc}\}),$$
$$(\{(\texttt{lapt}, \iota), (\texttt{ex}, \iota), (\texttt{sol}, \iota), (\texttt{memo}, \iota), (\texttt{usb}, \iota), (\texttt{pr sol}, \iota)\}, \{\texttt{enc}\}),$$
$$(\{(\texttt{lapt}, \iota), (\texttt{ex}, \iota), (\texttt{sol}, \iota), (\texttt{memo}, \iota), (\texttt{usb}, \iota), (\texttt{usb}, \gamma)\}, \{\texttt{enc}\})\}.$$

The different attack options implement distinct ways of storing the exam and the solution files, and depend on whether the solution file is encrypted or not. The first four options correspond to the situation where the teacher can use the encryption, because the student is prepared to break it. The last four cases model that, in addition to the actions listed in the first set, the student should also stop the teacher from encrypting the solution file.

The use of sets (instead of multisets) ensures that accessing the laptop is performed only once. However, thanks to the use of different indices (ι and γ) saving the exam and the solution files on a usb represent two different actions.

Quantitative analysis. If α is an attribute, the function β_α is still of the form $\beta_\alpha \colon \mathbb{B} \to D_\alpha$, i.e., it does not take the indices into account, so two twin nodes having the same goal will get the same value by β_α. This way, the computational burden of estimating values for similar basic actions is omitted. To ensure a correct handling of the cloned nodes, the value of attribute α must now be evaluated on the semantics of the tree. Let $A_\alpha = (D_\alpha, \text{OR}_\alpha^\text{p}, \text{AND}_\alpha^\text{p}, \text{OR}_\alpha^\text{o}, \text{AND}_\alpha^\text{o}, \text{C}_\alpha^\text{p}, \text{C}_\alpha^\text{o})$ be an attribute domain for α. If the propositional semantics (resp. the set semantics) is used, then the evaluation of the tree whose interpretation is given by formula (3) (resp. (4)) proceeds as follows

$$\alpha(T) = (\text{OR}_\alpha^\text{p})_{i=1}^l \left(\text{C}_\alpha^\text{p}((\text{AND}_\alpha^\text{p})_{j=1}^{n_i} \beta_\alpha(\mathbf{p}_{ij}), (\text{OR}_\alpha^\text{o})_{j=1}^{m_i} \beta_\alpha(\mathbf{o}_{ij})) \right). \tag{5}$$

Example 9. Let us make use of the set semantics to evaluate the minimal time for the exam attack on the well-formed tree from Fig. 7. We use the basic assignment from Example 4, except for the two print nodes that now represent distinct basic actions. We set $\beta_\alpha(\texttt{print exam}) = 6$ and $\beta_\alpha(\texttt{print sol}) = 2$, to model that printing a longer document will take more time. The minimal time corresponding to each attack option is as follows

$(\{(\mathtt{lapt}, \iota), (\mathtt{ex}, \iota), (\mathtt{sol}, \iota), (\mathtt{memo}, \iota), (\mathtt{break}, \iota), (\mathtt{pr\ ex}, \iota), (\mathtt{pr\ sol}, \iota)\}, \emptyset) \mapsto 171,$

$(\{(\mathtt{lapt}, \iota), (\mathtt{ex}, \iota), (\mathtt{sol}, \iota), (\mathtt{memo}, \iota), (\mathtt{break}, \iota), (\mathtt{pr\ ex}, \iota), (\mathtt{usb}, \gamma)\}, \emptyset) \mapsto 170,$

$(\{(\mathtt{lapt}, \iota), (\mathtt{ex}, \iota), (\mathtt{sol}, \iota), (\mathtt{memo}, \iota), (\mathtt{break}, \iota), (\mathtt{usb}, \iota), (\mathtt{pr\ sol}, \iota)\}, \emptyset) \mapsto 166,$

$(\{(\mathtt{lapt}, \iota), (\mathtt{ex}, \iota), (\mathtt{sol}, \iota), (\mathtt{memo}, \iota), (\mathtt{break}, \iota), (\mathtt{usb}, \iota), (\mathtt{usb}, \gamma)\}, \emptyset) \mapsto 165,$

$(\{(\mathtt{lapt}, \iota), (\mathtt{ex}, \iota), (\mathtt{sol}, \iota), (\mathtt{memo}, \iota), (\mathtt{pr\ ex}, \iota), (\mathtt{pr\ sol}, \iota)\}, \{\mathtt{enc}\}) \mapsto +\infty,$

$(\{(\mathtt{lapt}, \iota), (\mathtt{ex}, \iota), (\mathtt{sol}, \iota), (\mathtt{memo}, \iota), (\mathtt{pr\ ex}, \iota), (\mathtt{usb}, \gamma)\}, \{\mathtt{enc}\}) \mapsto +\infty,$

$(\{(\mathtt{lapt}, \iota), (\mathtt{ex}, \iota), (\mathtt{sol}, \iota), (\mathtt{memo}, \iota), (\mathtt{usb}, \iota), (\mathtt{pr\ sol}, \iota)\}, \{\mathtt{enc}\}) \mapsto +\infty,$

$(\{(\mathtt{lapt}, \iota), (\mathtt{ex}, \iota), (\mathtt{sol}, \iota), (\mathtt{memo}, \iota), (\mathtt{usb}, \iota), (\mathtt{usb}, \gamma)\}, \{\mathtt{enc}\}) \mapsto +\infty.$

According to the formula from Eq. (5), we obtain that the time of the shortest attack is $\min\{171, 170, 166, 165, +\infty\} = 165$, in contrast to 210 min obtained for the non well-formed tree in Fig. 3. The reason is that the action of accessing the laptop is now counted only once. This comparison shows that distinguishing between different types of repeated nodes improves the accuracy of the attack–defense tree analysis. We finally remark that every attack option where the second set is not empty gets value $+\infty$. This models that these options do not represent successful attacks, as they cannot be performed in finite time.

6   Back to Civilization: Conclusion

The goal of the work presented in this paper was to provide guidelines for properly handling attack–defense trees where several nodes have the same label. A thorough analysis of numerous examples of such trees resulted in a classification of the repeated nodes into two categories: cloned nodes and twin nodes. These two kinds of nodes must be treated differently, because activating a cloned node activates all other ones having the same label, while activating one of the repeated twin nodes does not have any influence on the other ones.

To formally capture the difference between the two cases, we have proposed a new labeling scheme which complements the node's goal with the information regarding which repeated nodes are cloned, and which ones are twins. Furthermore, we have extended the classical grammar that generates ADTrees in a way that includes the labels of the refined nodes. This enabled us to define well-formed ADTrees, and formally specify their semantics. The definition of well-formedness ensures that the trees are not only well-typed (with respect to the actions of the proponent and the opponent), but also that they do not suffer from common mistakes or omissions often made during the tree creation process.

Since attack trees are special cases of ADTrees, the solution elaborated in this work directly applies to classical attack trees. We therefore hope that our survival kit will be a valuable and practical help to security experts making use of attack(–defense) trees to model and evaluate the security of their systems.

Repeated labels are just a special case of a much larger problem of dependencies between nodes in ADTrees. In practice, different attacks may share some but not all of the necessary actions, they may involve temporal or causal dependencies between the actions of the two actors, etc. We are currently working on extending the ADTree model with such dependencies in order to be able to analyze scenarios involving sequences (instead of sets of) actions, as well as distinguishing between preventive and reactive countermeasures.

Another aspect that we would like to study is the formulation of the goals in ADTrees. Due to their conciseness, the labels are often imprecise or misleading. In addition, several formulations in the natural language might correspond to the same goal. A methodology to devise precise labels and to decide which formulations are equivalent should be developed, so that the nodes with different but equivalent labels can be treated in the same, and if possible automated, way.

Acknowledgments. We would like to thank Wojciech Wideł for the very fruitful discussions on the meaning of countermeasures in ADTrees, which allowed us to improve the approach developed in this paper.

References

1. Aslanyan, Z., Nielson, F.: Pareto efficient solutions of attack-defence trees. In: Focardi, R., Myers, A. (eds.) POST 2015. LNCS, vol. 9036, pp. 95–114. Springer, Heidelberg (2015). https://doi.org/10.1007/978-3-662-46666-7_6
2. Aslanyan, Z., Nielson, F., Parker, D.: Quantitative verification and synthesis of attack-defence scenarios. In: CSF, pp. 105–119. IEEE Computer Society (2016)
3. Audinot, M., Pinchinat, S., Kordy, B.: Is my attack tree correct? In: Foley, S.N., Gollmann, D., Snekkenes, E. (eds.) ESORICS 2017. LNCS, vol. 10492, pp. 83–102. Springer, Cham (2017). https://doi.org/10.1007/978-3-319-66402-6_7
4. Bagnato, A., Kordy, B., Meland, P.H., Schweitzer, P.: Attribute decoration of attack-defense trees. IJSSE **3**(2), 1–35 (2012)
5. Gadyatskaya, O., Harpes, C., Mauw, S., Muller, C., Muller, S.: Bridging two worlds: reconciling practical risk assessment methodologies with theory of attack trees. In: Kordy, B., Ekstedt, M., Kim, D.S. (eds.) GraMSec 2016. LNCS, vol. 9987, pp. 80–93. Springer, Cham (2016). https://doi.org/10.1007/978-3-319-46263-9_5
6. Katz, P.: PKZIP 6.0 Command Line User's Manual. PKWare, Inc. (2002). https://pkware.cachefly.net/webdocs/manuals/win6_cli-usersguide.pdf
7. Kordy, B., Mauw, S., Radomirovic, S., Schweitzer, P.: Attack-defense trees. J. Log. Comput. **24**(1), 55–87 (2014). http://dx.doi.org/10.1093/logcom/exs029
8. Kordy, B., Mauw, S., Schweitzer, P.: Quantitative questions on attack–defense trees. In: Kwon, T., Lee, M.-K., Kwon, D. (eds.) ICISC 2012. LNCS, vol. 7839, pp. 49–64. Springer, Heidelberg (2013). https://doi.org/10.1007/978-3-642-37682-5_5
9. Kordy, B., Piètre-Cambacédès, L., Schweitzer, P.: Dag-based attack and defense modeling: don't miss the forest for the attack trees. Comput. Sci. Rev. **13–14**, 1–38 (2014)
10. Kordy, B., Pouly, M., Schweitzer, P.: Computational aspects of attack–defense trees. In: Bouvry, P., Kłopotek, M.A., Leprévost, F., Marciniak, M., Mykowiecka, A., Rybiński, H. (eds.) SIIS 2011. LNCS, vol. 7053, pp. 103–116. Springer, Heidelberg (2012). https://doi.org/10.1007/978-3-642-25261-7_8
11. Kordy, B., Wideł, W.: How well can i secure my system? In: Polikarpova, N., Schneider, S. (eds.) IFM 2017. LNCS, vol. 10510, pp. 332–347. Springer, Cham (2017). https://doi.org/10.1007/978-3-319-66845-1_22

12. Mauw, S., Oostdijk, M.: Foundations of attack trees. In: Won, D.H., Kim, S. (eds.) ICISC 2005. LNCS, vol. 3935, pp. 186–198. Springer, Heidelberg (2006). https://doi.org/10.1007/11734727_17
13. Paul, S.: Towards automating the construction & maintenance of attack trees: a feasibility study. In: GraMSec@ETAPS. EPTCS, vol. 148, pp. 31–46 (2014)
14. Roy, A., Kim, D.S., Trivedi, K.S.: Attack countermeasure trees (ACT): towards unifying the constructs of attack and defense trees. Secur. Commun. Netw. **5**(8), 929–943 (2012)
15. Schneier, B.: Attack trees. Dr Dobb's J. Softw. Tools **24**, 21–29 (1999)
16. Vigo, R., Nielson, F., Nielson, H.R.: Automated generation of attack trees. In: CSF, pp. 337–350. IEEE Computer Society (2014)
17. Wesley, K.J., Anbiah, R.R.J.: Cracking PKZIP files' password. A to Z of C, pp. 610–615 (2008)

Visualizing Cyber Security Risks
with Bow-Tie Diagrams

Karin Bernsmed[1], Christian Frøystad[1], Per Håkon Meland[1,3(✉)],
Dag Atle Nesheim[2], and Ørnulf Jan Rødseth[2]

[1] SINTEF Digital, Trondheim, Norway
{karin.bernsmed,christian.froystad,per.h.meland}@sintef.no
[2] SINTEF Ocean, Trondheim, Norway
{dag.atle.nesheim,ornulfjan.rodseth}@sintef.no
[3] Norwegian University of Science and Technology, Trondheim, Norway

Abstract. Safety and security risks are usually analyzed independently, by different people using different tools. Consequently, the system analyst may fail to realize cyber attacks as a contributing factor to safety impacts or, on the contrary, design overly secure systems that will compromise the performance of critical operations. This paper presents a methodology for visualizing and assessing security risks by means of bow-tie diagrams, which are commonly used within safety assessments. We outline how malicious activities, random failures, security countermeasures and safety barriers can be visualized using a common graphical notation and propose a method for quantifying risks based on threat likelihood and consequence severity. The methodology is demonstrated using a case study from maritime communication. Our main conclusion is that adding security concepts to the bow-ties is a promising approach, since this is a notation that high-risk industries are already familiar with. However, their advantage as easy-to-grasp visual models should be maintained, hence complexity needs to be kept low.

Keywords: Security · Safety · Risk assessment · Bow-tie diagrams
Maritime communication

1 Introduction

One of the least understood challenges for cyber physical systems (CFS) is uncertainty in the environment, cyber attacks and errors in connected physical devices [46]. The tight coupling between the cyber and physical world leads to new forms of risks that have not been considered adequately, such that the cyber element adversely affects the physical environment [4]. Safety risks, where the system can harm the environment in which it operates, and security risks, where the environment (e.g. malicious actors and other systems) can harm the system, tend to be analyzed independently [42], by different people using different standards, tools and notations. As pointed out by Sun et al. [50], safety

© Springer International Publishing AG 2018
P. Liu et al. (eds.): GraMSec 2017, LNCS 10744, pp. 38–56, 2018.
https://doi.org/10.1007/978-3-319-74860-3_3

and security goals interact synergistically or conflictingly, and should therefore be evaluated together. If not, conflicts can result in either (a) overly secure systems that compromise the reliability of critical operations or (b) create insecure systems where back-doors are easily found.

An inherent challenge when combining safety and security in an analysis is the increased complexity. Graphical visualizations are helpful when you want to make complex problems easier to understand and navigate [20]. The purpose of this paper is to bridge the gap between safety and security during risk assessment by utilizing the graphical bow-tie diagram methodology [11,14,15,25]. Bow-tie diagrams are very suitable for communicating the results of a risk assessment to different stakeholders within an organization due to the clear diversification of causes and effects for a given unwanted event, and to clarify which barriers have (or have not) been implemented. Bow-tie analysis, which includes the generation of one or more bow-tie diagrams, is a common approach to map the risks associated with unwanted events in, for example, the oil and gas industry. Our approach is to take advantage of the familiarity of this graphical notation among industry experts, analyze use cases within the safety-critical maritime sector, and try to answer the following research questions:

1. How can bow-tie diagrams be extended to include security considerations in addition to safety considerations?
2. How can the likelihood of cause and severity of cyber attacks be visualized in bow-tie diagrams?

In order to answer these questions, we apply a *design science* research methodology [48], with focus on the extended bow-tie diagram methodology as an artefact with a high priority on relevance for the cyber physical domain. Evaluation is done through analysis of descriptive, constructed use cases for maritime service scenarios to demonstrate its utility [21].

Our goal has not been to create yet another theoretical model for risk assessment, but to propose a solution to a real, existing problem we experience in the maritime domain when introducing new technology that may have effect both safety and security. This follows the research paradigm of *pragmatism* [19], which is associated with action, intervention and constructive knowledge. Furthermore, it should be based on real problems and have practical usefulness beyond the specific case studies.

This paper is organized as follows. Section 2 presents related work. In Sect. 3, we introduce the marine communication case study in which we have developed the proposed methodology. Section 4 explains the concepts and terminology that we use and Sect. 5 presents the proposed bow-tie risk assessment methodology, which is exemplified in Sect. 6. Finally, in Sect. 7 we discuss the results and Sect. 8 concludes the paper.

2   Related Work

The most common way of documenting and visualizing risks is in a risk matrix, where the seriousness of the evaluated risks can be easily compared based on the combination of likelihood and consequence. The US Air Force developed the Risk Matrix Approach (RMA) [18] in 1995, and after that it has spread out to a multitude of domains, such as weapons manufacturing, finance, transport and project management [38]. Still, RMA is a very simplistic notation that does not properly visualize the causes of the risks, and how to address them.

Within the field of security, there are many more specialized modelling notations that are in general concerned about *"identifying system behavior, including any security defenses; the system adversary's power; and the properties that constitute system security"* [5]. Security modelling comes in many different forms and flavors, but they all share the common aim of understanding security issues so they can be dealt with effectively. Which one to choose usually depends on what the analyst wants to focus on, level of abstraction/details and personal preference (e.g. familiarity). To quote Shostack [47]: *"different diagrams will help in different circumstances"*. For instance, an attack tree [31,45] is a tree-based notation showing how an adversary can choose among different paths or branches to obtain an overall attack goal. The attack-defense trees [26] extend this notation by also adding preventive nodes, which again can be attacked by attack nodes. Attack graphs [40] and vulnerability cause graphs [8] are examples of a graph-based notation used for analyzing vulnerabilities, and CORAS [30] contains several graphical notations for a risk analysis process. There also exist different types of security extensions to more general purpose graphical modelling notations, such as Data flow diagrams [47], UML [24,49] and BPMN [32].

For safety, there are many notations that go even further back in history. The fault-tree analysis (FTA) method was developed in the 1960s for safety and reliability [29], and a recent survey of usage is provided by Ruijters and Stoelinga [43]. Event tree analysis (ETA) is an established technique originating from the nuclear industry [3], and is used to analyze how a series of events can lead to a potential accident scenario. Similarly to ETA, cause-consequence diagrams (CCA) [39] are also used to analyze safety causes.

When considering safety and security in combination, there have been quite a few related studies. For instance, Winther et al. [52] show how to handle security issues as part of HAZOP studies, which is a systematic analysis on how deviations from the design specifications in a system can arise, and whether these deviations can result in hazards. Raspotnig et al. [42] have use UML-based models within a combined safety and security assessment process to elicitate requirements. Bieber and Brunel [7] show how common system models for security and safety can be used for airworthiness certification within aviation. Kumar and Stoelinga [28] have married fault and attack trees so that both safety and security can be considered in combination. Further examples of methods, models, tools and techniques in the intersection of safety and security can be found in the surveys by Zalewski et al. [53], Piètre-Cambacédès and Bouissou [41], Chockalingam et al. [12], as well as Kriaa et al. [27].

There have been several efforts by practitioners related to the use of bow-tie diagrams for cyber security, but they differ from what we are presenting in this paper in several ways. For instance, a report from SANS Institute [35] outlines how a bow-tie risk assessment methodology can be applied to conduct a cyber security risk assessment in an engineering environment. There is no change to the diagram notation as such, but they argue that *"the first step towards obtaining Engineering community buy-in"* is to compare concepts from security to bow-tie, and basically evaluate cyber threats in the same manner as hazards. They also include considerations related to actors and motivation, but this is done in order to reduce the number of possible scenarios before modelling, and not part of the notation itself. A report from DNV-GL [16] also proposes the use of bow-tie diagrams as a key component in a cyber security assessment program for the maritime sector. Here, standard safety notation is used, and the focus is on visualization of barriers. Quantitative indicators are explicitly left out, and even though vulnerability consideration is central in the overall assessment process, this is not included as diagram concepts. Similarly, the *Bow Tie for Cyber Security* series [22] at PI Square gives numerous examples where the standard notation is used for security. The US Coastguard has also published a report [34] on how to use bow-ties to identify preventive and responsive responses to cyber attacks for marine transportation systems. Their examples are on a very high abstraction level, where causes are for instance *hactivists, technical errors* and *insider threats*. Two additional examples of bow-tie diagrams that visualize IT security risks are provided in [10]. The focus here is more on chains of barriers, although it seems like vulnerabilities are represented as escalation factors.

3 Case Study: Maritime Communication

In order to give a better understanding of the methodology and examples used in the later sections, we would like to explain our maritime case study and why security is a growing concern intertwined with safety in this domain.

Shipping has become increasingly dependent on digital data exchanges. As dependence grows and the functions supported becomes more entangled in the ship operations and critical interactions with on-shore authorities, the need to consider consequences of digital attacks on the data exchanges also increases. This calls for a more systematic approach to maritime cyber security.

In 2011, ENISA pointed out [13] that the *"awareness on cyber security needs and challenges in the maritime sector is currently low to non-existent"*. Come 2015, the Lysne commission of Norway [2] reaffirmed this message. The lack of general awareness regarding cyber security, makes the industry more vulnerable to attacks.

Maritime navigational systems of today rely heavily on Global Navigation Satellite Systems (GNSS), such as GPS and GLONASS, to navigate safely, avoid collisions or groundings and for voyage optimization. The GNSS signals available for civilians are unencrypted and unauthenticated and are easily jammed or even spoofed [6]. Automatic Identification System (AIS) is used to identify other ships and their intentions, but can also be used to transmit short safety messages, e.g. to act as virtual aids to navigations. AIS is becoming part of the more extensive VHF Data Exchange System (VDES), which will extend the use of AIS to include even more digital information exchanges. The AIS messages are unencrypted and unauthenticated, and relatively easy to jam or spoof. Furthermore, IOActive [44] conducted tests on SATCOM firmware from multiple vendors and found vulnerabilities such as hardcoded credentials, undocumented protocols, insecure protocols, backdoors, and weak password reset. Our attention is on digital data exchanges between ships and between ship and shore and the possible consequences of cyber-attacks on these exchanges.

Ships spend most of their time at sea with a minimal crew, and remote monitoring and maintenance is becoming more and more common. If not organized in an appropriate way, this could allow an attacker extensive and easy access to the systems on the ship. Additionally, there are multiple actors connected to the network on-board a ship, including passengers, crew, and operational systems. These actors have different requirements regarding safety, security and separation. For instance, some vessels have physically separated networks, while others only provide logically separated networks. The mechanisms for logical separation of networks vary, but are often just a simple firewall.

4   Concepts and Terminology of Bow-Ties

A bow-tie diagram is shaped like a bow-tie, where the central *knot* typically represent an accident scenario, or as we will later refer to, an unwanted event. The diagram can be seen as a combination of a fault tree and an event tree [17], where the left side shows which causes can lead up to the accident, and the right side the potential effects once the accident has occurred. As pointed out by the tool provider CGE Risk Management[1], the power of this diagram is that it gives a clear distinction between proactive and reactive risk management, in combination with an overview of multiple plausible scenarios.

To combine security with bow-tie safety assessment, we need to synchronize the terminology and concepts from the safety and security domains. The bow-tie diagram in Fig. 1 shows the traditional layout, notation and concepts from safety assessments in the upper left horizontal part (*cause, barrier, escalation factor*), with concepts we introduce from security in the lower left horizontal part (*threat, security control*). *Hazard* and *unwanted event* are mainly from safety, while *asset* comes from security. On the right side of the figure, the *consequence* concept is shared between safety and security, and can be remedied with safety barriers and security controls, often in combination. We describe these concepts further below.

As defined by International Maritime Organization (IMO) [23], the first step in a Formal Safety Assessment (FSA) [23] is to identify all potential hazards that can contribute to accidents. A *hazard* is a potential to threaten human life, health, property or the environment. Examples of maritime hazards are off-shore operations, hazardous substances and sources of ignition onboard and external hazards, such as storms, lightening and other ships. Hazards may give rise to scenarios in which people, the environment or property will be damaged. The list

---

[1] https://www.cgerisk.com/knowledge-base/risk-assessment/thebowtiemethod.

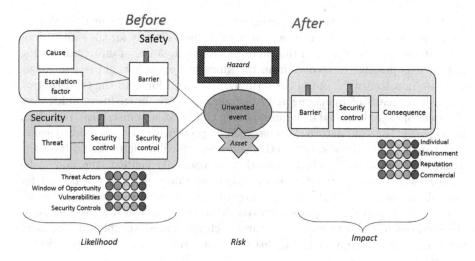

Fig. 1. Our combined approach for modelling safety and security in a bow-tie diagram.

of identified hazards and their associated scenarios will be used as input to the safety risk assessment. Basically, a hazard can be anything with the potential to cause harm, but which is also necessary to perform business. From a risk analysis perspective, the hazard needs to be controlled so that unwanted events will not occur.

An *unwanted event* in safety assessment, also known as top event, loss event, or loss of control, represents what will happen if one loses control over a hazard, which again can have severe *consequences*. An unwanted event is typically caused by an accident, or a random failure. In security assessments, the equivalent is often called *incident*, something that typically affects the confidentiality, integrity or availability of a critical system, data, or processes necessary for the operation of the business. Such incident may have malicious or accidental causes. In our model, we are using the term unwanted event for anything that can cause harm to the asset(s) associated to the hazard, regardless if they stem from safety or security causes. In real life, it is often a combination of different causes that lead to unwanted events, therefore we want to evaluate them together.

Related to security, an *asset* is anything that has value to an organization. The ISO/IEC 27005 standard [1] distinguishes between primary assets, which are core business processes and their corresponding information, whilst supporting assets are those required to be in place to support the activities of the primary assets. Typical examples of (primary) assets in a maritime context are Maritime Safety Information (MSI), ship certificates, and electronic nautical charts. Asset is not a concept that is used in traditional safety assessment, but is usually the first thing to identify when it comes to security assessments. Therefore, we include a mapping between hazard and which assets will be damaged in case the unwanted event occurs.

A *threat* is anything that can potentially cause an unwanted event [1]. Within safety assessments, the term *cause* is very often used directly for the same meaning. A *barrier* is a mechanism that aims to interrupt causes of unwanted events, or that it is possible to recover from the unwanted event without severe consequences. In a security context, the term barrier corresponds to the term *control*, which is a means of managing risk, including policies, procedures, guidelines, practices or organizational structures, which can be of administrative, technical, management, or legal nature [1]. These can be preventive controls used to avoid, detect or mitigate threats, or reactive controls, which are intended to limit the damage caused by an incident. Note that in a security context, the word safeguard, mitigations, or countermeasure, are sometimes used as a synonym for control. An *escalation factor* is anything that may cause a safety barrier to fail. There is no one-to-one mapping between this concept and security terminology, however, to succeed with a threat, a threat actor will need to exploit one or more vulnerabilities, which often is only feasible at a certain point of time (window of opportunity).

In our model, we use threats to explicitly represent malicious activities, while causes are related to traditional safety accidents. We continue to use both barrier and security control for both sides of the bow-tie, though they may have the same implementation (e.g. through redundancy). Note that there can be chains of both barriers or security controls (the latter is illustrated in Fig. 1). Such chains follow the principle of *defence in depth* - if the first barrier fails or control is circumvented, there is another one still operating.

We also introduce a set of color coded indicators for each threat branch on the left side, and for each consequence branch on the right side of the diagram. These indicators are meant to help visualize the likelihood of an unwanted event, and the severity of a consequence in similar manner that is used for risk matrices. This allows us to adopt the RMA framework as described in Sect. 2 as apart of the notation, and make use of the color indicators that the industry community is already familiar with. For a threat branch, we associate indicators related to *threat actors, window of opportunity, vulnerabilities* and *security controls*. For instance, the threat actors indicator informs whether or not it is likely that there exists groups or individuals who have the competence, resources and motivation necessary to perform an attack and instantiate the threat. Similarly, we indicate the likely existence of the other indicators. For a consequence branch, the indicators represent the severity of the impact related to *individuals*, the *environment*, the *reputation* of a company and *commercial* (monetary) loss.

In the next section, we focus on how to identify what color should be used for each indicator, and how to quantify the overall risk of a bow-tie diagram for an unwanted event.

5   Risk Assessment

As illustrated in Fig. 1, the risk of an unwanted event will be a combination of the likelihood and the impact of the unwanted event. Our contribution in this paper focuses on a subset of all potential unwanted events, which are those caused by hostile cyber attacks. In our model, an unwanted event U will be a function of one or more threats. Each unwanted event will lead to one or more consequences C, where each identified consequence is associated with a corresponding impact (i.e. severity, or loss,) value L. The risk R associated with a certain unwanted event U, which we denote $R(U)$, will then be approximated as the probability that the unwanted event occurs, i.e. $p(U)$, multiplied with the worst-case consequence impact value that has been identified, which we denote L_C, and the likelihood that this consequence occurs, i.e. $p(C)$. The formal expression for this is

$$R(U) \approx p(U) \times L_C \times p(C) \tag{1}$$

To quantify the risk of an unwanted event, we hence need to assess (1) the probability of the unwanted event (as a function of one or more identified threats) and (2) the impact value and probability of the worst-case consequence of the unwanted event.

5.1   Assessing the Left Side of the Bow-Tie (Cause)

Assessing the probability of a cyber attack is a notoriously difficult problem. In our model, we assume that all the threats are *mutually independent*. This means that all the identified cyber attacks will be executed independently of each other and that any of them can manifest itself and cause the unwanted event during the time for which the system, or service, is being assessed. Under this assumption, the probability of the unwanted event U can be computed as

$$p(U) = p(at\ least\ one\ T_i\ occurs) = 1 - \prod_{i=1}^{n}(1 - p(T_i)) \tag{2}$$

where $p(T_i)$, $i = 1 \ldots n$, is the probability of threat T_i. The problem will hence be reduced to assessing the probabilities, or likelihoods, of the individual threats that have been identified.

Compared to more simplistic probability models, in which the threats are modelled as mutually exclusive (i.e. $p(U)$ will be computed as a sum of the individual threats), the proposed Eq. 2 is much more realistic, since it allows more threats to manifest within the same time interval, which corresponds more closely to the real world. By using Eq. 2, we can also model cases in which multiple attackers work simultaneously to exploit different vulnerabilities, and cases where one attacker exploits all the vulnerabilities he can find. However, the assumption that all the threats are independent may not always be true. In particular, it is questionable whether one can model scenarios in which an attacker is aware of all the potential threats that can be carried out, since this may affect the probabilities of the individual threats, hence violating the independence assumption. Another issue may be that, for some unwanted events, once the unwanted event has happened, it will be less likely to happen again due to increased awareness. This is a common situation in an security context, where threats are manifesting themselves through the actions of human beings rather than through random failures, and the malicious actors will lose their *element of surprise*.

Another characteristic of Eq. 2 is that the more threats one identifies, the higher the probability of the unwanted event. A side effect of using this model could therefore be that a more thorough risk assessor, who manages to identify more threats, will also end up with a higher probability of the unwanted event. However, the influence of the number of identified threats will be negligible, as long as both the threat probabilities and the number of identified threats are sufficiently small (which is the case in most real-life scenarios).

In our opinion, in spite of the aforementioned issues, this is the simplest and most straightforward alternative we have for computing the probability of an unwanted event $p(U)$ as a function of the identified threats. This same model is frequently used in system reliability analysis, in which a system analysis models the system as a set of components, assesses the individual failure rates of the components and evaluates the effect of the total system reliability. In our case, we model malicious threats rather than random failures, however, the underlying line of thought is similar; we are considering multiple sources of error that can cause the system, or service, to fail, regardless of cause. Note that, when using this approach, care must be taken to ensure that all the identified threats are independent and, as explained above, the risk assessor must understand the characteristics of the underlying mathematical model.

Assessing the Threat Actors, Window of Opportunity, Vulnerabilities and Security Countermeasures. We move on to describe how factors, such as the actors who pose the threat, the needed window of opportunity for the threat to be successful and any vulnerabilities and security countermeasures present in the system can be assessed and visualized. As explained in Sect. 4, we use color coded indicators to represent these factors in the graphical model.

Threat Actors. Threat actors are the attackers who will represent a security risk against the system that is being assessed. Threat actors can be classified in terms of characteristics, such as skill, capabilities, resources, intent and access [9]. The risk assessor can estimate the threat actors by using the values of Table 1.

Window of Opportunity. The "window of opportunity" depends on how often/long the threat actor theoretically could gain access to the target (system or data) and how often/long the target of interest is within reach of the attacker. The risk assessor can estimate the window of opportunity by using Table 2.

Vulnerabilities. No system is perfect, nor are the security measures that are put in place to prevent the threat from manifesting itself. Vulnerabilities can range from simple programming errors to large design flaws of software, hardware and processes. The presence of vulnerabilities increases the likelihood of a threat manifesting. The risk assessor can estimate the existence of vulnerabilities by using Table 3.

Table 1. Color coding for representing the threat actors

Threat actors

Dangerousness	Description	Color coding
Severe	There are threat actors highly capable of pursuing this threat	
High	There are threat actors capable of pursuing this threat	
Moderate	There are threat actors somewhat capable of pursuing this threat	
Low	There are threat actors interested in pursuing this threat, but their capability is limited	
None	There are threat actors interested in pursuing this threat, but they are not capable of acting on this interest	

Table 2. Color coding for representing the window of opportunity

Window of opportunity

Window	Description	Color coding
Always	This threat is always possible.	
Frequent	This threat is frequently possible (there will be an opportunity about once every week).	
Rare	This threat is rarely possible (there will be an opportunity about once every year).	
Extremely rare	This threat is extremely rarely possible (there will be an opportunity about once every 10th year).	
Never	This threat is never possible.	

Table 3. Color coding for representing the presence of vulnerabilities

Vulnerabilities

Vulnerability	Description	Color coding
Known easy	One or more known vulnerabilities exist, which are easy to exploit.	
Known-difficult	One or more known vulnerabilities exist, but they are either not publicly known, or they are difficult to exploit.	
Unknown	No known vulnerabilities exist, however, vulnerabilities are expected to appear in the near future.	
Very unlikely	It is very unlikely that the system has, or will have, any vulnerabilities in the near future.	
Formally proven absence	Formal methods, or the like, have been applied to demonstrate that no vulnerabilities exist. It is extremely unlike that vulnerabilities will appear in the near future.	

Security Controls. Finally, the risk assessor will need to input information about the existence of security control and assess their effectiveness (Table 4).

Assessing the Threats. For each threat T_i and preventive security controls $Ctrl_1 \ldots Ctrl_m$, the risk assessor choose values for *Threat Actors*, *Window of Opportunity*, *Vulnerabilities* and *Security Controls* according to Tables 1, 2, 3 and 4. This is visualized as extended traffic lights as shown in Fig. 2. In addition to the traffic lights, the relevant controls for each threat are shown as separate boxes to give an overview of which threats are mitigated by which controls.

The visualization in Fig. 2 serves as domain specific assistance to the risk assessor when assessing $p(T_i)$, $i = 1 \ldots n$, i.e. the probability of each of the identified threats. We do not dictate exactly how this estimation should be done in practice, as there are different ways of doing threat prediction, and any model depends a lot on the available information used as input. When working with maritime threat scenarios, we have been using averages from generic threat intelligence data, and then adjusted these based on the case specific domain data using expert opinions.

5.2   Assessing the Right Side of the Bow-Tie (Consequence)

The consequence of an evaluated risk can manifest itself in many ways. FSA normally only consider individual risk and societal risk which represents the main scope of the Maritime Safety Committee in IMO where the FSA was developed. We have found it useful to also include other aspects, such as the environmental (pollution), commercial (monetary losses) and reputational (loss of confidence by e.g. customers, business partners, bank, insurance, regulatory bodies) damage caused by each identified unwanted event in our model. As an example of

Table 4. Color coding for representing the effectiveness of security controls

Security controls

Control	Description	Color coding
Known to be ineffective	No security countermeasure exists, or, one or more security countermeasures exists but they are known to be ineffective.	
Probably not effective	One or more security countermeasures exists but they can be circumvented.	
Effective	One or more security countermeasures exists, which are believed to be effective.	
Very effective	One or more security countermeasures exists, which are very effective.	
Formally proven effective	Formal methods, or the like, have been applied to demonstrate that existing security mechanisms are sufficient and work as intended.	

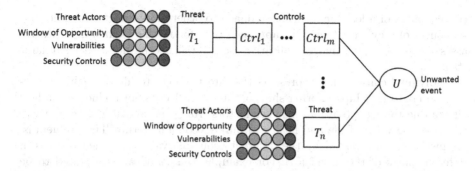

Fig. 2. The relation between an unwanted event, threats, threat actors, window of opportunity, vulnerabilities and (preventive) security controls

reputational damage, the Paris MoU[2] publishes a black list for all ships depending on results from Port State Controls. Once your ship is on this list, you are much more eligible for inspections and your operation may suffer.

Table 5. Consequence type and severity level

Consequences

Level	Individual	Environment	Reputation	Commercial	Color coding
Cata-strophic	Multiple deaths	Uncontained release with potential for very large environmental impact	International coverage, unrecoverable damage	$ 50 000 k	
Critical	One death	Uncontained release with potential for major environmental impact	National and some international coverage, impact lasting more than a year	$ 5 000 k	
Moderate	Multiple severe injuries	Uncontained release with potential for moderate environmental impact	National media coverage, impact lasting more than 3 months	$ 500 k	
Negligible	One minor injury	On site release contained without external assistance	Local complaint/ recognition, impact less than one month	$ 5 k	
None	No injuries	No effect	No damage	$ 1 k or less	

The risk assessor can estimate the consequence of each identified unwanted event using Table 5. One obvious problem with comparing these different outcomes is to compare consequences for life and health with purely economic or environmental damages. However, it is possible to compare the economic

---

[2] https://www.parismou.org/.

consequences of a lost life or health damage to other more direct economic consequences of a cyber attack. Our approach is to follow this (semi-) quantitative assessment, and leave a more qualitative societal risk acceptance analysis to later stages.

Individual consequence represents the direct danger to life or health of persons on board the ship, on other ships or on shore. It does not include secondary effects due to, e.g. pollution or other factors. As noted above, it is not trivial to assess the value of life and health in purely economic terms. The problem is, for instance, complicated by the different economic values assigned to lives in different parts of the world [51]. For example, this value was estimated to be at USD 0.8 million in South Korea in the year 2000, and at USD 9.7 million in Japan the same year. In our model, we will use the mean value of USD 5 million for one life as baseline. This represents the mean value from [51], but not weighted according to population in the different areas.

We follow the defined severity levels for economical loss as shown in Table 5. This maps critical to the above value corresponding to loss of one life and adjusts other levels accordingly.

The inclusion of reputational and economical loss in the risk assessment has been a matter of some discussion. Our rationale for doing this and not only focusing on individual and environmental risks, is that in many cases the motivation for and the consequences of a successful cyber-attack is likely to be much higher in the commercial domain than in the general safety domains. This assumption is strengthened by todays ship bridge operational regime where all received information must be checked against other sources of information, including making visual assessment of the ships situation. Thus, including commercial consequences will likely lead to more risks being assessed as not acceptable and by that lead to a higher overall safety level.

6   Use Case Example: Navigational Information Update

In this section, we demonstrate the use of our proposed methodology to represent unwanted events in a bow-tie diagram and to assess the corresponding risk. The context is cyber security threats in the maritime communication case study introduced in Sect. 3. The use case we investigate is called *Navigational Information Update*. The objective here is to illustrate the visualization, and not to present the complete description.

Ships are required to keep critical electronic databases up to date. Such databases include electronic charts and lists of navigation signals. Updating can be done by requesting updates as the voyage progresses and getting data from the chart provider. In the near future, this will be implemented over an Internet based service via satellite or other high capacity carriers. Failing to get the right data can cause safety hazards as well as a danger of detention by the Port State Control in the next port. In addition, some of this information is provided by commercial companies that need to protect the supplied information from copying to non-paying ships.

In this example, we address electronic ship navigation as a potential hazard and we want to assess the risk of the unwanted event "Ship receives incorrect updates". The affected asset is the navigation data that is being transferred. Figures 3 and 4 illustrate the identified threats, security controls and potential consequences that we have identified in our analysis.

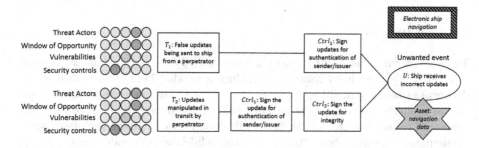

Fig. 3. The left hand threat side with preventive controls for the unwanted event "Ship receives incorrect updates"

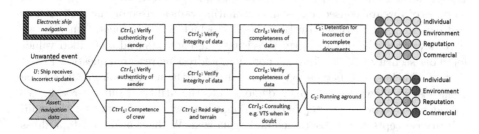

Fig. 4. The right hand consequence side with reactive controls for the unwanted event "Ship receives incorrect updates"

To compute the risk, we need to assess the probabilities of all the identified threats, as well as the impact value and probability of the worst-case consequence identified for this unwanted event. The assessment of a risk assessor, who has considered the threat actors, window of opportunity, vulnerabilities and security controls, is used as a source for this threat prediction. If we for instance set probability of threat $T_1 = 0.45$ and probability of threat $T_2 = 0.23$, and then apply Eq. 2, we can compute the probability of the unwanted event:

$$p(U) = 1 - (1 - p(T_1)) \times (1 - p(T_2)) = 1 - (1 - 0.45) \times (1 - 0.23) \approx 0.57 \quad (3)$$

Furthermore, let's assume the consequence $C_1 = 0.3$, $p(C_1) = 0.5$, $C_2 = 0.7$ and that $p(C_2) = 0.2$. By applying Eq. 1, we find that the risk of the unwanted event to be:

$$R(U) \approx 0.57 \times 0.7 \times 0.2 \approx 0.08 \quad (4)$$

This number does not mean much by itself, but can be used as a relative number when comparing with other unwanted events, and to justify the addition of barriers/controls.

As illustrated by this simple example, the bow-tie diagram provides an illustrative overview over the identified threats, security controls and potential consequences of the unwanted event.

7   Discussion

To make useful cyber security visualizations with bow-tie diagrams, we needed to identify which security concepts to include and what kind of quantified input data would be meaningful as input to the diagrams. In our case, we have done this in separate processes, one for each side of the diagrams. For the left side (potential causes and threats, including likelihood), security and domain experts participated in a workshop setting (n = 10), while the right side (consequences and their severity) was evaluated by representatives from maritime industry and coastal authorities through an online survey (n = 18). Both groups were working with the same set of seventeen service scenarios for maritime communication, and twenty use cases that overlapped between the services. Note that none of these groups worked directly with bow-ties as a graphical notation, but were focused on types of threats, consequences and estimating values based on their experience and expert opinion. Based on these results, which are documented in [36], we have developed the methodology for visualizing concepts and quantified values for cyber security with the bow-tie notation, addressing research question 1 from Sect. 1. This has then been applied to a sample of the use cases from the service scenarios, as shown in Sect. 6, to demonstrate the utility of our approach. We consider this to be a first step of evaluation, where we have shown that the main security concepts can be contained and visualized. We have also tried to address research question 2 by adding color coded indicators to the diagrams, which are there to justify the likelihood and impact of an unwanted event. However, further work is needed to do in-depth evaluation on how this is perceived and found useful by other analysts, stakeholders from the maritime domain, as well as stakeholders from other safety domains.

Some general observations we have made when working with bow-tie modelling is that they are very suitable to show the broadness and distribution of different causes and consequences for unwanted events, along with protective and reactive barriers. However, this approach also has its limitations. For instance, a bow-tie diagram will struggle to represent the depth and details of how attacks can be performed. Furthermore, a single cause or threat can lead to different unwanted events, therefore, there can easily be repetition/redundancy between a collection of bow-ties addressing different hazards. We therefore recommend that the diagrams are complemented with more established methods for threat modelling, and that these are reused and referred to from nodes within the bow-ties. This can for instance be fault-trees for safety, or generic attack trees or misuse cases for security, that Meland et al. [33] have already showed can be shared and reused between different projects, organizations or domains with benefit. A prerequisite to realize this would be modelling tool support beyond simple drawing tools, as well as collaboration and willingness to share knowledge between risk analyst addressing both safety and security.

To capture more security related information within a bow-tie, it is also possible to add specific nodes in the model for concepts such as threat actors and vulnerabilities. We believe that this would lead to an unnecessary complexity of the diagram, and it would lose some of its advantage as an easy to grasp graphical representation. The number and types of nodes would increase, and there would in many cases be many-to-many relationships between threat actors, threats, vulnerabilities, and security controls. Therefore, we rather use the more simplified notation of indicators related threat and consequence branches, that sums up for instance whether it is likely there are many relevant threat actors.

8 Conclusion

Safety assessments with bow-tie diagrams give a good pictorial understanding of major risks and how they are controlled. This is a technique that many of the high-risk industries are already familiar with, such as oil and gas, mining, aviation, maritime and public health services [37]. Due to the increasing connectivity of cyber physical systems, these are the same industries that are now becoming more and more exposed to cyber attacks. To avoid conflicting goals and requirements between safety and security, we believe that adding security to the bow-tie notation is more accommodating than inducing yet another specialized, separate modelling technique that tries to capture all aspects of safety and security. Bow-tie diagrams are meant to be easy to understand, and by combining a minimal set of security concepts along with associated indicators, we can show both safety and security considerations without overflowing the diagrams.

Acknowledgments. The research leading to these results has been performed as a part of the Cyber Security in Merchant Shipping (CySiMS) project, which received funding from the Research Council of Norway under Grant No. 256508, and the SafeCOP-project, which received funding from the ECSEL Joint Undertaking under Grant No. 692529. We appreciate all the feedback and comments from Professor Guttorm Sindre at NTNU and anonymous reviewers that helped us improve this paper.

References

1. ISO/IEC 27005 Information technology - Security techniques - Information security risk management. Technical rep. (2008). http://www.iso.org/iso/catalogue_detail? csnumber=56742
2. Digitale Sarbarheter Maritim Sektor: Technical rep. (2015). https://www. regjeringen.no/contentassets/fe88e9ea8a354bd1b63bc0022469f644/no/sved/7.pdf
3. Andrews, J.D., Moss, T.R.: Reliability and Risk Assessment. Wiley-Blackwell, Hoboken (2002)

4. Banerjee, A., Venkatasubramanian, K.K., Mukherjee, T., Gupta, S.K.S.: Ensuring safety, security, and sustainability of mission-critical cyber-physical systems. Proc. IEEE **100**(1), 283–299 (2012)
5. Bau, J., Mitchell, J.C.: Security modeling and analysis. IEEE Secur. Priv. **9**(3), 18–25 (2011)
6. Bhatti, J., Humphreys, T.: Hostile control of ships via false GPS signals: demonstration and detection. Navigation **64**(1), 51–66 (2016)
7. Bieber, P., Brunel, J.: From safety models to security models: preliminary lessons learnt. In: Bondavalli, A., Ceccarelli, A., Ortmeier, F. (eds.) SAFECOMP 2014. LNCS, vol. 8696, pp. 269–281. Springer, Cham (2014). https://doi.org/10.1007/978-3-319-10557-4_30
8. Byers, D., Ardi, S., Shahmehri, N., Duma, C.: Modeling software vulnerabilities with vulnerability cause graphs. In: Proceedings of the International Conference on Software Maintenance (ICSM 2006), pp. 411–422 (2006)
9. Casey, T.: Threat agent library helps identify information security risks (2007). https://communities.intel.com/docs/DOC-1151
10. CGE Risk Management Solutions: Using bowties for it security (2017). https://www.cgerisk.com/knowledge-base/risk-assessment/using-bowties-for-it-security
11. Chevreau, F.R., Wybo, J.L., Cauchois, D.: Organizing learning processes on risks by using the bow-tie representation. J. Hazard. Mater. **130**(3), 276–283 (2006)
12. Chockalingam, S., Hadziosmanovic, D., Pieters, W., Teixeira, A., van Gelder, P.: Integrated safety and security risk assessment methods: a survey of key characteristics and applications. arXiv preprint arXiv:1707.02140 (2017)
13. Cimpean, D., Meire, J., Bouckaert, V., Vande Casteele, S., Pelle, A., Hellebooge, L.: Analysis of cyber security aspects in the maritime sector. ENISA, 19 December (2011). https://www.enisa.europa.eu/publications/cyber-security-aspects-in-the-maritime-sector-1
14. Cockshott, J.: Probability bow-ties: a transparent risk management tool. Process Saf. Environ. Prot. **83**(4), 307–316 (2005)
15. De Dianous, V., Fiévez, C.: Aramis project: a more explicit demonstration of risk control through the use of bow-tie diagrams and the evaluation of safety barrier performance. J. Hazard. Mater. **130**(3), 220–233 (2006)
16. DNV-GL AS: Recommended practice. Cyber security resilience management for ships and mobile offshore units in operation (2016). DNVGL-RP-0496
17. Ferdous, R., Khan, F., Sadiq, R., Amyotte, P., Veitch, B.: Analyzing system safety and risks under uncertainty using a bow-tie diagram: an innovative approach. Process Saf. Environ. Prot. **91**(1), 1–18 (2013)
18. Garvey, P.R., Lansdowne, Z.F.: Risk matrix: an approach for identifying, assessing, and ranking program risks. Air Force J. Logistics **22**(1), 18–21 (1998)
19. Goldkuhl, G.: Pragmatism vs interpretivism in qualitative information systems research. Eur. J. Inf. Syst. **21**(2), 135–146 (2012)
20. Hall, P., Heath, C., Coles-Kemp, L.: Critical visualization: a case for rethinking how we visualize risk and security. J. Cybersecurity **1**(1), 93–108 (2015)
21. Hevner, A.R., March, S.T., Park, J., Ram, S.: Design science in information systems research. MIS Q. **28**(1), 75–105 (2004). http://dl.acm.org/citation.cfm?id=2017212.2017217
22. Paul, H.: Security: Bow Tie for Cyber Security (0x01): Ho... — PI Square (2016). https://pisquare.osisoft.com/groups/security/blog/2016/08/02/bow-tie-for-cyber-security-0x01-how-to-tie-a-cyber-bow-tie
23. IMO: Revised guidelines for Formal Safety Assessment (FSA) for use in the IMO rule-making process (2013)

24. Jürjens, J.: UMLsec: extending UML for secure systems development. In: Jézéquel, J.-M., Hussmann, H., Cook, S. (eds.) UML 2002. LNCS, vol. 2460, pp. 412–425. Springer, Heidelberg (2002). https://doi.org/10.1007/3-540-45800-X_32
25. Khakzad, N., Khan, F., Amyotte, P.: Dynamic risk analysis using bow-tie approach. Reliab. Eng. Syst. Saf. **104**, 36–44 (2012)
26. Kordy, B., Mauw, S., Radomirović, S., Schweitzer, P.: Foundations of attack–defense trees. In: Degano, P., Etalle, S., Guttman, J. (eds.) FAST 2010. LNCS, vol. 6561, pp. 80–95. Springer, Heidelberg (2011). https://doi.org/10.1007/978-3-642-19751-2_6
27. Kriaa, S., Pietre-Cambacedes, L., Bouissou, M., Halgand, Y.: A survey of approaches combining safety and security for industrial control systems. Reliab. Eng. Syst. Saf. **139**, 156–178 (2015)
28. Kumar, R., Stoelinga, M.: Quantitative security and safety analysis with attack-fault trees. In: 2017 IEEE 18th International Symposium on High Assurance Systems Engineering (HASE), pp. 25–32. IEEE (2017)
29. Lee, W.S., Grosh, D.L., Tillman, F.A., Lie, C.H.: Fault tree analysis, methods, and applications; a review. IEEE Trans. Reliab. **34**(3), 194–203 (1985)
30. Lund, M.S., Solhaug, B., Stølen, K.: Model-Driven Risk Analysis: The CORAS Approach. Springer, Heidelberg (2010). https://doi.org/10.1007/978-3-642-12323-8
31. Mauw, S., Oostdijk, M.: Foundations of attack trees. In: Won, D.H., Kim, S. (eds.) ICISC 2005. LNCS, vol. 3935, pp. 186–198. Springer, Heidelberg (2006). https://doi.org/10.1007/11734727_17
32. Meland, P.H., Gjære, E.A.: Representing threats in BPMN 2.0. In: 2012 Seventh International Conference on Availability, Reliability and Security (ARES), pp. 542–550. IEEE (2012)
33. Meland, P.H., Tøndel, I.A., Jensen, J.: Idea: reusability of threat models – two approaches with an experimental evaluation. In: Massacci, F., Wallach, D., Zannone, N. (eds.) ESSoS 2010. LNCS, vol. 5965, pp. 114–122. Springer, Heidelberg (2010). https://doi.org/10.1007/978-3-642-11747-3_9
34. Michel, C.D., Thomas, P.F., Tucci, A.E.: Cyber Risks in the Marine Transportation System. The U.S. Coast Guard Approach
35. Mohr, R.: Evaluating cyber risk in engineering environments: a proposed framework and methodology. SANS Institute (2016). https://www.sans.org/reading-room/whitepapers/ICS/evaluating-cyber-risk-engineering-environments-proposed-framework-methodology-37017
36. Nesheim, D., Rødseth, Ø., Bernsmed, K., Frøystad, C., Meland, P.: Risk model and analysis. Technical rep., CySIMS (2017)
37. NevilleClarke: Taking-off with BowTie (2013). http://www.nevilleclarke.com/indonesia/articles/topic/52/title/
38. Ni, H., Chen, A., Chen, N.: Some extensions on risk matrix approach. Saf. Sci. **48**(10), 1269–1278 (2010)
39. Nielsen, D.S.: The cause/consequence diagram method as a basis for quantitative accident analysis. Technical rep., Danish Atomic Energy Commission (1971)
40. Phillips, C., Swiler, L.P.: A graph-based system for network-vulnerability analysis. In: Proceedings of the 1998 Workshop on New Security Paradigms, pp. 71–79. ACM (1998)
41. Piètre-Cambacédès, L., Bouissou, M.: Cross-fertilization between safety and security engineering. Reliab. Eng. Syst. Saf. **110**, 110–126 (2013)

42. Raspotnig, C., Karpati, P., Katta, V.: A combined process for elicitation and analysis of safety and security requirements. In: Bider, I., Halpin, T., Krogstie, J., Nurcan, S., Proper, E., Schmidt, R., Soffer, P., Wrycza, S. (eds.) BPMDS/EMMSAD -2012. LNBIP, vol. 113, pp. 347–361. Springer, Heidelberg (2012). https://doi.org/10.1007/978-3-642-31072-0_24

43. Ruijters, E., Stoelinga, M.: Fault tree analysis: a survey of the state-of-the-art in modeling, analysis and tools. Comput. Sci. Rev. **15**, 29–62 (2015)

44. Santamarta, R.: A wake-up call for satcom security. Technical White Paper (2014)

45. Schneier, B.: Attack trees. Dr. Dobbs J. **24**(12), 21–29 (1999)

46. Sha, L., Gopalakrishnan, S., Liu, X., Wang, Q.: Cyber-physical systems: a new frontier. In: IEEE International Conference on Sensor Networks, Ubiquitous and Trustworthy Computing, SUTC 2008, pp. 1–9. IEEE (2008)

47. Shostack, A.: Threat Modeling: Designing for Security. Wiley (2014)

48. Simon, H.A.: The Sciences of the Artificial. MIT Press, Cambridge (1996)

49. Sindre, G., Opdahl, A.L.: Eliciting security requirements with misuse cases. Requirements Eng. **10**(1), 34–44 (2005)

50. Sun, M., Mohan, S., Sha, L., Gunter, C.: Addressing safety and security contradictions in cyber-physical systems. In: Proceedings of the 1st Workshop on Future Directions in Cyber-Physical Systems Security (CPSSW 2009) (2009)

51. Viscusi, W.K., Aldy, J.E.: The value of a statistical life: a critical review of market estimates throughout the world. J. Risk Uncertainty **27**(1), 5–76 (2003)

52. Winther, R., Johnsen, O.-A., Gran, B.A.: Security assessments of safety critical systems using HAZOPs. In: Voges, U. (ed.) SAFECOMP 2001. LNCS, vol. 2187, pp. 14–24. Springer, Heidelberg (2001). https://doi.org/10.1007/3-540-45416-0_2

53. Zalewski, J., Drager, S., McKeever, W., Kornecki, A.J.: Towards experimental assessment of security threats in protecting the critical infrastructure. In: Proceedings of the 7th International Conference on Evaluation of Novel Approaches to Software Engineering, ENASE 2012, Wroclaw, Poland (2012)

CSIRA: A Method for Analysing the Risk of Cybersecurity Incidents

Aitor Couce-Vieira[1,3]([✉]), Siv Hilde Houmb[2], and David Ríos-Insua[3]

[1] Universidad Rey Juan Carlos, Madrid, Spain
am.couce@alumnos.urjc.es, aitor.couce@icmat.es
[2] Secure-NOK AS, Stavanger, Norway
sivhoumb@securenok.com
[3] Consejo Superior de Investigaciones Científicas,
Instituto de Ciencias Matemáticas, Madrid, Spain
david.rios@icmat.es

Abstract. Analysing risk is critical for dealing with cybersecurity incidents. However, there is no explicit method for analysing risk during cybersecurity incidents, since existing methods focus on identifying the risks that a system might face throughout its life. This paper presents a method for analysing the risk of cybersecurity incidents based on an incident risk analysis model, a method for eliciting likelihoods based on the oddness of events and a method for categorising the potential ramifications of cybersecurity incidents.

Keywords: Cybersecurity · Risk analysis · Incident risk analysis
Decision support

1 Introduction

Cybersecurity incidents happen in a context of uncertainty in which incident responders have to analyse the potential uncertainties around the incident and the potential consequences in the system and on the assets. The earlier signs of one of these events are, typically, suspicious anomalies that could also be caused by legit actions by the system or users. Here, the analysis focuses on identifying what could have caused the anomalous event, and what events might follow. For instance, a new connection within a network could be caused by a maintenance laptop or an unauthorised party accessing the network. Additionally, if a specific attack or problem has been identified, then the analysis focuses on identifying the consequences of the threat, how likely they are or how the potential countermeasures would change the risk. For example, analysing the presence of malware in an industrial controller would deal with aspects such as whether it is harmful to the controller or the current industrial process, whether it can spread to other devices or what the consequences of removing the malware or changing the device are.

P. Liu et al. (eds.): GraMSec 2017, LNCS 10744, pp. 57–74, 2018.
https://doi.org/10.1007/978-3-319-74860-3_4

Methods for cybersecurity risk analysis may be classified into three approaches: upstream, downstream and combined. Upstream methods, such as attack trees [1], fault trees or probabilistic attack graphs [2], identify the causes of the main incident. Downstream methods, such as FMECA[1] [3] or event trees [4], identify the consequences of the main incident. Combined methods, such as bow-ties [5,6] and risk matrices [7], cover both upstream and downstream analysis. A bow-tie combines an upstream tree for the causing events of the main incident and a downstream tree for its consequences. Risk matrices assign an ordinal value to the likelihood and to the severity of a risk, and then derive an ordinal risk rating from both values. Other relevant combined methods are CORAS [8] and FAIR [9]. Most of the existing methods, especially upstream and downstream ones, concentrate on risk description[2] [10] rather on risk evaluation.

Risk matrices are the most popular risk analysis method, but its limitations [7] are even more problematic when it comes to analysing incidents. First, combining the qualitative interpretations of likelihood in a chain of events would become meaningless, since they do not follow probability axioms. Second, analysing the impact over assets with them also present problems. On the other hand, risk matrices are very suggestive on what stakeholders should value as most frameworks using them provide a supporting table identifying some impact categories (e.g., people, property, reputation) and the corresponding severity level. In addition, they are also very suggestive on how should stakeholders evaluate the risk, since most frameworks provide an already coloured matrix to categorise risks.

This paper presents a method for analysing the risk of cybersecurity incidents, hereafter called CSIRA. The method combines a general model for incident risk analysis, a model for categorising the ramifications of cybersecurity incidents and a minimal method for eliciting likelihoods based on the oddness of events. These methods are introduced in Sect. 2. Section 3 introduces CSIRA, supported by an example of its application in Sect. 4. Finally, Sect. 5 briefly discusses our contributions and future work.

2   Base Models

2.1   GIRA: A General Model for Incident Risk Analysis

Figure 1 depicts a general model for incident risk analysis (GIRA), represented as an influence diagram. GIRA [11] combines risk information from upstream and downstream risk descriptions, as well as risk evaluation. As an influence diagram, GIRA provides a visualisation of the cause-effect relations of the risk, and the capability of processing quantitative and qualitative elicitations of it (this last one through a semi-quantitative procedure).

---

[1] Failure mode, effects and criticality analysis.
[2] In ISO terminology, risk description is named risk analysis whereas risk analysis is named risk assessment.

In an influence diagram, ovals represent events with uncertain states ('what could happen?'). Double-lined nodes represent events with deterministic/known states ('what would happen?'). Rectangles represent a set of alternative actions that decision-makers can take ('what we can do?'). Hexagons represent a set of preferences over the outcomes of a node ('how we value what could happen?'). Arcs represent conditional relations between nodes ('if this happens in the antecedent, then that happens in the consequent'). Stacked nodes represent that for certain node types, there could be several of them.

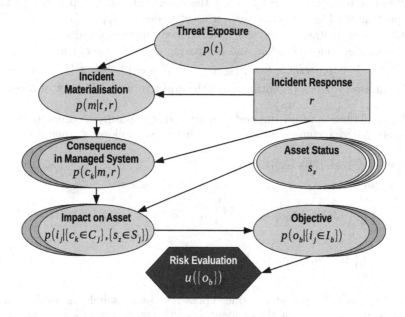

Fig. 1. GIRA depicted as an influence diagram.

The *threat exposure* node represents the likelihood that a threat is present in, or targeting, the system that the incident handlers are in charge of protection (MS, the managed system). Mathematically, it is represented by the probability distribution $p(t)$. The *incident response* node represents the alternative actions that the incident handlers could implement to avoid or mitigate the incident. The variable representing these actions is r. The *incident materialisation* node represents the likelihood that the threat materialises as an incident in the MS, taking into account the response of incident handlers. This is the first conditional node, $p(m|t,r)$, which means that the probability of incident materialisation depends on the threat presence and the response. The *consequences in the managed system* nodes represent the likelihood that an incident or its response cause further negative events in the MS. Its distribution is modelled as $p(c_k|m,r)$. There could be multiple nodes of this type, so we define the set of consequence nodes as $\{c_k\} = \{c_1, \ldots, c_K\}$, being K the total number of consequences.

An asset is any element affected by the incident and valuable to the stakeholders. The *impact on asset* nodes provide the likelihood that a consequence in the MS leads to impacts over the assets of the MS or other systems, or over any other stakeholders' interests. This node takes into account the current *asset status*, which might enable or escalate the impacts of the incident. An asset status is represented as s_z and the set of asset status nodes as $\{s_z\} = \{s_1, \ldots, s_Z\}$. An impact on asset node is represented as $p\left(i_j | \{c_k : \exists\, c_k \rightarrow i_j\}, \{s_z : \exists\, s_z \rightarrow i_j\}\right)$, being $\{c_k : \exists\, c_k \rightarrow i_j\}$ the set of consequence nodes parenting the j-th impact node[3] and, similarly, $\{s_z : \exists\, s_z \rightarrow i_j\}$ the asset status nodes parenting the j-th impact node. The set of impact on asset nodes is $\{i_j\} = \{i_1, \ldots, i_J\}$. The *objective* nodes synthesise impacts in a reduced number of objectives to facilitate stakeholders understanding and comparing the outcome of the incident. An objective node is represented as $p\left(o_b | \{i_j : \exists\, i_j \rightarrow o_b\}\right)$, being $\{i_j : \exists\, i_j \rightarrow o_b\}$ impact on assets nodes parenting the b-th objective node. The set of objective nodes is $\{o_b\} = \{o_1, \ldots, o_B\}$.

The combination of all the nodes, from threat exposure to objective nodes, represents *risk description*, which is modelled by the following equation:

$$p\left(\{o_b\}, \{i_j\}, \{s_z\}, \{c_k\}, m, r, t\right) =$$
$$= p(o_1, \ldots, o_B, i_1, \ldots, i_J, s_1, \ldots, s_Z, c_1, \ldots, c_K, m, r, t) =$$
$$= \left[\prod_{b=1}^{B} p\left(o_b | \{i_j : \exists\, i_j \rightarrow o_b\}\right)\right] \left[\prod_{j=1}^{J} p\left(i_j | \{c_k : \exists\, c_k \rightarrow i_j\}, \{s_z : \exists\, s_z \rightarrow i_j\}\right)\right]$$
$$\times \left[\prod_{k=1}^{K} p(c_k | m, r)\right] p(m | t, r)\, p(t). \tag{1}$$

Finally, the *risk evaluation* node represents the stakeholders' evaluation of the risk scenarios caused by the incident. It can be modelled, following the multi-attribute utility theory paradigm [12], as $u\left(\{o_b\}\right) = u(o_1, \ldots, o_B)$. The actual risk evaluation is based on the expected utility when response r is implemented,

$$\psi(r) = \int \ldots \int u\left(\{o_b\}\right) p\left(\{o_b\}, \{i_j\}, \{c_k\}, m, t\right)\ dt\ dm\ dc_K \ldots do_1. \tag{2}$$

From this equation, we can obtain the maximum expected utility response, by calculating $r^* : \max \psi(r)$.

Another aspect to consider is the time frame of the risk analysis. Specifically, the *expiration time* (e) of GIRA is the estimated moment of the earliest relevant change in any of the elements that participate in the incident (e.g., threat, system, assets). The expiration time could also be a specific time frame set by the analyst. The analysts should refer likelihoods to such time frame.

---

[3] More properly, the set of consequence nodes for which there exist an arc (directed edge as a graph) directed to the impact node i_j.

2.2   Eliciting the Likelihood Based on the Oddness of the Event

The quality of risk analysis relies on how well it considers uncertainty [13]. This is achieved by using suitable and well-processed data, if available, or in the partial or complete support of expert knowledge [14] or other elicitation methods [15]. However, this information might not be available during the time frame of the incident, in which the analysts do not have access to data or experts.

Analysing the likelihood of events using a qualitative interpretation could be arbitrary, but a meaningful yet practical approach is basing this splitting on a qualitative interpretation of probability ranges: *certain* for $p(e) = 1$, *possible* for $p(e) = (t, 1)$, *rare* for $p(e) = (0, t)$ and *impossible* for $p(e) = 0$. Any event x that clearly has a likelihood below the interpretative oddness threshold t is defined as rare, whereas the events with a likelihood around or above t are defined as possible. This simple method can be extended with several levels of *oddness*. Interpretatively, this means that rare would change to $p(e) = (t_2, t_1)$ and could be conceived as *rare (oddness 1)*, and that we could define a new *rarer than rare/rare (oddness 2)* event with $p(e) = (t_3, t_2)$. We can continue this process until a *are (oddness i)* event, which might be useful for comparing the likelihoods of different events, although it would become more and more difficult to interpret in absolute terms.

Additionally, we can establish a rule for the likelihood of a chains of n events, based on the accumulated oddness, i.e.,

$$p(e_n|e_{n-1}|\ldots|e_1) = (t_{l-1}, t_l) : l = \sum_i^n \mathrm{odd}(e_i),$$

being $\mathrm{odd}(e_i)$ the oddness of the event. Certain and possible events have an oddness of zero. Additionally, any chain with at least one impossible event is automatically impossible, and any chain with all of its events certain is automatically certain.

Following this rules we have that a chain o possible and certain events is possible, a chain with a rare event would be rare (one event with oddness 1), a chain with two rare events would be a rarer than rare event (two events with oddness (1), a chain with a rarer than rare event would be a rarer than rare event too (one event with oddness (2). For instance, in industrial cybersecurity, an analyst could interpret that the event of an attacker manipulating a controller is rare and that, given such a manipulation, the event of a controlled sabotage by the attacker is rare. Therefore, this chain of events would be elicited as 'rarer than rare event'.

Table 1 summarises these concepts. It also shows the numerical implementation in a Bayesian network like GIRA, which can take the qualitative likelihood as a numerical input to populate the probabilities of nodes and, vice versa, translate the overall probabilities calculated by the network into the qualitative interpretation again. These values are defined based on practical purposes. First, a probability range of 2 orders of magnitude, e.g. $(1 \times 10^{-2}, 1)$, allows us to model dozens of states. The differences among the magnitudes of the various probability ranges are established in a way so that a chain with a rare event will always

Table 1. Table with the probabilistic interpretation of qualitative likelihoods.

Qualitative likelihood	Probabilistic interpretation	Numerical input to GIRA Bayesian network	Numerical output from GIRA Bayesian network
Certain	1	1	1
Possible	$(t_1, 1)$	$(1 \times 10^{-2}, 1)$	$(1 \times 10^{-10}, 1)$
Rare (oddness 1)	(t_2, t_1)	$(1 \times 10^{-12}, 1 \times 10^{-10})$	$(1 \times 10^{-20}, 1 \times 10^{-10})$
Rarer than rare (oddness 2)	(t_3, t_2)	$(1 \times 10^{-22}, 1 \times 10^{-20})$	$(1 \times 10^{-30}, 1 \times 10^{-20})$
...	...	...	...
Impossible	0	0	0

have a lower probability than a chain without it. In the case of GIRA, we have a chain of 5 nodes and, taking into account that we use probability ranges of 2 orders of magnitude, the difference between probability ranges must be, at least, 10. This way, by multiplying the probabilities of the chain of events, we will get as output the overall probabilities, with their different orders of magnitude.

2.3 Understanding Potential Ramifications of Cybersecurity Incidents

Multiple guidelines and taxonomies exist for identifying and categorising cybersecurity risks. We can distinguish two groups. One group at the technical level, the larger in the literature, deals with the categorisation of cyber attacks and their effects on digital systems. These guidelines might be useful for identifying elements related to threats, incidents, and system consequence. The other group deals with the impact that cybersecurity risks might have on assets, value or risk objectives. Examples of widely used methods are COBIT [16] or FAIR [9]. However, the majority of the categories for impacts and assets have a perspective that pivots on a business/organisational interpretation of assets and stakeholders. Although most risk management happens in organisational settings (e.g., business or public agencies), a more broad perspective is feasible when thinking about cybersecurity risk impacts, i.e., asset as something with value for somebody and stakeholder as somebody that might be affected by the incident.

A thorough categorisation model would require a combination of IT, OT, cyber-phisical and cyber-psychological risks, an analysis of their impact at microsocial and macrosocial level and an analysis of what new cyber risks would emerge in the future (e.g. what risks the pervasive use of virtual reality will bring and how they could become cybersecurity risks). There is no scientific or technical literature so comprehensive. However, a simplified model for quick elicitation may be established. Figure 2 depicts a graphical model for categorising the potential ramifications of cybersecurity incidents. In the context of GIRA, this model might be helpful for identifying the consequences and impacts nodes.

The starting point is the MS, in which the analysed cybersecurity incident happens. The primordial risks of cybersecurity incidents are those involving the processing, storage and transmission of digital data. For example, ransomware, denial of service or man-in-the-middle attacks. These events could happen in the MS or other digital systems managed by the organisation dealing with the incident or third parties.

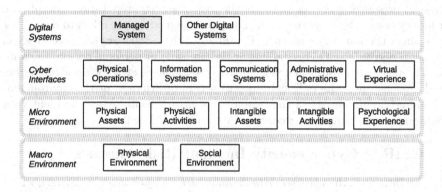

Fig. 2. Categories that classify the ramifications of cybersecurity risks

However, the importance of cyber risks resides, mostly, in the ramifications to other organisational or physical systems and assets that depend on, or can be affected by, the compromised digital systems. The most direct ramifications are the incidents grouped in the broad category of cyber interfaces. Physical operations refer to the interactions between physical reality and digital systems, such as input and output devices (e.g., keyboards, screens, printers, mouses, USB ports) or the actuators and sensors of industrial control systems. Examples of risks here involve unauthorised cyber-physical actions like the ones executed by Stuxnet [17] (manipulation of nuclear plant centrifuge speeds) or the malicious hijacking of laptop cameras. Information systems refer to the actual information contained in the digital systems (e.g., documents, pictures). An example risk in this case is the stealing of secret documents. Communication systems refer to the actual communication facilitated by the digital systems (e.g., chats, video conferences). Examples of risks here are the interference with a video conference or even the dissemination of false information through vulnerabilities in social networks (e.g., Twitter bots). Administrative operations refer to the affairs conducted with the digital systems (e.g., invoicing or buying online). An example risk in this area is the hijacking of an e-banking account. The virtual experience refers to the human experience in the reality created by the digital system (e.g., user experience in an application, human interaction in a social network). Examples of this type of risk are the exposure of personal information or sensitive images in social networks.

The indirect ramifications are categorised in a micro- and a macro-environment that refer to non-digital and non-cyber consequences. The micro-environment refers to risks at the particular or organisational level, as well as risks with organisations and people with a relatively direct relationship (e.g., customers and suppliers for a business, family and friends for a person). The first type of risks are in physical assets (e.g., machinery, personnel) and activities (e.g., manufacturing and transporting items). An example risk could be the sabotage by Stuxnet of the facility centrifuges (asset) and the enrichment of uranium (activity). Intangible assets refer to any characteristic or thing without physical presence. Example risks are the loss of secrets, reputation, compliance or money caused by a cyber attack. The psychological aspect refers to how cyber risks affect the human experience. Examples of these risks are the psychological problems derived from cyber-bulling or the exposure or personal data to the public. The macro-environment refers to the consequences at a social or ecosystem level. For instance, the political impact on Iran of Stuxnet, or the environmental and economic impact in the case a cyber attack facilitates an accident with contaminants or dangerous materials in an industrial facility.

3   CSIRA: Cybersecurity Incident Risk Analysis

Now we introduce the *cybersecurity incident risk analysis model (CSIRA)*, which aims at providing a paradigm practicable as a quick risk analysis method during cybersecurity incidents. CSIRA combines GIRA, the oddness method for likelihood elicitation, the graphical model for brainstorming cybersecurity incident ramifications and a simplified method for risk evaluation based on comparing the outcomes of different incident responses.

First, CSIRA uses GIRA (Sect. 2.1) as the risk analysis model, so that a high-level but comprehensive method is applied to the cybersecurity incident assessment. As argued previously, risk matrices oversimplify many risks components and other methods are more focused on the technical side (e.g. bow-ties). It is feasible to combine the use of a more detailed technical model for the cyber attack (e.g., attack tree) and the consequences (e.g., fault tree) with the use of GIRA for the impact and objective analysis.

Second, CSIRA uses a simplified interpretation of likelihood (Sect. 2.2), so that the elicitation is quick but at least implementable numerically. The qualitative scale of risk matrices cannot be applied to a chain of events nor be interpreted easily as a probability range. We also assume that a quantitative or semi-quantitative elicitation is not feasible in real-time. If so, then it would also be feasible to directly use GIRA, with quantitative data or expert elicitation.

Third, CSIRA uses a simplified model for eliciting the ramifications of cybersecurity incidents (Sect. 2.3), so that all feasible types of incidents are thought about. This intends to facilitate brainstorming, based the contextual knowledge of the user undertaking the analysis. We think that this approach is more feasible and useful in real time than presenting a general catalogue of impacts.

Fourth, GIRA would need the elicitation of the preferences and risk attitudes of the stakeholders, following the standard process in influence diagram building.

However, this would require time and support from experts. For CSIRA, we establish a faster alternative method, desicribed in Sect. 4.4: Once the users build the risk description part, they could obtain the total likelihoods of the risk problem. From the decision-making perspective, the only comparison they have to make is how the responses to the incident, and inaction, affect risk objectives.

CSIRA does not contain any knowledge base or any process to build one. For that to be useful, it would be necessary with very tailored information adapted to the specific systems, assets and stakeholders of the organisation. Indeed, rather than the potential incorporation of cybersecurity knowledge, we would recommend the use of a collection of cybersecurity standards. The most relevant one in this case is the NIST Cybersecurity Framework [18], which provides (1) the most comprehensive structuring of the aspects that should be taken into account in cybersecurity management and (2) specific chapters that deal with these topics in other relevant collections of standards (e.g., NIST, ISO, COBIT). Nor do we provide any automatic reasoning mechanism besides the Bayesian calculation of likelihoods. Although automation would reduce human task load, it would also take decision-making from the users. Indeed, the intention is the opposite: providing a risk analysis model that explicitly relies, as much as possible, on human interpretation and decision-making.

4   An Example Cybersecurity Risk Analysis

This section introduces the steps for using CSIRA, supported by an example. Our intention is not to undertake a realistic risk analysis but to provide an example to show CSIRA. First, we cover risk description, which consists in three steps. The first step, in Sect. 4.1, is risk identification using the graphical model presented in Sect. 2.3 for identifying cybersecurity incident ramifications. The second step is risk elicitation (Sect. 4.2), using GIRA as the base risk model (presented in Sect. 2.1) with the elicitation method presented in Sect. 2.2 to generate the likelihoods of different events. The final step of the risk description is risk calculation, using also the mentioned elicitation method. The outcome of risk description are the relevant risk scenarios for decision-making: the potential results of the different incident responses regarding their relevant risk objectives. The risk analysis finalises with the risk evaluation of Sect. 4.4.

The example case is applied to the industrial control systems (ICS) of an oil and gas drilling rig, as this facility is a paradigmatic case of the physical and organisational ramifications that a cybersecurity incident could have. The incident would be the presence of a wiper malware in the system in charge of drilling the well. This kind of malware is capable of erasing data in the operating system (OS) boot records or critical files. Interestingly [19] some of the most notorious wiper cyber attacks, like Shamoon and BlackEnergy, targeted the oil and gas industry. The human-machine interfaces (HMI) of industrial systems are typically installed on top of popular OS like Windows. Therefore, a disruption in the HMI caused by a wiper might affect, to some extent, the industrial operation that the HMI helps to control. This involves that incident handlers should think about the ramifications of the incident on industrial operations and assets.

4.1   Risk Description: Identification

Figure 3 depicts the consequences and impacts of cybersecurity incidents, applying the method of Sect. 2.3 to our scenario of a wiper in a drilling rig. The
managed system is the drilling ICS. The initial incident is the presence of the
threat, i.e., the presence of the wiper malware in the ICS. The exposure to this
threat could lead to the main incident, which is the execution of the wiper in
the PC hosting the HMI software. The square represents the potential response
of the incident handler. Given that a wiper could be a sophisticated tool, a full
fresh re-installation of the HMI PCs would be a prudent response.

In case the wiper is successfully running in an HMI PC, the next consequence
could be the disruption of the OS of the HMI PC. In addition, the incident
response has also a consequence: a fresh installation of the HMI PCs would
need to put the ICS under maintenance for 24 h. The next step is to identify
the ramifications that the disruption could have beyond the ICS. The first one
is the disruption in the human-machine interface, i.e., the disruption of the
interaction between operator, ICS and industrial operation. This could lead to a

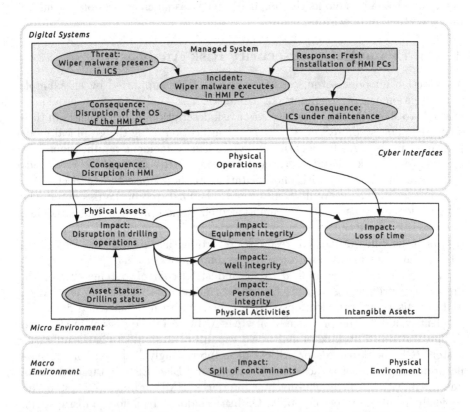

Fig. 3. Graphical representation of potential risks of a wiper in a drilling rig. Rounded
nodes represent uncertain events. Rectangles represent incident handler decisions.
Double-rounded circles represent known states.

disruption of the drilling operations, which in turn might lead to incidents with equipment, the oil well or personnel. In addition, an incident involving the well integrity might lead to a spill involving hydrocarbons or other contaminants into the rig floor or the sea. An additional consequence, very relevant in oil platforms, is the loss of time, which can be caused by both the disruption in the drilling operations and the maintenance of the ICS (in the case of re-installing the HMI OS). However, one important element affects the disruption of the drilling operations: whether the platform is drilling or performing other activity.

4.2   Risk Description: Elicitation

Figure 4 illustrates the influence diagram of our example, using the likelihood elicitation of Sect. 2.2, and derived from the risks identified in Sect. 4.1.

The uppermost node is the *threat exposure*. It represents the uncertainty about the presence of the wiper. In this case, the analysts considered that the presence is possible (represented as P in the graph). Its complementary state (no presence of wiper) is also possible. Additionally, the *incident response* node represents the actions that the incident handler can take. In our case, the re-installation of the HMI OS with a fresh and updated version or the option of leaving the system as is.

The *incident materialisation* node represents the main incident: the execution of the wiper in the HMI PC. It has two uncertain states: whether the wiper runs in the PC or not. However, these events are conditioned by two factors. First, whether the wiper presence is a false alarm (threat exposure node). Second, whether the incident handlers re-install the HMI PCs. This is reflected in the likelihood assigned. If the wiper is present and the incident handlers leave the system as is, then it is possible that the wiper would run in the HMI PC. Otherwise, the wiper would not run (in the graph, 0 represents impossible and 1 represents certain).

There are two *consequence in the managed system* nodes. The first one represents the event of the wiper actually disrupting the OS of the HMI. In case the wiper is running in the HMI PC, then the likelihood of the HMI disruption is rare (as established earlier, rare (oddness 1), represented in the graph as R1) and the likelihood of its opposite is, thus, possible. In case the wiper is not running, then the certain event is the correct status. The second consequence node represents the event of putting the system under maintenance caused by the re-installation of the HMI PCs.

There are several *impact on asset* nodes. They represent most of the incident ramifications outside the managed system we identified in the previous section, except the disruption of drilling operations. The reason is that such disruption acts as an 'intermediate' risk, i.e., its risks are reflected on other assets, like the integrity of the different assets, the loss of time or the spill of contaminants. These nodes are preceded by the asset status node informing whether the platform is drilling. In addition, the impact nodes should summarise the likelihood of the chain of events that do not happen in the MS but may lead to those impacts. This means that given a consequence in the MS and the status of some asset,

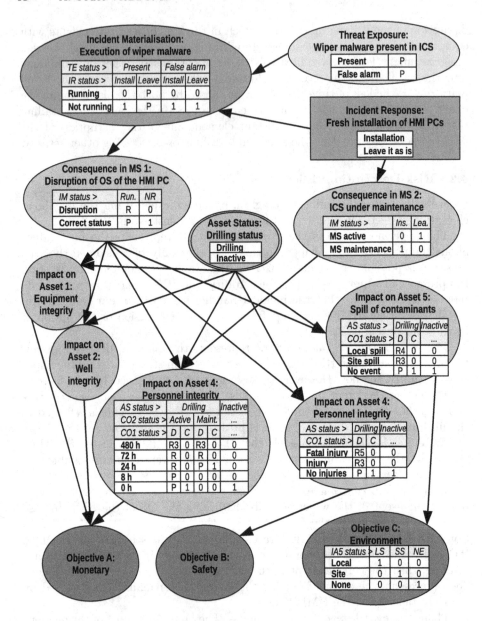

Fig. 4. Influence diagram representing the risk analysis for the wiper incident in a drilling control system. When it comes to the likelihoods, a sure event is represented with 1, an impossible event with 0, a possible event with P, a rare event with R, a rarer than rare event with R2, and so on.

they should reflect the likelihood of the different impact levels attainable. For instance, in case the impact 5 'spill of contaminants' we have that, given that the asset status is drilling and that the HMI PC has been disrupted, the likelihood of a local spill is rare (oddness 4), the likelihood of a site spill is rare (oddness 3) and the likelihood of the no spill event is possible.

It is necessary to analyse the chain of events to determine whether one event is clearly rarer than other, as in Sect. 2.2. For instance, the event of a fatal personnel injury is established as clearly rarer than a non-fatal injury and than a local spill. Then, we establish that the event of a local spill is clearly rarer than a site spill. Following this procedure, we assign the different oddness to different events.

A final aspect to take into account is the expiration time of this risk analysis. Most of the events described have no clear time boundary. However, one of the nodes of our example stands out as the compass of timely risk response: the asset status node. First, all of the relevant impacts happen when the platform is drilling. Second, the incident handlers are able to know whether the platform is drilling or not and when this status would change. For instance, drilling might be scheduled for turns lasting several hours in the upcoming weeks. As an example, the expiration time for the analysis could be 8 h.

4.3   Risk Description: Calculation

Following the procedure for likelihood calculation in Sect. 2.2, we can calculate the final conditional probabilities of the different nodes of the influence diagram. Figure 5 displays the calculation for the case in which the incident response 'leave the MS as is' is selected and taking into account that the current asset status is 'drilling'.

The logic of the influence diagram allows us to disregard infeasible and impossible events. For instance, the stricken out text in grey cells highlights infeasible events (e.g., in the consequence 2 node, it is infeasible any event that is conditioned by the incident response event of 'installation') or impossible events (once again, in the consequence 2 node, the event of 'maintenance' is impossible, given that the incident response event is 'leave the system as is'). This kind of reasoning propagates through the diagram.

Additionally, the oddness method of likelihood propagation allows us to replicate conditional probability. For instance, in the incident materialisation node, the marginal likelihood of the event 'wiper not running', given the events 'false alarm' in the threat exposure node and 'leave it as is' in the incident response, is certain. However, its conditional probability is possible, since its materialisation is a chain of a possible event ('false alarm') and a certain event ('wiper not running, given the false alarm and the leaving of the system as is'). This procedure propagates through the diagram. Additionally, when an event can happen through multiple event chains, then the likelihood of the likeliest one is selected. For example, in the impact on asset 5, the event 'no spill event' is rare if it comes from the chain with the consequence 1 event 'disruption', and it is possible if it comes from the chain with the consequence 1 event 'correct status'. Since the event is, overall, at least possible, this is the likelihood passed to the child event 'none' in the objective C node.

70   A. Couce-Vieira et al.

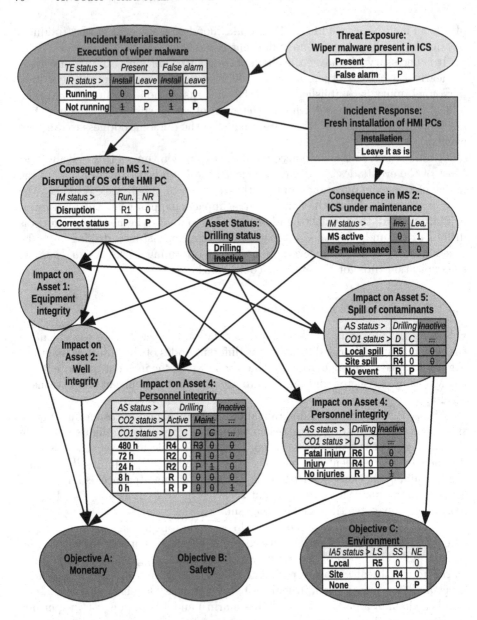

Fig. 5. Influence diagram representing the total conditional likelihoods for the risk analysis problem. Grey cells with the text stricken out represent infeasible or impossible events. Likelihoods in bold highlight that the conditional likelihood differs from the marginal one in Fig. 4.

4.4 Risk Evaluation

From an evaluative point of view risks and, specifically, impacts over value are incommensurable, i.e., they cannot, or ought not, be objectively evaluated in a single severity scale [20]. Therefore, a single scale, like the severity level of risk matrices, leads to a high level of incommensurability. On the other hand, it is recommendable to limit the number of elements to compare to facilitate decision-making. Multiple methods exist for evaluating risk, for instance, if the analyst has time and access to subject-matter experts, it is recommendable to use a method for preference and risk attitude elicitation, e.g. multi-attribute utility theory [21]. The rationality axioms make sense for generating a transparent and

Asset Status:		Rig is drilling		
Response:		Leaving the MS as is		
Likelihood		Objective A: Monetary	Objective B: Safety	Objective C: Environment
Certain		-	-	-
Possible		€ 0	No injuries	No spill
Rare		€ 80,000	-	-
Rarer than rare		€ 240,000 € 720,000	-	-
Oddness 3 or higher		€ 2,000,000 [R3] € 4,800,000 [R4] € 5.000.000 [R5] € 6,800,000 [R7] € 9,800,000 [R9] € 11,800,000 [R12]	Injuries [R4] Fatal injury [R6]	Site spill [R4] Local spill [R5]

Asset Status:		Rig is drilling		
Response:		Fresh installation of HMI PCs		
Likelihood		Objective A: Monetary	Objective B: Safety	Objective C: Environment
Certain		€ 240,000	No injuries	No spill
Possible		-	-	-
Rare		-	-	-
Rarer than rare		-	-	-
Oddness 3 or higher		-	-	-

Fig. 6. Tables representing the likelihood of different risk objectives when the incident handlers leave the wiper in the MS (upper table) and when they decide to do a fresh installation of the affected computers (lower table). Events with an oddness of 3 or higher contain their specific likelihood with squared brackets.

logical evaluation of the risk scenarios. Utility functions are flexible enough to represent multiple types of preference and risk attitudes and they offer strong analytical and mathematical properties. In addition, it is possible to avoid re-eliciting preferences as long as there are no changes in preferences.

The outcome of the risk description part is a set of scenarios representing how risk objectives could be affected by an incident, given the incident response. As depicted in Fig. 4, we created three objective nodes: monetary, safety and environment. The monetary node synthesises the cost that an incident in the assets might cause. On the other hand, the safety and environment nodes are practically direct translations of their precedent impact on asset nodes, as they have only one parent node.

As a decision problem, risk analysis is undertaken with the purpose of clarifying what are the best options to counter a risky situation. In our case, this involves that the main components to be evaluated are the potential responses of the incident handlers regarding risk objectives.

Tables in Fig. 6 display the relevant information that CSIRA presents to the stakeholders so that they are able to compare what different events regarding risk objectives, and their likelihood, might happen if they implement a response. In this case, the alternatives are either assuming a cost €240,000, caused by the lost time of maintaining the MS or face the rare event of losing €80,000, or the rarer than rare events of losing €240,000 or €720,000. If they disregard the even more rare events (oddness 3 or greater), then it seems a simple comparison between a certain lost of €240,000 and a loss three times greater but many more times less likely. However, should the stakeholders take into account the most rare events, then the comparison would become less clear.

5 Discussion

We have presented CSIRA, a model for building a high-level cybersecurity incident risk analysis. CSIRA is based on an influence diagram that provides a more comprehensive risk analysis than risk matrices. Realising the fact that risk quantification is practically infeasible in real time, we have implemented an alternative qualitative method that is at least implementable in an influence diagram to follow the basic logic of probability. We have put a special emphasis on what stakeholders value (impact nodes), how to synthesize these impacts over value (objective nodes) and how do stakeholders evaluate potential responses with respect to these risk objectives (risk evaluation). These axiological aspects require, rather than plain business impact scales, decision analysis modelling, so that value aspects are better formalised [22].

We present our method as an alternative to risk matrices rather than to more technical methods like attack or failure trees. Namely for two reasons, matrices use a single severity scale to merge their different categories of impact, in contrast to our approach or a more granular identification of impacts and their synthesis in a reduced number of risk objectives. Additionally, our likelihood elicitation method is as simple as the risk matrices (and it shares its limitations) but is designed to follow probability axioms, so that it could be applied to chains of events.

Upcoming work will focus on the implementation of CSIRA. Provide a more detailed specification of GIRA and the likelihood elicitation method. The main aspect is its software implementation. The R environment offers an ideal platform for elaborating a framework for the generation of CSIRA risk analysis case studies. Alternative, a Python implementation would facilitate the creation of an small application to undertake a CSIRA analysis. Besides the implementation of the influence diagram, that requires statistical and graph visualisation packages, it is also important to define a semantic model of CSIRA that captures the input from the users. Additionally, the elicitation method presented here would require a set of functions that transforms the user input (e.g., possible, oddness-1 rare event) into the marginal probabilities of the Bayesian nodes, and a set of functions that transforms the calculated probabilities into the 'oddness' language again. Future work after the implementation shall focus on test-based improvements of CSIRA and the construction of guidelines for its use.

Acknowledgements. The authors are grateful to the support of the MINECO MTM2014-56949-C3-1-R project, the AXA-ICMAT Chair in Adversarial Risk Analysis, the Regional Forskingsfond Vestlandet project 245291 Cybersecurity Incident Response Framework, and the COST IS1304 Action on Expert Judgement.

References

1. Schneier, B.: Attack trees. Dr. Dobb's J. **24**(12), 21–29 (1999)
2. Singhal, A., Ximming, O.: Security Risk Analysis of Enterprise Networks Using Probabilistic Attack Graphs. National Institute of Standards and Technology, Gaithersburg (2011). https://doi.org/10.6028/nist.ir.7788
3. Department of Defense: MIL-STD-1629A, Procedures for Performing a Failure Mode, Effect and Criticality Analysis. Department of Defense, Washington DC, USA (1980)
4. Clemens, P.L., Simmons, R.J.: System Safety and Risk Management: A Guide for Engineering Educators. National Institute for Occupational Safety and Health, Cincinnati (1998)
5. International Association of Drilling Contractors: Health, Safety and Environment Case Guidelines for Mobile Offshore Drilling Units, Issue 3.6. International Association of Drilling Contractors, Houston, TX, USA (2015)
6. International Organisation for Standardization: ISO 17776:2000, Petroleum and Natural Gas Industries – Offshore Production Installations – Guidelines on Tools and Techniques for Hazard Identification and Risk Assessment. International Organisation for Standardization, Geneva, Switzerland (2000)
7. Cox, L.A.: What's wrong with risk matrices? Risk Anal. **28**(2), 497–512 (2008). https://doi.org/10.1111/j.1539-6924.2008.01030.x
8. Lund, M.S., Solhaug, B., Stølen, K.: Model-Driven Risk Analysis: The CORAS Approach. Springer, Heidelberg (2011). https://doi.org/10.1007/978-3-642-12323-8
9. The Open Group: Risk Taxonomy. The Open Group, Reading, UK (2009)

10. Cherdantseva, Y., Burnap, P., Blyth, A., Eden, P., Jones, K., Soulsby, H., Stoddart, K.: A review of cyber security risk assessment methods for SCADA systems. Comput. Secur. **56**, 1–27 (2016). https://doi.org/10.1016/j.cose.2015.09.009

11. Couce-Vieira, A., Insua, D.R., Houmb, S.H.: GIRA: a general model for incident risk analysis. J. Risk Res. (2017). Advance online publication https://doi.org/10.1080/13669877.2017.1372509

12. Keeney, R.L., Raiffa, H.: Decisions with Multiple Objectives. Cambridge University Press, Cambridge (1993). https://doi.org/10.1017/CBO9781139174084

13. European Food Safety Authority: Guidance on Uncertainty in EFSA Scientific Assessment. European Food Safety Authority, Parma, Italy (2016)

14. European Food Safety Authority: Guidance on Expert Knowledge Elicitation in Food and Feed Safety Risk Assessment. European Food Safety Authority, Parma, Italy (2014). https://doi.org/10.2903/j.efsa.2014.3734

15. Renooij, S.: Probability elicitation for belief networks: issues to consider. Knowl. Eng. Rev. **16**(3), 255–269 (2001). https://doi.org/10.1017/s0269888901000145

16. ISACA: COBIT 5: A Business Framework for the Governance and Management of Enterprise IT. ISACA, Rolling Meadows, IL, USA (2012)

17. Langner, R.: Stuxnet: dissecting a cyberwarfare weapon. IEEE Secur. Priv. **9**(3), 49–51 (2011). https://doi.org/10.1109/msp.2011.67

18. National Institute of Standards and Technology. Framework for Improving Critical Infrastructure Cybersecurity (2014)

19. Industrial Control Systems Cyber Emergency Response Team. Destructive Malware. National Cybersecurity and Communications Integration Center (US) (2014)

20. Espinoza, N.: Incommensurability: the failure to compare risks. In: The Ethics of Technological Risk, pp. 128–143. Earthscan, London (UK) (2009)

21. Reichert, P., Langhans, S.D., Lienert, J., Schuwirth, N.: The conceptual foundation of environmental decision support. J. Environ. Manage. **154**, 316–332 (2015). https://doi.org/10.1016/j.jenvman.2015.01.053

22. Gregory, R., Failing, L., Harstone, M., Long, G., McDaniels, T., Ohlson, D.: Structured Decision Making: A Practical Guide to Environmental Management Choices. Wiley, Hoboken (2012)

Quantitative Evaluation of Attack Defense Trees Using Stochastic Timed Automata

René Rydhof Hansen[1], Peter Gjøl Jensen[1], Kim Guldstrand Larsen[1],
Axel Legay[2], and Danny Bøgsted Poulsen[3(✉)]

[1] Department of Computer Science, Aalborg University, Aalborg, Denmark
[2] INRIA - Rennes, Rennes, France
[3] Christian Albrechts Universität, Kiel, Germany
dbp@informatik.uni-kiel.de

Abstract. Security analysis is without doubt one of the most important issues in a society relying heavily on computer infrastructure. Unfortunately security analysis is also very difficult due to the complexity of systems. This is bad enough when dealing with ones own computer systems - but nowadays organisations rely on third-party services - *cloud services* - along with their own in-house systems. Combined this makes it overwhelming difficult to obtain an overview of possible attack scenarios. Luckily, some formalisms such as attack trees exist that can help security analysts. However, temporal behaviour of the attacker is rarely considered by these formalisms.

In this paper we build upon previous work on attack-defence trees to build a proper temporal semantics. We consider the attack-defence tree a reachability objective for an attacker and thereby separate the attacker logic from the attack-defence tree. We give a temporal stochastic semantics for arbitrary attackers (adhering to certain requirements to make the attacker "sane") and we allow annotating attacker actions with time-dependent costs. Furthermore, we define what we call a cost-preserving attacker profile and we define a parameterised attacker profile. The defined semantics is implemented via a translation to UPPAAL SMC. Using UPPAAL SMC we answer various questions such as the expected cost of an attack, we find the probability of a successful attack and we even show how an attacker can find an optimal parameter setting using ANOVA and Tukeys test.

1 Introduction

Society is in increasing fashion relying on computer systems to support it in every-day life and users are as such depending on computer systems to store their personal data to automate tasks: companies may store information about customers e.g. addresses for billing purposes and credit card information for automatic payment. The more information stored in computer systems, the higher

Work partially Supported by the BMBF through the ASSUME (01IS15031J) project, and the chist-era project success.

P. Liu et al. (eds.): GraMSec 2017, LNCS 10744, pp. 75–90, 2018.
https://doi.org/10.1007/978-3-319-74860-3_5

the need for protecting these data. History has however shown that making systems inpenetrable is extremely difficult and we have witnessed several security breaches. The IT-infrastructure of today is complex and gaining a high-level overview of how attacks may occur is extremely difficult for all but the simplest infrastructures - a problem worsened by the fact that organisations nowadays heavily rely on *Cloud Services*. A tool that has been developed for battling this complexity is *Attack-trees* [8,10]. Attack-trees is a tree-based formalism in which an overall attack on an organisation may be refined into sub-attacks - or different ways of achieving an attack. This formalism provides a security specialist a quick way of describing the possible ways that he sees an attack can happen. Attack trees were originally introduced by Schneier [12] and since given a formal semantics by Mauw and Oostdijk [10] - an overview of attack-trees is given by Kordy et al. [9]. Basic quantitative analysis is possible on the attack-tree formalism (with some annotations regarding costs and probabilities) in a bottom-up fashion (i.e. costs for leaf nodes are propagated up the attack-tree to calculate the cost of individual sub-attacks) [4]. In addition also various extensions have been considered in order to improve the analysis of attacks. Given an overview of possible attacks, it is intuitively straightforward to connect the attack nodes with possible defence measures, allow defence measures to be split into sub-tasks, and allow defences to be countered by other attack options which gives us the *Attack-Defence-trees* (AD-tree) formalism [2,8]. These trees allow analysis of the interplay between the attacker and defender and by doing so give better understanding of possible attack-defence scenarios [4,8]. An Attack-defence tree describes a game between two players but most analyses are still based on a bottom-up-propagations [2] approach. Two recent works by Hermanns et al. [7] and Gadyatskaya et al. [6] develop a temporal and stochastic semantics for attack-defence scenarios. Hermanns et al. [7] develops their own formalism *Attack-Defence-Diagrams* (ADD) highly inspired by attack-defence trees. A problem with ADDs, in our view, is that while giving a stochastic semantics they also compromise the simplicity of attack-defence trees by requiring the user to consider things like *reset*-gates. The work by Gadyatskaya et al. [6] on the other hand take their outset on the attack-defence trees and build the semantics directly on top of these - thus a security specialist may do their modelling exactly as usual and let a tool translate this to a stochastic semantics. Both Hermanns et al. [7] and Gadyatskaya et al. [6] translated their respective formalism to timed automata [1] with stochastic interpretations. Another recent work concerned with temporal ordering of events is that of Aslanyan et al. [3] which adds a sequential sequence operator to the syntax of attack-defence trees. This logically split the tree into sub-attack-defence-trees which are processed in sequence. They then use this split into sub-trees to develop a game semantics playing out as follows: first the defender selects defence measures for the first tree, then the attacker selects attacks and a result for the first tree is found (using a probabilistic outcome of the attackers selected attacks). The result of the first tree is then propagated onwards to the second subtree - and so it continues till the last sub-tree. Unlike Hermanns et al. [7] and Gadyatskaya et al. [6] the attacker is not allowed to retry failed attacks.

In this paper we expand upon the work of Gadyatskaya et al. [6] by firstly allowing the cost of an attack to be a function of time instead of a constant cost per atomic attack attempt. Secondly, we introduce the concept of parameterised attackers and show how we can find attacker-parameters that minimise cost by applying Analysis Of VAriance (ANOVA). The entire modelling framework is translated into a UPPAAL SMC model automatically by a python script. All the user needs to provide is a textual description of the AD-tree, the description of the cost per atomic attack and the duration interval for each atomic attack.

In Sect. 2 we introduce the attack-defence tree formalism and define our stochastic semantics with costs. We also present attacker and defender questions and describe how these may be solved. In Sect. 3 we instantiate our framework with a parameterised attacker. In Sect. 4 we discuss a translation of Sect. 3 into UPPAAL SMC timed automata and show how to use UPPAAL SMC to answer the questions of Sect. 2.

2   Attack-Defence Trees

In this section we first present the traditional "static" attack-defence-trees, followed by an extension to a temporal semantics following the work of Gadyatskaya et al. [6]. A stochastics semantics is on top the temporal semantics by defining success probabilities for attacker actions and by associating a time distribution to atomic attacks. As a final part of this section, and a main contribution of the paper, we present a parameterised attacker model.

At the simplest a static attack-defence tree (AD-tree) is a propositional formula with propositions split into attacker propositions (A_a) and defender propositions (A_d).

Definition 1 (AD-tree). *An AD-tree over the attacker actions A_a and defender actions A_d is generated by the syntax $t:: = p \mid t \wedge t \mid t \vee t \mid \sim t$ where $p \in A_a \cup A_d$. We denote by $\mathcal{L}(A_a, A_d)$ all AD-trees over A_a and A_d.*

For an AD-tree $\psi \in \mathcal{L}(A_a, A_d)$ and selected attacker actions $A \subseteq A_a$ and selected defence measures $D \subseteq A_d$, we inductively define $[\![\psi]\!]A, D$ as follows

- $[\![p]\!]A, D = \mathtt{tt}$ if $p \in A \cup D$, $\mathtt{ff}$ otherwise
- $[\![\psi_1 \wedge \psi_2]\!]A, D = ([\![\psi_1]\!]A, D) \wedge ([\![\psi_2]\!]A, D)$
- $[\![\psi_1 \vee \psi_2]\!]A, D = ([\![\psi_1]\!]A, D) \vee ([\![\psi_2]\!]A, D)$
- $[\![\sim \psi]\!]A, D = \neg([\![\psi]\!]A, D)$

We depict an AD-tree by its parse tree as shown in Fig. 1. The particular AD-tree in Fig. 1 models how an attacker may substitute an RFID-tag in a shop [2,6]. One way involves threatening the employees; another involves bribing a subject - which also requires identifying the subject before-hand.

The syntax given in Definition 1 is overly liberal in what AD-trees it allows. In particular, it allows defining trees in which an actor may do actions helping the opponent - for instance $\mathtt{StealCreditCard} \wedge \neg\mathtt{LooseCreditCard}$ would express

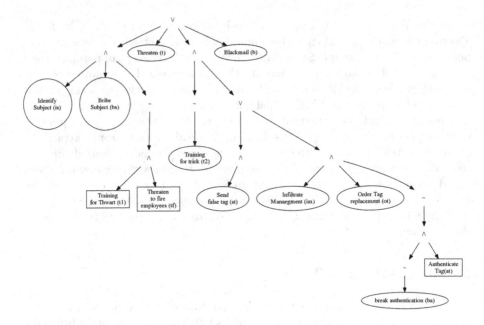

Fig. 1. An Attack-Defence Tree. Circles denote attacker actions, squares defender actions.

that the attacker achieve an attack if he steals a credit cards and does not loose it again. We consider that the attacker does things actively and thus would have chosen to loose the credit card. To avoid this problem we follow along [2] and impose a type-system that disallows such trees. The type system has two types a and d, denoting attacker and defender respectively and is given in Fig. 2.

$$\frac{}{\mathsf{A}_d, \mathsf{A}_a \vdash p : a}, p \in \mathsf{A}_a \qquad \frac{}{\mathsf{A}_d, \mathsf{A}_a \vdash p : d}, p \in \mathsf{A}_d \qquad \frac{\mathsf{A}_d, \mathsf{A}_a \vdash \psi_1 : r \quad \mathsf{A}_d, \mathsf{A}_a \vdash \psi_2 : r}{\mathsf{A}_d, \mathsf{A}_a \vdash \psi_1 \wedge \psi_2 : r}$$

$$\frac{\mathsf{A}_d, \mathsf{A}_a \vdash \psi_1 : r \quad \mathsf{A}_d, \mathsf{A}_a \vdash \psi_2 : r}{\mathsf{A}_d, \mathsf{A}_a \vdash \psi_1 \vee \psi_2 : r} \qquad \frac{\mathsf{A}_d, \mathsf{A}_a \vdash \psi_1 : r}{\mathsf{A}_d, \mathsf{A}_a \vdash \sim \psi_1 : r^{-1}}, r^{-1} = \begin{cases} a & \text{if } r = d \\ d & \text{if } r = a \end{cases}$$

Fig. 2. Type system to make attack-defence trees well-formed

For the remainder of this paper we only consider well-formed AD-trees with respect to the type-system in Fig. 2. Since we are interested in analysing possible attacks, we restrict our attention to AD-trees, ψ, for which $\mathsf{A}_d, \mathsf{A}_a \vdash \psi : a$. From now on let $\mathcal{L}^w(\mathsf{A}_a, \mathsf{A}_d) = \{\psi \in \mathcal{L}(\mathsf{A}_a, \mathsf{A}_d) \mid \mathsf{A}_a, \mathsf{A}_d \vdash \psi : a\}$.

A key question for AD-trees is whether an attacker for any set of defence measures can select a set of atomic attacks such that an attack will be successful.

In a similar fashion, the defender is interested in finding defence measures that guarantee an attack can never occur.

Attacker Question 1. *Given an AD tree $\psi \in \mathcal{L}^w(\mathsf{A}_a, \mathsf{A}_d)$ and a $D \subseteq \mathsf{A}_d$ does there exist an $A \subseteq \mathsf{A}_a$ such that $[\![\psi]\!]A, D = \mathtt{tt}$.*

Defender Question 1. *Given an AD tree $\psi \in \mathcal{L}^w(\mathsf{A}_a, \mathsf{A}_d)$ does there exist a $D \subseteq \mathsf{A}_d$ such that for any $A \subseteq \mathsf{A}_a$, $[\![\psi]\!]A, D = \mathtt{ff}$.*

2.1 Temporal Semantics

Our temporal semantics consist of four components: the tree, the attacker, the defender and an environmental model. The tree component defines a finite graph with vertices containing successful atomic attacks and the currently selected defense measures. The attacker is a mapping from the tree-vertices to actions he may choose to perform. The actual outcome of performing an action is simultaneously selected by the environment component.

Definition 2 (Tree-Graph). *Let $\psi \in \mathcal{L}^w(\mathsf{A}_a, \mathsf{A}_d)$ be an AD-tree, then the tree-graph over ψ, denoted $\mathtt{Graph}(\psi)$, is a tuple $(\mathcal{V}^t, \mathcal{V}^t_\dagger, v^{t^0}, \mathsf{E}, \mathsf{E}_d)$ where*

- $\mathcal{V}^t = 2^{\mathsf{A}_a} \times 2^{\mathsf{A}_d}$ *is a set of vertices,*
- $\mathcal{V}^t_\dagger \subseteq \{(A, D) \in \mathcal{V}^t \mid [\![A, D]\!]\psi = \mathtt{tt}\}$ *is a set of final vertices,*
- $v^{t^0} = (\emptyset, \emptyset)$ *is the initial vertex,*
- $\mathsf{E} \subseteq \mathcal{V}^t \times \mathsf{A}_a \times \mathcal{V}^t$ *is a set of edges where $((A, D), a, (A \cup \{a\}, D)) \in \mathsf{E}$ if $a \notin A$ and $[\![\psi]\!]A, D = \mathtt{ff}$,*
- $\mathsf{E}_d = \{(v^0, D, S) \mid D \subseteq \mathsf{A}_d \wedge S = (\emptyset, D)\}$ *is the defence select edges.*

An attacker looks into the state of the tree-graph and based on this information selects a set of actions that are feasible for him to perform. Likewise, a defender maps the initial vertex of the graph to possible subsets of defenses to perform. In the following, assume there is a special symbol $\dagger \notin \mathsf{A}_a$ used by an attacker to signal he will not do any action.

Definition 3. *Let $\psi \in \mathcal{L}^w(\mathsf{A}_a, \mathsf{A}_d)$ be an AD-tree and let its associated tree-graph be $\mathtt{Graph}(\psi) = (\mathcal{V}^t, \mathcal{V}^t_\dagger, v^{t^0}, \mathsf{E}, \mathsf{E}_d)$. An attacker is a function $\mathtt{Att} : \mathcal{V}^t \to 2^{\mathsf{A}_a} \cup \{\{\dagger\}\}$ with the restriction that if $a \in \mathtt{Att}((A, D))$ then $a \notin A$ and either $(A, D) \notin \mathcal{V}^t_\dagger$ or $a = \dagger$. We call $\mathtt{Att}$ deterministic if for all $v^t \in \mathcal{V}^t$, $|\mathtt{Att}(v)| = 1$ - otherwise it is non-deterministic.*

The requirement on the attacker function is expressing that the attacker can only choose to do an action if that action has not previously succeeded and the tree is not already true.

Definition 4. *Let $\psi \in \mathcal{L}^w(\mathsf{A}_a, \mathsf{A}_d)^w$ be an AD-tree and let its associated tree graph be $\mathtt{Graph}(\psi) = (\mathcal{V}^t, \mathcal{V}^t_\dagger, v^{t^0}, \mathsf{E}, \mathsf{E}_d)$. A defender is a function $\mathtt{Def} : \{v^{t^0}\} \to 2^{2^{\mathsf{A}_d}}$. We call $\mathtt{Def}$ determinstic if $|\mathtt{Def}(v^{t^0})| = 1$ - otherwise it is non-deterministic.*

The temporal semantics we consider is based on the idea that a defender selects his defence measures once, followed by the attacker selecting atomic attacks in a step-wise fashion.

Remark 1. The choice of letting the defender select defence measures once is contrasting the work of Hermanns et al. [7] that considers a semantics where defender and attacker can do actions interchangeably. We believe it is a more realistic scenario that a defender choose actions to prevent attacks and not actively work against an attacker.

Definition 5. *Let $\psi \in \mathcal{L}(A_a, A_d)^w$ be an AD-tree, $\mathtt{Graph}(\psi) = (\mathcal{V}^t, \mathcal{V}^t_\dagger, v^{t0}, \mathrm{E}, \mathrm{E}_d)$ be its associated tree-graph, $\mathtt{Def}$ be a defender and let $\mathtt{Att}$ be an attacker. Then the transition system over ψ with attacker $\mathtt{Att}$ and defender $\mathtt{Def}$, denoted $\mathtt{LTS}(\psi|\mathtt{Att}|\mathtt{Def})$, is a tuple $(\mathcal{V}, \mathcal{V}_\dagger, v^0, \rightarrow, \rightarrow_\neg, \rightarrow_\dagger, \dashrightarrow)$ where*

- $\mathcal{V} = \mathcal{V}^t$ *is a set of states,*
- $\mathcal{V}_\dagger \subseteq \mathcal{V}^t_\dagger \cup \{v \in \mathcal{V} \mid \mathtt{Att}(\mathcal{V}) = \dagger\}$ *is a set of dead-end states,*
- $v^0 = v^{t0}$ *is the initial state,*
- $\rightarrow \subseteq \mathcal{V} \times A_a \times \mathcal{V}$ *is a set of transitions where $(v, a, v') \in \rightarrow$ if $a \in \mathtt{Att}(v)$ and $(v, a, v') \in \mathrm{E}$,*
- $\rightarrow_\neg \subseteq \mathcal{V} \times A_a \times \mathcal{V}$ *is a set of transitions where $(v, a, v) \in \rightarrow_\neg$ only if $(v, a, v') \in \rightarrow$,*
- $\rightarrow_\dagger = \{(v, \dagger, v) | v \in \mathcal{V} \wedge \dagger \in \mathtt{Att}(v)\}$ *is the do-no-attack transition relation, and*
- $\dashrightarrow \subseteq \{(v^0, D, v) \mid D \in \mathtt{Def}(v^0) \wedge (v^0, D, v) \in \mathrm{E}_d\}$ *is the defence select transitions.*

As per tradition we write $v \xrightarrow{a} v' (v \xrightarrow{\neg a} v')$ in lieu of $(v, a, v') \in \rightarrow ((v, a, v') \in \rightarrow_\neg)$ and generalises this to $\dashrightarrow$ and $\rightarrow_\dagger$. We write $v \rightarrow^* v'$ if there is a sequence of transitions emanating from v and ending in v' and denote by $\mathtt{Reach}(v) = \{v'|v \rightarrow^* v'\}$. A run over $\mathtt{LTS}(\psi|\mathtt{Att}|\mathtt{Def})$ is a sequence

$$(v^0, D)(v_1, \alpha_1)(v_2, \alpha_2) \ldots (v_{n-1}, \alpha_{n-1})(v_n, \dagger)v_n$$

where $v^0 \xdashrightarrow{D} v_1$ and for all $1 \leq i < n$, $\alpha_i \in \{a, \neg a \mid a \in A_a\}$, $v_i \xrightarrow{\alpha_i} v_{i+1}$ and finally $v_n \xrightarrow{\dagger} v_n$. We denote by $\Omega(\psi|\mathtt{Att}|\mathtt{Def})$ all runs over ψ.

Obviously, as an attacker, we would be interested in for any D to find a run $(v^0, D)(v_1, \alpha_1)(v_2, \alpha_2) \ldots (v_n, \dagger)v_n$ where $v_n \in \mathcal{V}_\dagger$ and $[\![\psi]\!]v_n = \mathtt{tt}$ whereas a defender wishes to find a D' such that all runs end in a state $v'_\dagger$ where $[\![\psi]\!]v'_\dagger = \mathtt{ff}$.

Attacker Question 2. *Given an AD tree $\psi \in \mathcal{L}^w(A_a, A_d)$, an attacker $\mathtt{Att}$, non-deterministic defender $\mathtt{Def}$ is it the case for all D that there exists a run $(v^0, D)(v_1, \alpha_1)(v_2, \alpha_2) \ldots (v_n, \dagger)v_n \in \Omega(\psi|\mathtt{Att}|\mathtt{Def})$ such that $[\![\psi]\!]v_n = \mathtt{tt}$.*

Defender Question 2. *Given an AD tree $\psi \in \mathcal{L}^w(A_a, A_d)$, attacker $\mathtt{Att}$, non-deterministic defender $\mathtt{Def}$ does there exists a $D \subseteq A_d$ such that for any run $(v^0, D)(v_1, \alpha_1)(v_2, \alpha_2) \ldots (v_n, \dagger)v_n \in \Omega(\psi|\mathtt{Att}|\mathtt{Def})$, $[\![\psi]\!]v_n = \mathtt{ff}$.*

Technique 1. *The verification technique that may be used to answer Attacker Question 2 and Defender Question 2 is model checking. Consider we are given an AD-tree $\psi \subseteq \mathcal{L}^w(\mathsf{A}_a, \mathsf{A}_d)$, an attacker* Att *and non-deterministic defender* Def *and want to answer Attacker Question 2. Let* $\mathrm{LTS}(\psi|\mathtt{Att}|\mathtt{Def}) = (\mathcal{V}, \mathcal{V}_\dagger, v^0, \rightarrow,$ $\rightarrow_\neg, \rightarrow_\dagger, \dashrightarrow)$ *and let* $\mathcal{V}_D = \{v \in \mathcal{V} \mid v^0 \overset{D}{\dashrightarrow} v\}$ *be the set of states reached by the defender doing an action. Then the straightforward approach for answering Attacker Question 2 is to do a reachability search from all of the states in* $\mathcal{V}_D$ *for a state* $v \in \mathcal{V}_\dagger$ *where* $[\![v]\!]\psi = \mathtt{tt}$. *That is, if for all vertices* $v \in \mathcal{V}_D$ *the set* $R_v = \{v' \in \mathtt{Reach}(v) \mid [\![v']\!]\psi = \mathtt{tt}\}$ *is non-empty then Attacker Question 2 is true. On the other hand, if for some* v, R_v *is empty we have found an answer for Defender Question 2.*

The possibility of an attack is interesting in its own right, but disregards how long time an attack may take. In the real world, an attacker may only be interested in attacks that are executable within a given time horizon. Likewise, the defender could possibly be happy as long he can guarantee a successful attack can only occur after a specific time. To incorporate timing information, consider that each atomic attack is assigned a duration interval by a function $\Delta : \mathsf{A}_a \rightarrow \mathcal{B}(\mathbb{R})$ - where $\mathcal{B}(\mathbb{R})$ denotes all possible intervals over $\mathbb{R}$. A timed attacker is thus a tuple $\mathtt{Att}^\tau = (\mathtt{Att}, \Delta)$ where Att is an attacker and Δ is defined as above.

With a timed attacker $(\mathtt{Att}, \Delta)$ and defender Def define a timed run as a sequence

$$(v^0, D)(v_1, d_1, \alpha_1)(v_2, d_2, \alpha_2) \ldots (v_n, \dagger)v_n$$

where

$$(v^0, D)(v_1, \alpha_1)(v_2, \alpha_2) \ldots (v_n, \dagger)v_n$$

is a run and for all $1 \leq i < n$, $d_i \in \Delta(c(\alpha_i))$ where $c(a) = c(\neg a) = a$. For the remainder of this paper we let $\Omega^\tau(\psi|\mathtt{Att}^\tau|\mathtt{Def})$ be all timed runs over timed attacker $\mathtt{Att}^\tau$ and defender Def.

Attacker Question 3. *Given an AD tree* $\psi \in \mathcal{L}^w(\mathsf{A}_a, \mathsf{A}_d)$, *a time horizon* τ, *timed attacker* $\mathtt{Att}^\tau$, *non-deterministic defender* Def *does there for all* D *exist a timed run* $(v^0, D)(v_1, d_1, \alpha_1)(v_2, d_2, \alpha_2) \ldots (v_n, \dagger)v_n \in \Omega^\tau(\psi|\mathtt{Att}^\tau|\mathtt{Def})$ *such that* $[\![\psi]\!]v_n = $ *and* $\sum_{i=1}^{n-1} d_i \leq \tau$.

Defender Question 3. *Given an AD tree* $\psi \in \mathcal{L}^w(\mathsf{A}_a, \mathsf{A}_d)$, *timed attacker* $\mathtt{Att}^\tau$, *a time horizon* τ *and non-deterministic defender* Def *does there exists a* D *such that for all timed runs* $(v^0, D)(v_1, d_1, \alpha_1)(v_2, d_2, \alpha_2) \ldots (v_n, \dagger)v_n \in \Omega^\tau(\psi|\mathtt{Att}|\mathtt{Def})$ *either* $[\![\psi]\!]v_n = \mathtt{ff}$ *or* $\sum_{i=1}^{n-1} d_i > \tau$.

Technique 2. *For answering Attacker Question 3 for* $\psi \in \mathcal{L}^w(\mathsf{A}_a, \mathsf{A}_d)$ *with timed attacker* $\mathtt{Att}^\tau = (\mathtt{Att}, \Delta)$ *and non-deterministic defender* Def *we will consider a symbolic transition system with states of the form* (v, I) *where* $v \in \mathcal{V}$ *and* I *is an interval of* $\mathbb{R}_{\geq 0}$ *and initial state* $(v^0, [0, 0])$. *From a symbolic state* (v, I) *we can do a symbolic transition* $(v, I) \overset{a}{\rightsquigarrow} (v', I + I')$ *if (and* $(v, I) \overset{\neg a}{\rightsquigarrow} (v, I + I')$

if $a \neq \dagger$) and $I' = \Delta(a)$ ($I' = [0,0]$ if $a = \dagger$). Similarly to the traditional semantics we define Reach$((v, I))$ *to be the set of reachable symbolic states from* Reach$((v, I))$. *Answering Attacker Question 3 with a time bound τ is now a matter of generating the sets $R_v\{(v', [a, b]) \in$* Reach$((v^0, [0,0]))|a \leq \tau \wedge [\![v']\!]\psi =$ tt$\}$ *where $v \in \{v' \mid v^0 \overset{D}{\dashrightarrow} v'\}$ and verifying they are all non-empty. Conversely if one of them is empty, we have found a solution to Defender Question 3.*

2.2 Stochastic Semantics

Our end goal is to have a fully stochastic model. For the defender part of the transition system we let the choice of defence measures be selected according to a probability mass function $\gamma_{\text{Def}} : 2^{A_d} \to [0,1]$. A stochastic defender is thus a tuple $\text{Def}^S = (\text{Def}, \gamma_{\text{Def}})$ where Def is a defender and $\gamma_{\text{Def}}(D) \neq 0 \implies D \in \text{Def}(v^{t^0})$. A stochastic attacker for ψ is a tuple $\text{Att}^S = (\text{Att}^\tau, \gamma_{\text{Att}}, \delta)$ where $\text{Att}^\tau = (\text{Att}, \Delta)$ is a timed attacker, $\gamma_{\text{Att}} : \mathcal{V} \to A_a \cup \{\dagger\} \to \mathbb{R}$ assigns a probability mass function to each state for selecting the action to perform and $\delta : A_a \to \mathbb{R} \to \mathbb{R}$ assigns a probability density to the possible execution times of each action. A few requirements must be stated here

1. if $\gamma_{\text{Att}}(v^t)(a) \neq 0$ then $a \in \text{Att}(v^t)$ and
2. if $\delta(a)(r) \neq 0$ then $r \in \Delta(a)$.

The first requirement is simply expressing that the stochastic attacker may only select actions defined by the timed attacker while the second requirement expresses that only execution times inside the interval defined by Δ should be given a density. The final component we need before giving the stochastic semantics is a an environment Env that assigns success probabilities to the execution of individual atomic actions: formally for each action we let $\text{Env}_a : \{a, \neg a\} \to]0,1[$ be a probability mass function assigning a non-zero probability of succeeding an atomic attack.

Forming the core of a probability measure over runs of LTS$(\psi|\text{Att}^\tau|\text{Def})$ with a stochastic attacker $\text{Att}^S = (\text{Att}^\tau, \gamma_{\text{Att}}, \delta)$ and stochastic defender $\text{Def}^S = (\text{Def}, \gamma_{\text{Def}})$, we define a measure over a structure $\pi = (v_0, I_0, \alpha_0)$ $(v_0, I_0, \alpha_0) \dots (v_n, \dagger)v_n$ where for all i, I_i is an interval and $\alpha_i \in \{a, \neg a \mid a \in A_a\}$ from v inductively as follows:

$$G_v^{\text{Att}^S|\text{Def}^S|\text{Env}}(\pi) = (v_0 \overset{?}{=} v) \cdot \gamma_{\text{Att}}(v)(c(\alpha_0)) \cdot$$
$$\left(\int_{I_0} (\delta(c(\alpha_0))(\tau)) \, d\tau \right) \cdot \text{Env}_{c(\alpha)}(\alpha_0) \cdot G_{v'}^{\text{Att}^S|\text{Def}^S|\text{Env}}(\pi^1),$$

where, $v_0 \overset{?}{=} v$ is 1 if $v_0 = v$ and zero otherwise, $v \overset{\alpha_0}{\longrightarrow} v'$, $c(a) = c(\neg a) = a$ and base case $G^{\text{Att}^S|\text{Def}^S|\text{Env}}(v_n v_n) = \gamma_{\text{Att}}(v_n)(\dagger)$. As we will notice, the structure π does not include defence measures and thus we are lacking the probabilistic behaviour of the defender. For taking this into account, we instead consider structures like $\Pi = (v^0, D)\pi$ to which we can easily assign a probability measure as follows $F_{v^0}^{\text{Att}^S|\text{Def}^S|\text{Env}}(\Pi) = \gamma_{\text{Def}}(D) \cdot G_v^{\text{Att}^S|\text{Def}^S|\text{Env}}(\pi)$ where $v^0 \xrightarrow{D} v$. We will usually omit the v^0 subscript and thus whenever we write $F^{\text{Att}^S|\text{Def}^S|\text{Env}}$ we really mean $F_{v^0}^{\text{Att}^S|\text{Def}^S|\text{Env}}$.

With a measure over timed runs, we are now ready to define the probability of a successful timed attack: let $\omega = (v^0, D)(v_1, d_1, \alpha_1)(v_2, d_2, \alpha_2) \ldots (v_n, \dagger)v_n$ be a timed run, then we define the indicator function for ψ and time bound τ as

$$1_{\psi,\tau}(\omega) = \begin{cases} 1 & \text{if } [\![\psi]\!]v_n \text{ and } \sum_{i=1}^{n-1} d_i \leq \tau \\ 0 & \text{otherwise} \end{cases}.$$

Integrating $1_{\psi,\tau}$ over all runs yields the probability of a successful attack.

$$\mathbb{P}^{\text{Att}^S}(\psi, \tau) = \int_{\omega \in \Omega^\tau(\psi)} 1_{\psi,\tau} \mathrm{d}F^{\text{Att}^S|\text{Def}^S}$$

Attacker Question 4. *Given an AD-tree, a stochastic attacker, a stochastic defender and time bound τ; what is the probability of a succesful attack.*

Technique 3. *The technique we shall later apply for answering Attacker Question 4 is statistical model checking. This technique relies on having a simulator for the stochastic semantics that can generate timed runs up to a time bound τ. Each run is now either a succesful attack or a failed attack i.e. a Bernoulli experiment. Generating several runs we can, using classic statistical methods, estimate the probability with some confidence.*

2.3 Adding Cost

In the running example, we note that some of the attacks naturally will result in some cost for the attacker. The most obvious one being the "bribe" option. Therefore researchers started augmenting their modelling languages with costs [2,6,7] . In this paper we are also considering a cost-based semantics but instead of a fixed cost per atomic attack a, we define a cost rate C_a and define the cost of a timed run $\omega = (v^0, D)(v_1, d_1, \alpha_1)(v_2, d_2, \alpha_2) \ldots (v_n, \dagger)v_n$ as $\mathsf{C}(\omega) = \sum_{i=1}^{n-1} C_{c(\alpha_i)} \cdot d_i$. Given a time bound τ we define, in the style of Gadyatskaya et al. [6], the cost of a timed bounded run to be the accumulated cost up to reaching the time bound or the accumulated cost before reaching a successful state. Formally, if $\omega = (v^0, D)(v_1, d_1, \alpha_1)(v_2, d_2, \alpha_2) \ldots (v_n, \dagger)v_n$ and $i = \max\{i \mid [\![\psi]\!]v_n = \mathtt{ff} \wedge \sum_{j=1}^{i-1} d_j \leq \tau\}$ then we we define $\mathsf{C}^\tau(\omega) = \sum_{j=1}^{i-1} C_{c(\alpha_j)} \cdot d_j$. For a stochastic attacker, Att^S, we can now define his expected cost of an attempted attack against a stochastic defender Def^S within a time bound τ as

$$\mathbb{E}^{\text{Att}^S|\text{Def}^S|\text{Env}}(\psi, \tau) = \int_{\omega \in \Omega^\tau(\psi)} \mathsf{C}^\tau(\omega) \, \mathrm{d}F^{\text{Att}^S|\text{Def}^S|\text{Env}}$$

Attacker Question 5. *Given an AD-tree* ψ, *a stochastic attacker* Att^S, *a stochastic defender* Def^S *and a time bound* τ, *what is the expected cost of an attack? That is, calculate* $\mathbb{E}^{\text{Att}^S|\text{Def}^S}(\psi, \tau)$.

Technique 4. *As for Attacker Question 4 we answer Attacker Question 5 by applying statistical model checking. The approach is intuitively simple: generate a set of sample runs* $\omega_1, \dots \omega_n$, *for all* i *calculate* $c_{\omega_i} = \mathbb{E}^{\text{Att}^S|\text{Def}^S|\text{Env}}(\psi, \tau)$. *The* $c_{\omega_i}s$ *are random variables from the same underlying distribution and thus we can estimate their expected value.*

For the remainder of the paper we require on-the-fly information of the cost of runs; which means that we need to annotate our states with cost-information. Let $\text{LTS}(\psi|\text{Att}^\tau|\text{Def}) = (\mathcal{V}, \mathcal{V}_\dagger, v^0, \to, \to_\neg, \to_\dagger, \dashrightarrow)$ then a cost-annotated state is a tuple $c(v, r)$ where $v \in \mathcal{V}$ and $r \in \mathbb{R}$. We let $\mathcal{C}$ denote all cost-annotated states; and we say a cost-annotated-run is a sequence

$$\omega = ((v^0, c_0), D)((v_1, c_1), d_1, \alpha_1)((v_2, c_2), d_2, \alpha_2) \dots (v_n, c_n)(v_n, c_n)$$

where $c_o = c_1 = 0, (v^0, D)(v_1, d_1, \alpha_1)(v_2, d_2, \alpha_2) \dots (v_n, \dagger)v_n$ is a timed run and for all $2 \leq i \leq n$, $c_i = c_{i-1} + (\frac{1}{C_{c(\alpha_{i-1})}} \cdot d_{i-1})$. Lastly, for the remaining part of this paper we will have γ_{Att} map from cost-annotated states thus $\gamma_{\text{Att}} : \mathcal{C} \to \mathbb{A}_a \to \mathbb{R}$. In addition we let $\mathcal{S}(\psi)$ be the set of all possible stochastic attackers for the AD-tree ψ.

2.4   Parameterised Attacker

The framework so far defines the interaction between a specific stochastic attacker and a specific stochastic defender. However, attackers may be defined in terms of parameters that define their stochastic behaviour. Formally, a parameterised attacker is a tuple $(\mathcal{P}, \mathcal{D}, B)$ where $\mathcal{P} = \{p_1, p_2, \dots, p_n\}$ is a list of parameters each with finite domain D_i given by $\mathcal{D} : \mathcal{P} \to 2^{\cup_{i=1}^n D_i}$ and $B : \times_{i=1}^n D_i \to \mathcal{S}(\psi)$ gives the stochastic attacker corresponding to a given parameter setting.

Attacker Question 6. *Let* ψ *be an attack defence-tree,* Def^S *be a stochastic defender,* Env *be an environment, and let* t $(\mathcal{P}, \mathcal{D}, B)$ *be a parameterised attacker where* $\mathcal{P} = \{p_1, \dots, pn\}$ *and for all* i, $\mathcal{D}(p_i) = D_i$.
    Find $Q = \arg\min_{q \in \times_{i=0}^n D_i} \mathbb{E}^{B(q)|\text{Def}^S|\text{Env}}(\psi)$.

Technique 5. *For answering our final question of optimising parameters we will apply the statistical method ANalysis Of VAriance (ANOVA).*

ANOVA. Analysis of variance is a collection of statistical tests developed to compare whether one or more discrete *factors* has a significant effect on a continuous *response* variable. In the following we consider the one-factor design where we only have one factor and wishes to determine if this factor affects the response [11]. Consider we have a single factor with k levels, then for each level

i we associate a random variable $\mathcal{X}_i$ giving the response values. Then an anova analysis tests the hypothesis that $\mathbb{E}(\mathcal{X}_0) = \mathbb{E}(\mathcal{X}_1) \cdots = \mathbb{E}(\mathcal{X}_n)$ i.e. whether the mean response is the same for all the levels. For each level i we obtain samples $X_i = \{x_0^i, x_1^i, \ldots x_m^i\}$ and denote by $\bar{X}_i = \sum_{k=0}^m \frac{1}{m} x_k^i$ the mean of these and by $\bar{X} = \frac{1}{n*m} \sum_{l=0}^n \sum_{k=0}^m x_k^l$ the average of all samples.
ANOVA now calculates what is called the F-statistic

$$F = \frac{(\frac{1}{n-1}) \sum_{i=0}^n (\bar{X}_i - \bar{X})^2}{\frac{1}{m-n}(\sum_{i=0}^n \sum_{k=0}^m (x_k^i - \bar{X})^2)}$$

which if the hypothesis is true should follow a F-distribution with $n-1$ and $m-n$ degrees of freedom. Now, as usual with hypothesis, we can calculate a value p which characterises how likely it is to obtain a value of F if the hypothesis is true. If p is less than some predetermined α then we reject the hypothesis. ANOVA is only capable of determining whether there is a difference between the levels, but is inadequate for finding which level is the one being different. For finding the different one we need to apply a *post-hoc* test that will perform a comparison between all the pairs. One such test is Tukeys-Test which will compare all pair-wise means and return whether they are different - with some significance.

Optimising with ANOVA. The approach we take for finding the optimal parameter for minimising the expected cost of an attack is to iteratively generate samples for each configuration until a significant difference of α is found using ANOVA. Afterwards we apply Tukeys test - and for each pair of configurations that are significantly different from each other we remove the one with the smallest mean. In Algorithm 1 `Simulate`(ψ,c,τ) simulates the AD-tree ψ with the configuration c and returns the cost over that run, `Anova`(*simulations*) runs the anova analysis and returns the $p-$value, `FilterTukey`(*simulations*) runs Tukeys test and filter out the configuration with smallest cost for each significantly different pairs of configurations.

A small caveat with Algorithm 1 is that it may spin into an infinite loop if ANOVA determines there is significant difference while Tukeys-Test find no different pairs. In this case no filtering occurs and thus the algorithm will continue generating samples (and as ANOVA already determined there is a difference, α will never get larger than $1 - \alpha$ to terminate. In practice we overcome this problem by limiting the number of times the algorithm can determine there is a difference without removing a configuration.

3   Instantiating the Framework

The preceding section has defined a general modelling framework for attackers and defenders. In this section we present one way of defining a parameterised attacker. The first parameter we consider adding is a cost budget which is the maximal amount of resources an attacker can use during an attack. Given a cost budget variable, B, we define a cost-preserving stochastic attacker as one

Data: Set of configurations C, a time bound τ and an AD-tree ψ, samples per iteration x
foreach $c \in$ C **do**
| $simulations[c] = \emptyset$;
end
while $\neg conf$ **do**
   foreach $c \in$ C **do**
     foreach $i \in \{0, 1, \ldots, x\}$ **do**
     | $simulations[c] = simulations[c] \cup$ Simulate(ψ,c,τ)
     end
   end
   $a =$Anova($simulations$);
   if $a > 1 - \alpha$ **then**
   | $conf =$ tt;
   end
   else if $a < \alpha$ **then**
   | $C =$FilterTukey($simulations$)
   end
end
return C

Algorithm 1. Parameter Optimisation Algorithm.

that assign higher probabilities to atomic attacks that preserve most of the cost budget.

In the following we let $\mathtt{Att}^{nd}$ be the fully non-deterministic attacker - i.e. if $\psi \in \mathcal{L}(\mathtt{A}_a, \mathtt{A}_d)$ then $\mathtt{Att}((A, D)) = \mathtt{A}_a \setminus A$ if $[\![D, a]\!]\psi = $ ff otherwise †.

Definition 6. *Let* $\psi \in \mathcal{L}(\mathtt{A}_a, \mathtt{A}_d)$, *let B be a cost budget and let C be the cost-annotated states; then a cost-preserving stochastic attacker is a stochastic attacker* $\mathtt{Att}^S(B) = (\mathtt{Att}^\tau, \gamma^C_{\mathtt{Att}}, \delta)$ *with* $\mathtt{Att}^\tau = (\mathtt{Att}^{nd}, \Delta)$ *where*

- $\delta(a)$ *is a uniform distribution over* $\Delta(a)$,
- $\gamma^C_{\mathtt{Att}}((v, c))(a) = \frac{W(a)}{\sum_{b \in \mathtt{A}_a} W(b)}$ *where*
  - $W(a) = \frac{B - (c + C_a \cdot d_h)}{B}$ *with* $\Delta(a) = [d_l, d_h]$ *if* $B - (c + C_a \cdot d_h) > 0$ *and* $a \in \mathtt{Att}(v)$ *- otherwise* 0.
  if $a \in \mathtt{A}_a$ *and* $W(a) \neq 0$,
- $\gamma^C_{\mathtt{Att}}((v, c))(†) = 1 - \sum_{a \in \mathtt{A}_a} \gamma^C_{\mathtt{Att}}((v, c))(a)$ *and*
- $\delta((v, c))(r) = \frac{1}{d_h - d_l}$ *if* $r \in [d_l, d_h]$ *and* $\Delta(a) = [d_l, d_h]$.

Table 1. Parameters of the running example: the Cost column is the cost-rate of attack; while probability is success probability of the attack.

Attack	Cost rate	Probability
is	4	0.80
bs	5	0.70
t	5	0.70
b	5	0.70
st	2.5	0.50
ba	4.25	0.60
im	3.5	0.50
ot	0	0.60

It is not unreasonable to think that some attackers may have higher tendency to perform some attacks - even though they are more costly. Based on this thought we adapt the cost-preserving attacker to one with multiple parameters - one for each atomic attack. We call these parameters for likeliness-parameters.

Definition 7 (Parameterised-Attacker). *Let* $\psi \in \mathcal{L}(\mathtt{A}_a, \mathtt{A}_d)$ *where* $\mathtt{A}_a = \{a_1, \ldots, a_n\}$ *be an AD-tree, let B be a cost budget, let* $\mathtt{Att}^S(B) = (\mathtt{Att}^\tau, \gamma^C_{\mathtt{Att}}, \delta)$ *be the cost-preserving stochastic attacker, let C be the cost-annotated states and let* $D \subseteq \mathbb{R}_{\geq 0}$ *be some finite domain. Then we define our parameterised attacker*

$\mathtt{Att}^{SP}(B) = (\mathcal{P}, \mathcal{D}, B)$ *where* $\mathcal{P} = \{p_a | a \in A_a\}$, $\mathcal{D}(p_a) = D$ *for all* $a \in A_a$, *and*
$B(p_{a_1}, \ldots, p_{a_n}) = (\mathtt{Att}^\tau, \gamma^P_{\mathtt{Att}}, \delta)$ *where*

- $\gamma^P_{\mathtt{Att}}((v, c))(a) = \frac{W(a)}{\sum_{b \in A_a} W(b)}$ *where* $W(d) = p_d \cdot \gamma^C_{\mathtt{Att}}(d)$ *for* $a \in A_a$ *and*
- $\gamma^P_{\mathtt{Att}}((v, c))(\dagger) = 1 - \sum_{b \in A_a} \gamma^P_{\mathtt{Att}}((v, c))(b)$

Example 1. As an example of how the parameters may affect expected cost of an attacker we consider four different configurations for our running example (see Table 1 for the cost and success probabilities); namely (1) all likeliness parameters are 1, (2) all likeliness parameters are 1500, (3) all likeliness parameters are 1 except for *threaten* which is 1500 and (4) all likeliness parameters are 1 except for *threaten* and *Bribe* which are 1500.

Estimating the expected cost for these different configurations with a time limit of 1000 yield expected cost 229 ± 35 for Item 1, 208 ± 33 for Item 2, 120 ± 20 for Item 3 and finally for Item 4 we get 102 ± 20. All of the estimates were computed using 30 simulations.

4 Experiments

The framework developed has been translated into a UPPAAL SMC [5] timed automata model based on a textual description of the AD-tree, the cost parameters and their timing intervals. Also the textual description includes the probabilities of an atomic attack to be successful. In the following we will use these scripts in conjunction with UPPAAL to answer the questions raised throughout the running text.

4.1 Encoding

Although this encoding is specific for the instantiation of Sect. 3 we note that it shows the applicability of UPPAAL SMC to encode the general framework from Sect. 2. The encoding of an AD-tree within UPPAAL SMC follows along the lines of [6] with one automaton modelling the defender, one automaton modelling the attacker, and one automaton modelling the environmental choice of an outcome for the execution of an atomic attack. To coordinate their behaviour the automata synchronise over channels for indicating what action the attacker wants to perform - and boolean variables to maintain the discrete state of the AD-tree (i.e. what atomic attacks and defenses are true at any given time). In the following paragraph double concentric circles denote the initial state of an automaton.

Defender. In Fig. 3 we present the template of the Defender Timed Automaton for an AD-tree with the defender actions $A_d = \{p1d, p2d, p3d\}$. The automaton initiates by selecting a subset of A_d and setting the corresponding boolean variables (e.g. b_p1d) to true. Afterwards, the

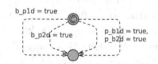

Fig. 3. The defender automaton

defender does nothing. Since there are no weights on the edges from the initial locations, the choice of an edge is a uniform choice - corresponding to the uniform choice in our stochastic semantics previously given.

Attacker. Let $\mathtt{Att}^{SP}(B) = (\mathcal{P}, \mathcal{D}, B)$ with $\mathcal{P} = \{p_{a\_1}, p_{a\_2}\}$ be a parameterised attacker with attacker actions $A_a = \{a1, a2\}$. Figure 4 shows how to encode the attacker given by $B(T1, T2)$. Here the AD-tree has $\Delta(ai) = [L\_ai, H\_ai]$ and a cost rate of C_ai/H_ai for executing a_i. The automaton keeps tracks of the currently used resources in the clock *usedRes*. Initially the automaton can go to a dead-end if one of two conditions

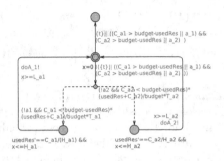

Fig. 4. The attacker automaton

are true: either (1) the tree is already true ($\{t\}$) or (2) for all atomic actions it is either the case that they cannot be performed without risking exceeding the budget (i.e. ($C\_ai > budget - usedRes$)) or they are already true. In case this edge is not enabled, the automaton instead transits to a probabilistic choice to choose what action to perform according to the weights previously described in Sect. 3. After selecting an attack a_i, the attacker goes to a location where a delay between $d \in [L\_ai, H\_ai]$ is selected and the clock *usedRes* is increased by $d \cdot (C\_a1/H\_a1)$. After this, the automaton synchronises on *doAi*! to tell the environment that he attempted to perform ai.

Environment. An example of an environment automaton is shown in Fig. 5. Initially it awaits *doA*? synchronisation from the attacker after which it instantly selects a result. A successful execution happens with probability p while an unsuccessful execution occurs with probability $1 - p$. If succesful the boolean variable b_A is set to true.

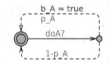

Fig. 5. The environment automaton

In practice there is one of these loops for each attacker proposition of the AD-tree.

4.2 Estimating Probability of Attack

Consider that we use the Cost-preserving attacker profile, and are given a time bound τ and consider the defender selects defence measures according to a uniform distribution; then we can answer Attacker Question 4 and Attacker Question 5 by using the statistical model checking capabilities of UPPAAL SMC. For Attacker Question 4 we simply ask the question $Pr[<=\tau]\{t\}$ which will return a confidence interval for performing a successful attack.

Table 2. Probability Estimates and expected cost for the Cost-preserving attacker for various time bounds.

Bound	Cost	Probability
10	34.78	0.08
50	143.28	0.52
100	221.64	0.84
200	192.70	0.95
400	232.75	0.95

For Attacker Question 5 we use the query $E[<=\tau; \text{nbRun}](\max : \text{usedRes}* (1 - \{t\}))$, where nbRun is the number of runs used by UPPAAL SMC to estimate the cost and *usedRes* is a UPPAAL variable counting the cost. The $(1 - \{t\})$ is a technicality to make sure *usedRes* stop increasing after the attack has been successful. In Table 2 we show the expected cost and probability of a successful attack. Estimating the cost was done with 500 runs in all cases.

4.3 Parameter Optimisation

We have applied Algorithm 1 (with UPPAAL SMC as a simulating backend) to our running example with the likeliness parameters obtaining values in the range $\{1, 150\}$ and with a time bound of 1000. The x in the algorithm was set to 10. The algorithm determined that 64 of the 256 configurations yield higher expected cost. The remaining ones are indistinguishable. In Fig. 6 we show boxplots for the various configurations ordered such that configurations deemed optimal by ANOVA are at the left while configurations yielding higher expected cost are to the right. Visually we notice that there is a seperation between these two groups.

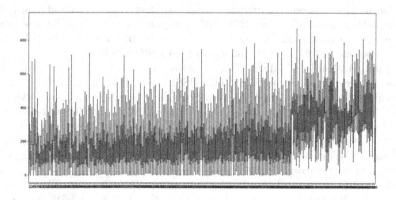

Fig. 6. Sampled data from the ANOVA analysis.

5 Conclusion

In this paper we have developed a temporal and stochastic semantics for attack-defense trees. The stochastic semantics distinguishes itself from similar work of [6] by allowing time-dependent cost functions. The attack-defense tree is translated into UPPAAL SMC stochastic timed automata, and it is shown how this translation may answer several of the questions stated throughout the running text: for instance how to estimate the expected cost of an attacker. This paper also includes a parameterised description of attackers which leads to the interesting question of finding optimal parameter settings. We develop a method based upon the statistical test ANOVA and observe that our algorithm found 64 out of 256 configurations to yield higher cost than the remaining ones.

In the future we plan to expand the expressive power of our framework, and we wish to handle temporal dependencies between attacker actions: currently, the attacker is capable of choosing to bribe a subject before actually having identified the subject. Another interesting work is to allow defenders to do counter measures while the attacker is attacking and create a more game-like feeling of the semantics. The definition of attackers are currently defined in terms of simple parameters, in the future will attempt creating a high-level for describing more complex attacker behaviours. Obtaining the probabilities and cost-functions that our framework depend on is a research topic in its own right.

References

1. Alur, R., Dill, D.: Automata for modeling real-time systems. In: Paterson, M.S. (ed.) ICALP 1990. LNCS, vol. 443, pp. 322–335. Springer, Heidelberg (1990). https://doi.org/10.1007/BFb0032042
2. Aslanyan, Z., Nielson, F.: Pareto efficient solutions of attack-defence trees. In: Principles of Security and Trust, vol. 9036, p. 95 (2015). https://doi.org/10.1007/978-3-662-46666-7_6
3. Aslanyan, Z., Nielson, F., Parker, D.: Quantitative verification and synthesis of attack-defence scenarios. In: IEEE 29th Computer Security Foundations Symposium, CSF 2016, Lisbon, Portugal, 27 June–1 July 2016, pp. 105–119. IEEE Computer Society (2016). https://doi.org/10.1109/CSF.2016.15
4. Bagnato, A., Kordy, B., Meland, P., Schweitzer, P.: Attribute decoration of attack-defense trees. Int. J. Secur. Soft. Eng. (IJSSE) **3**(2), 1–35 (2012)
5. David, A., Larsen, K.G., Legay, A., Mikucionis, M., Poulsen, D.B.: Uppaal SMC tutorial. STTT **17**(4), 397–415 (2015). https://doi.org/10.1007/s10009-014-0361-y
6. Gadyatskaya, O., Hansen, R.R., Larsen, K.G., Legay, A., Olesen, M.C., Poulsen, D.B.: Modelling attack-defense trees using timed automata. In: Fränzle, M., Markey, N. (eds.) FORMATS 2016. LNCS, vol. 9884, pp. 35–50. Springer, Cham (2016). https://doi.org/10.1007/978-3-319-44878-7_3
7. Hermanns, H., Krämer, J., Krčál, J., Stoelinga, M.: The value of attack-defence diagrams. In: Piessens, F., Viganò, L. (eds.) POST 2016. LNCS, vol. 9635, pp. 163–185. Springer, Heidelberg (2016). https://doi.org/10.1007/978-3-662-49635-0_9
8. Kordy, B., Mauw, S., Radomirović, S., Schweitzer, P.: Attack-defense trees. J. Logic Comput. **24**(1), 55–87 (2014)
9. Kordy, B., Piètre-Cambacédès, L., Schweitzer, P.: DAG-based attack and defense modeling: don't miss the forest for the attack trees. Comput. Sci. Rev. **13–14**, 1–38 (2014). https://doi.org/10.1016/j.cosrev.2014.07.001
10. Mauw, S., Oostdijk, M.: Foundations of attack trees. In: Won, D.H., Kim, S. (eds.) ICISC 2005. LNCS, vol. 3935, pp. 186–198. Springer, Heidelberg (2006). https://doi.org/10.1007/11734727_17
11. Montgomery, D.C.: Design and Analysis of Experiments. Wiley, Hoboken (2006)
12. Schneier, B.: Attack trees: Modeling security threats. Dr. Dobb's J. (1999)

Probabilistic Modeling of Insider Threat Detection Systems

Brian Ruttenberg[1]([⊠]), Dave Blumstein[1], Jeff Druce[1], Michael Howard[1],
Fred Reed[1], Leslie Wilfong[2], Crystal Lister[2], Steve Gaskin[3], Meaghan Foley[4],
and Dan Scofield[4]

[1] Charles River Analytics, Cambridge, MA 02138, USA
bruttenberg@cra.com
[2] Cognitio Corp., McLean, VA 22102, USA
[3] Applied Marketing Science, Waltham, MA 02451, USA
[4] Assured Information Systems, Rome, NY 13441, USA

Abstract. Due to the high consequences of poorly performing automated insider threat detection systems (ITDSs), it is advantageous for Government and commercial organizations to understand the performance and limitations of potential systems before their deployment. We propose to capture the uncertainties and dynamics of organizations deploying ITDSs to create an accurate and effective probabilistic graphical model that forecasts the operational performance of an ITDS throughout its deployment. Ultimately, we believe this modeling methodology will result in the deployment of more effective ITDSs.

Keywords: Insider threat · Probabilistic relational models

1 Introduction

Insider threats are a major source of concern for many Government agencies and private sector industries. For example, several recent high-profile incidents have revealed the severe damage that insiders can inflict on both Government and commercial organizations [7,14]. While human analysis and direct questioning may be the most accurate way to identify insiders, examining every individual in a large organization is infeasible and intrusive, and most organizations use automated methods to identify potential candidates for closer examination.

Automated insider threat detection systems (ITDSs) use information about the people, activities, and data from an organization to infer potential or active threats. Despite their widespread adoption, ITDSs tend to suffer from serious deficiencies [12]. First, most ITDSs are deployed in dynamic organizations and use uncertain or noisy data to make inferences; behavior changes over time, world events can temporarily (but significantly) disrupt activities, and logs used to infer threats may be imperfect or ambiguous. Second, the performance of deployed ITDSs can vary significantly from their initial testing, or change over time. Considering the high consequences of false negative detections, system

© Springer International Publishing AG 2018
P. Liu et al. (eds.): GraMSec 2017, LNCS 10744, pp. 91–98, 2018.
https://doi.org/10.1007/978-3-319-74860-3_6

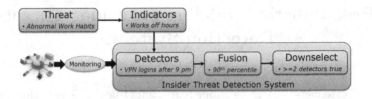

Fig. 1. An example functional architecture of an ITDS.

sensitivities are often increased, producing massive amounts of false positives that overwhelm human analysts. Finally, any post-deployment fixes on ITDSs is a time-consuming task and one that is often neglected due to cost.

One solution to these problems is to model a proposed ITDS *before* it is deployed in an organization. If such a model could account for the dynamics and uncertainties, one could predict the impact of deploying an ITDS, compute its sensitivity and robustness, or even use the model to optimize its performance. However, building and using such a model is a challenging endeavor, since organizations, people, and the ITDSs themselves are complex entities.

In this paper, we describe our efforts to build and use probabilistic and relational graphical models [3] to represent and reason about automated ITDS performance, quality and sensitivity. By representing the uncertainty in the threat system (e.g., non-deterministic detection algorithms) and in the organization, we have developed a powerful tool that gives ITDS analysts and designers the ability to understand *how* and *why* insider threat performance may change in deployed systems. Ultimately, we believe that our methodology will lead to the development of more robust, calibrated, and accurate insider threat systems.

This paper is organized as follows. In Sect. 2, we provide some background on insider threat systems and introduce notation on their structure and functions. In Sect. 3, we detail the design and implementation of a graphical model of ITDS. In Sect. 4, we present some applications and experiments using our system to demonstrate its benefits. Finally, we conclude in Sect. 5.

2   Insider Threat Systems

Although ITDSs vary in implementation, they typically share commonalities in their functional architecture, e.g., by decomposing the task of identifying malicious users into the identification of particular threat types. Threat types can include users exhibiting signs of leaving the organization, with newly abnormal work habits, or transferring an unusual amount of data. Because insiders act and behave relative to these threat types, the insider detection problem can be viewed as flagging users who exhibit *indicators* of a specific threat type.

To make these inferences, the ITDS uses *detectors* as numerical realizations of indicators. For example, consider the architecture of an ITDS shown in Fig. 1. The threat type of interest is "users who exhibit abnormal work habits", one indicator is "works off hours", and the detector for that indicator is "number of

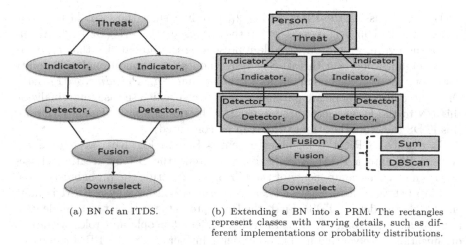

(a) BN of an ITDS.

(b) Extending a BN into a PRM. The rectangles represent classes with varying details, such as different implementations or probability distributions.

Fig. 2. The Bayesian network (BN) and probabilistic relational model (PRM) formulation of an ITDS.

days in a month with user VPN logins after 9 pm." The ITDS must also have an approach for issuing alerts from a potentially large number of detector values. This process can be thought of as being composed of *fusion* and *downselect* components; fusion merges detector outputs (e.g., counts the number of detectors for which a user was in the top 10% of all users), and downselect issues an alert if some criterion of the fusion is met (e.g., at least two detector values are true).

With complete information and perfect mappings from threat type to indicator to detector values, an ITDS would solve the insider threat detection problem. However, information gaps in the real world render perfect performance impossible. For example, actual threats vary in precisely which indicators they exhibit. Gaps also exist between indicators and detectors; "works off hours" may be a perfectly acceptable indicator, but "number of days in a month with VPN logins after 9 pm" may not accurately capture that concept. The net result is non-ideal performance in identifying threats, and potentially disastrous consequences for missed detections.

3 Graphical Models of Insider Threat Systems

3.1 Modeling Framework

Our goal under this effort is to create a flexible, adaptable, and rich framework for representing and reasoning on a variety of ITDS's deployed in a multitude of domains. Since these domains and ITSDs are uncertain and dynamic, we need a modeling representation that can accurately reflect these uncertainties yet still efficiently and effectively produce actionable results for a user. As such, we represent the ITDS and its domain as a *probabilistic relational model* (PRM) [3].

Before discussing the PRM, in Fig. 2(a) we first show the formulation of an ITDS described in Sect. 2 as a generative Bayesian network (BN) [6]. At the top of the figure, we have a variable representing the probability that a person in the organization is a threat. Successive nodes have conditional probability distributions of various components in the system, e.g., $P(Indicator_i|Threat)$. Once these distributions are parameterized for a specific use case, marginalizing this BN to the Downselect variable yields a distribution over the alert rate for this ITDS (among other things that can be computed).

In essence, a PRM is an object-oriented BN. In Fig. 2(b), we extend the original BN into a PRM. Specifically, we extend the BN by creating classes describing various components of the ITDS, and describe the probabilistic relationship between these classes. There are several reasons why a PRM is more effective for modeling ITDSs. First, the BN represents the threat as a single variable for an entire organization. In reality, different people and roles within an organization have varying likelihood of being insiders [1], and a PRM can easily represent this uncertainty in different classes (as shown by the Person class at the top of Fig. 2(b)). Second, ITDSs often flag people as potential threats when their behavior is different or anomalous compared to others in the organization or team. Hence, modeling the behaviors of a *group* of people can allow us to model algorithms that make relative comparisons (like dimensionality reduction or clustering). Finally, a PRM allows us to represent uncertainty over the structure of the ITDS itself, enabling us to characterize the performance of an ITDS that selects algorithms dynamically or non-deterministically. For example, Fig. 2(b) shows an ITDS where the choice of the fusion algorithm is either a simple sum operation or uses the clustering method DBScan [2]. As shown later, this representation can also allow one to optimize the ITDS to choose the best algorithm or parameter that maximizes performance.

3.2   Implementation

Implementing a large PRM for an ITDS with many users and complex constraints is challenging. To facilitate rapid construction, (re-)configuration, and reasoning, we build our framework using a probabilistic programming language (PPL) [9]. Probabilistic programming is a general approach to representation and reasoning that uses the flexibility and expressiveness of programming languages to create complex, rich, and realistic models of the world. Specifically, we use Figaro [8], an object-oriented PPL that allows us to express PRMs that are scalable (e.g., can be expanded to model complex, large organizations), uncertain (e.g., over user behavior), and incorporate complex modeling components (e.g., multifaceted tasks such as downselecting). Using Figaro also allows us to perform a variety of informative inference queries without constructing additional models, as will be discussed in Sect. 4. A full description of Figaro, downloadable code, and runnable examples are available at https://github.com/p2t2/figaro.

The most challenging task is the parameterization of the probabilistic and functional relationship between the variables, critical in describing uncertainty in an ITDS and the target organization. For example, conditional probability values such as $P(Indicator = True|Threat = True)$ must be chosen with respect to that indicator and the norms and expectations in a particular organizations. Full discussion of model parameterization is outside the scope of this paper. However, our team has proposed and explored several options for accurately representing parameters, including aggregation of collected statistics, using subject matter expertise, and deploying surveys to capture the organizational behaviors. For example, we deployed surveys that probed users about their email and internet usage habits, and used the results to estimate the value and uncertainty for parameter which can be directly incorporated into our model. Additional organization related parameters, e.g., prior threat probabilities, could be estimated from previous manual assessments of users, or approximated by parameters from similar organizations where these values are well known.

4   Experimentation

Once a model of an ITDS is defined, we can perform *inference* on the model. Here, we consider three realizations of inference: performance, sensitivity, and optimization, all performed on the *same* model. Because PPLs separate model representation from model inference [5], we only need to build a single model of the ITDS to perform a variety of queries. To test our approach, we model the performance of an ITDS running on a simulated organization consisting of four thousand employees, where users who are going to leave the company are considered threats, and our four indicators are associated with excessive webmail, login, and web-browsing activity. We obtain realistic detector data for these indicators from a CERT database [4]. The system recall (the fraction of true threats the system catches), the precision (the fraction of users the systems identifies as threats that are true threats), and the false positive rate (FPR- the fraction of users the system incorrectly identifies as threats) are considered.

4.1   Performance

Performance estimates are implemented as queries against the model for the distribution or expected value of metrics, conditioned on one or more other variables. For example, to measure the recall of an ITDS, we query the model for the conditional distribution $P(Downselect|Threat = true)$ (or the expectation with respect to this distribution). Similarly for precision, we query for $P(Threat|Downselect = true)$.

In addition to distributions or expectations, we can also produce confidence bounds on queries. That is, for some set of variables $\mathbb{V}$ in the model and some performance query Q (e.g., recall), we can compute $P(E[Q]|\mathbb{V})$, the distribution of the expected value of Q conditioned on $\mathbb{V}$. This has the benefit of conveying to the user the variation of system performance that one could expect when deploying the ITDS in the real world, with respect to some uncertain parameters (e.g., the prior over the threat rate). In Fig. 3(a), we compute the 60% confidence interval for 11 system performance metrics on our example ITDS model. The value

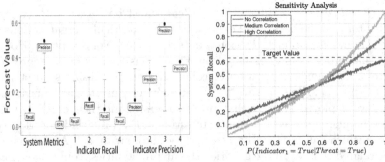

(a) Performance results, showing the predic- (b) Sensitivity analysis, varying a pa-
tion (circle), 60% interval, and ground truth rameter of the model $P(Indicator_1 =$
(dot) from a third–party evaluator. $true|Threat = true)$ for three different
levels of indicator correlation.

Fig. 3. Two illustrative examples of inference on an IEM.

of the first (left-most) query suggests that ITDS might detect fewer than 20% of
threats. However, system precision implies only one false positive for each true
positive, which appears to be an overly high precision for the ITDS application.
It is likely acceptable to release ten or more false alarms to every true threat-
assuming that would improve system recall-to the human screeners who are the
next step in the process.

4.2   Sensitivity

The sensitivity of the ITDS is also of interest to a system designer or analyst
who may want to understand the implications of incorrect assumptions or organizational changes over time. For example, suppose a slight perturbation in a
parameter leads to vastly different outcomes in the expected precision or recall of
the ITDS. Currently, sensitivity analysis is implemented using Figaro's existing
inference capabilities (i.e., vary each parameter and record the changes in performance). However, our ongoing research focuses on using more sophisticated
approaches, such as computing gradients of the queries via automatic differentiation [10].

Figure 3(b) illustrates how sensitivity analysis might inform an ITDS
designer. In this example, we computed the system recall for all possible values
of the parameter $P(Indicator_1 = True|Threat = True)$ for the ITDS pictured
in Fig. 2(b). In this experiment, we consider the additional (and often realistic) complexity that the indicators are correlated with three different degrees
strength. Interestingly, a perfect estimate (about 63%) cannot be realized by the
model with no correlation between the detectors, but can with the cases including correlation. However, the correlation cases induce more variation, and hence
less stability.

4.3 Optimization

Designers may also seek to improve the performance of an ITDS by investigating alternate configurations or algorithms, for example, by optimizing configuration parameters to maximize system metrics. Using the same model as in the other inference tasks, we frame optimization as a *decision-making* problem [13]. In this formulation, we define a set of utility variables $\mathbb{U}$ in the model (e.g., system precision or F_1 score) and a parameter to optimize P. The optimal parameter $\hat{P}$ is formulated as $\hat{P} = \underset{p \in P}{argmax} E[U|p]$ That is, select the value of P that produces the highest expected utility. Performing this optimization builds on the existing inference capabilities of Figaro that search the decision space over the parameters of interest to maximize the utility function [11]. Table 1 illustrates an experiment optimizing the configuration for six parameters in an ITDS, where the utility is defined as the sum of system precision and recall. The final column shows the incremental improvements to utility after each decision. This result suggests that the optimized design is nearly twice as good as the original baseline (with respect to the defined metrics).

Table 1. Results of an experiment optimizing configuration parameters to improve predicted performance.

Decision	Component	Original threshold	New threshold	Utility
1	Detector A	2000	2100	1.04
2	Detector B	3	1	1.12
3	Detector C	7	8	1.14
4	Detector D	3	7	1.11
5	Detector E	1	2	1.12
6	Downselect	2	3	1.89

5 Conclusion

In this paper, we detailed our work creating a probabilistic and relational graphical model of ITDSs. Using the inference capabilities of our model, ITDS designers can understand the performance and limitations of current and deployed systems, and eventually, build more effective systems to thwart damaging incidents.

Significant future directions exist for this work. While we have presented general capabilities of an ITDS model, there is still an open question of the best way to adapt these capabilities for a variety of organizations: e.g., transferring knowledge from one organization to another may be a feasible way to parameterize these models for new organizations. In addition, our framework allows a variety of model topologies that can change depending on the organization.

Acknowledgments. This work was supported by IARPA contract 2016-16031100002. The views expressed are those of the authors and do not reflect the official policy or position of the U.S. Government.

References

1. INSA's Security Policy Reform Council: Assessing the mind of the malicious insider. Technical report, Intelligence and National Security Alliance (2017). https://www.insaonline.org/
2. Ester, M., Kriegel, H.P., Sander, J., Xu, X., et al.: A density-based algorithm for discovering clusters in large spatial databases with noise. In: KDD, vol. 96, pp. 226–231 (1996)
3. Friedman, N., Getoor, L., Koller, D., Pfeffer, A.: Learning probabilistic relational models. In: IJCAI, vol. 99, pp. 1300–1309 (1999)
4. Glasser, J., Lindauer, B.: Bridging the gap: a pragmatic approach to generating insider threat data. In: Security and Privacy Workshops (SPW), pp. 98–104. IEEE (2013)
5. Goodman, N.D.: The principles and practice of probabilistic programming. In: Proceedings of the 40th Annual ACM SIGPLAN-SIGACT Symposium on Principles of Programming Languages, pp. 399–402. ACM (2013)
6. Jensen, F.V.: An Introduction to Bayesian Networks, vol. 210. UCL Press, London (1996)
7. NPR: Ex-NSA contractor accused of taking classified information is indicted (2013). http://www.npr.org/sections/thetwo-way/2017/02/09/514275544/ex-nsa-contractor-indicted-for-taking-classifed-information
8. Pfeffer, A.: Creating and manipulating probabilistic programs with Figaro. In: 2nd International Workshop on Statistical Relational AI (2012)
9. Pfeffer, A.: Practical Probabilistic Programming. Manning Publications, Cherry Hill (2016)
10. Rall, L.B. (ed.): Automatic Differentiation: Techniques and Applications. LNCS, vol. 120. Springer, Heidelberg (1981). https://doi.org/10.1007/3-540-10861-0
11. Ruttenberg, B.E., Pfeffer, A.: Decision-making with complex data structures using probabilistic programming. arXiv preprint arXiv:1407.3208 (2014)
12. Salem, M.B., Hershkop, S., Stolfo, S.J.: A survey of insider attack detection research. In: Stolfo, S.J., Bellovin, S.M., Keromytis, A.D., Hershkop, S., Smith, S.W., Sinclair, S. (eds.) Insider Attack and Cyber Security. Advances in Information Security, vol. 39, pp. 69–90. Springer, Boston (2008). https://doi.org/10.1007/978-0-387-77322-3_5
13. Shachter, R.D.: Evaluating influence diagrams. Oper. Res. **34**(6), 871–882 (1986)
14. New York Times: A lawsuit against Uber highlights the rush to conquer driverless cars (2017). https://nyti.ms/2kVzR8Z

Security Modeling for Embedded System Design

Letitia W. Li[1,2(✉)], Florian Lugou[1], and Ludovic Apvrille[1]

[1] Télécom ParisTech, Université Paris-Saclay,
450 route des Chappes, Sophia Antipolis, France
{letitia.li,florian.lugou,ludovic.apvrille}@telecom-paristech.fr,
letitia.li@vedecom.fr
[2] Institut VEDECOM, 77 rue des Chantiers, Versailles, France

Abstract. Among the many recent cyber attacks, the Mirai botnet DDOS attacks were carried out using infected IoTs. To prevent our connected devices from being thus compromised, their security vulnerabilities should be detected and mitigated early. This paper presents how the SysML-Sec Methodology has been enhanced for the evolving graphical modeling of security through the three stages of our embedded system design methodology: Analysis, HW/SW Partitioning, and Software Analysis. The security requirements and attack graphs generated during the Analysis phase determine the sensitive data and attacker model during the HW/SW Partitioning phase. We then accordingly generate a secured model with communication protection modeled using abstract security representations, which can then be translated into a Software/System Design Model. The Software Model is intended as the final detailed model of the system. Throughout the design process, formal verification and simulation evaluate safety, security, and performance of the system.

Keywords: Embedded systems · ProVerif · Formal verification

1 Introduction

To prevent the compromise of connected objects, their security vulnerabilities should be detected and mitigated, preferably as early as possible. Correcting these security flaws might be difficult once the system has been released - and sometimes impossible - if the flaws cannot be corrected by software update only. Furthermore, adding security mechanisms at the late stages of software development may change the performance of the system to render a selected architecture non-optimal.

Autonomous drones have been proposed for use in disaster relief efforts. However, insufficient security may allow an unauthorized attacker to gain control of the drone. Furthermore, disaster relief drones may carry sensitive data and images that should be kept confidential [15].

The SysML-Sec methodology was introduced to handle the design of such complex systems, in terms of safety, performance, and security [2]. SysML-Sec is an extension of UML for the design of embedded systems. It addresses system

© Springer International Publishing AG 2018
P. Liu et al. (eds.): GraMSec 2017, LNCS 10744, pp. 99–106, 2018.
https://doi.org/10.1007/978-3-319-74860-3_7

development starting from Requirements and Attacks analysis, progressing into Hardware/Software Partitioning, and finishing with Software/System Design. The entire design process is supported by TTool, a free, open-source, multi-profile toolkit [3].

The paper presents how security can be efficiently handled through the entire design process (see Fig. 1). Solid lines in the methodology represent manual steps to be performed by the designer, while dotted lines represent automatic steps performed by our toolkit. Our methodology starts with Requirements/Analysis phase, described in Sect. 2, which helps a designer consider the security requirements and possible attacks. Next, we describe the security-aware HW/SW Partitioning phase, where we model the abstract system architecture and behavior based on those requirements and risks. Section 4 describes the transition to the final Software Design phase. Next, we present the related work in Sect. 5. Finally, Sect. 6 concludes the paper.

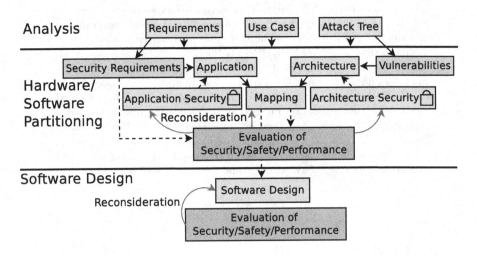

Fig. 1. Design methodology

2   Analysis: Security Requirements and Attack Trees

The methodology depicted in Fig. 1 starts with the Analysis phase (Step 1), which involves describing the requirements and use case of the system, and then considers the possible attacks that the system may face. This analysis is expected to prepare the verification phase, and to drive the two further steps (functional view, architecture view) with the selection of the components (functions, hardware elements) adapted to counter the listed attacks. The necessary iterations between requirements, attacks, and components of the system are not detailed in this paper, but are explained in [14].

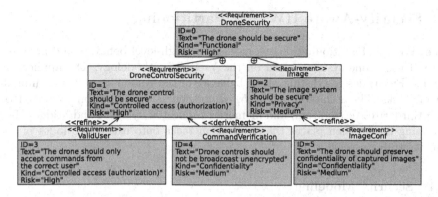

Fig. 2. Security-related Requirements Diagram for a drone

Figure 3 shows a high-level overview of one attack tree for gaining control of the drone. An attacker must understand how to forge commands, then gain remote access to the drone while denying access to the legitimate user controller. The avenues for gaining control include kicking the legitimate user and then connecting to the drone [6], or a Man-in-the-Middle (MITM) attack [13].

The Requirements Diagram includes the textual specifications regarding important properties of the system. Figure 2 shows an extract of the Security-related Requirements Diagram. These requirements may be continually refined with the details of their implementation. The requirement for the drone to be secure involves the sub-requirements that the drone should only accept commands from the authorized user, and that captured images should remain confidential.

After performing this analysis, we detail in the next section how to use these diagrams for security modeling in the HW/SW Partitioning phase.

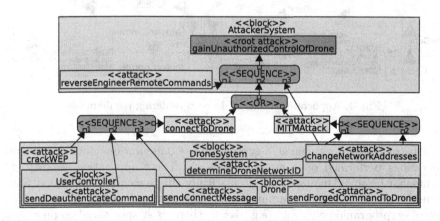

Fig. 3. Attack Tree for gaining unauthorized control of a drone

3   Security-Aware HW/SW Partitioning

The HW/SW Partitioning phases models the high-level behavior and architecture of the drone system, based on the Y-chart methodology. The application model (Fig. 4) designs the high-level behavior of the system as a set of communicating tasks. The architecture (Fig. 5) is modeled as the execution nodes (CPUs and Hardware Accelerators) and memories connected by buses and bridges. The mapping model then places the application tasks onto execution nodes of the architecture.

3.1   Security Modeling

Based on the security requirements described in the Analysis Phase, certain communications may be considered critical and must be secured. For example, since images taken by the camera and should be secure, we mark those communication channels with a grey lock to indicate that we should examine its security properties.

Attack Trees describing scenarios of attack also provide information on the attacker's actions and capabilities. In our attack tree, we assumed that the attacker could intercept the Wifi communications between the controller and Drone. On the other hand, since we assume the attacker has no physical access to the drone and cannot probe the internal drone bus, then we mark it as secure with the green shield.

In this sample mapping, mission commands are broadcast across a bus accessible to the attacker, so we must secure that communication.

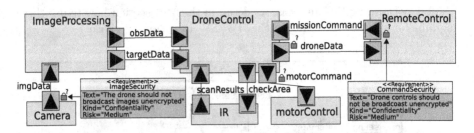

Fig. 4. Application model of drone considering requirements

Abstract operators named 'Cryptographic Configurations' indicate security operations performed on communications [9]. These application security elements may be added manually or automatically after a security verification. Since security operations can be computationally-intensive and require the secure storage of cryptographic elements (e.g., keys), there exist specialized co-processors Hardware Security Modules which perform cryptographic operations faster than a normal processor and store cryptokeys.

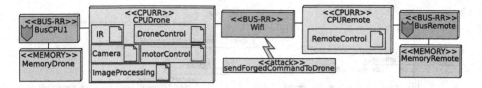

Fig. 5. Architecture model of drone considering attacks

To verify that these countermeasures are sufficient, our toolkit performs security verification automatically with ProVerif [12]. The verification results are backtraced automatically to our diagrams, by marking communications that are verified secure for a given mapping with a green lock, and marking insecure communications with a red lock. Once our mapping has been verified to meet all safety, security, and performance requirements, then the software of the system can be designed in detail, as described in the next section.

4 Security in Software Design

After HW/SW Partitioning has determined the architecture and mapping of the system, we design the software components of the application in greater detail. Our toolkit can generate a software design diagram automatically based on HW/SW Partitioning models. The details of the algorithms to be implemented must then be added by the designer. For example, the trajectory calculation algorithm should be added in place of the element indicating only its computational complexity. The generation saves the designer time, by creating the model blocks and framework.

Figure 6 shows the transition from the Activity Diagram in HW/SW Partitioning to the State Machine Diagram in Software Design for the drone controller. Cryptographic configurations are translated into software methods. The software modeling environment also offers primitives to closely model security protocols.

Verification of Software Design models is intended to verify the details of implementations of security. For example, the verification may concern the confidentiality of one given block attribute, or the authenticity of one given message exchanged between SysML block. On the contrary, verification at mapping stage concerns abstract data channel.

5 Related Work

[4] relies on Architecture Analysis and Design Language (AADL) models to consider architectural mapping during security verification. The authors note that a system must be secure on multiple levels: software applications must exchange data in a secure manner, and also execute on a secure memory space and communicate over a secure channel. Our approach, however, considers security regarding protection against external attackers instead of access control.

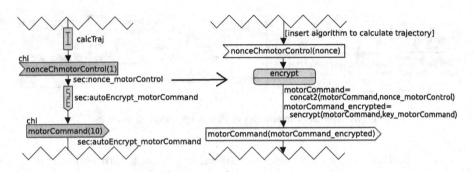

Fig. 6. Translation of activity diagrams to state machine diagrams

Another approach performs Design Space Exploration on a vehicular network protecting against replay and masquerade attacks [10]. The project evaluates possible security mechanisms, their effects on message sizes, and candidate architectures during the mapping phase. While their work targets automotive systems and network communications, our analysis may be applied more broadly for any embedded system.

Attack Defense Trees [7] analyze the possible attacks against a system, in conjunction with the defenses that the system may implement. The supporting toolkit ADTool analyzes attack scenarios to determine the cost, probability, time, etc., required for a successful attack.

The Knowledge Acquisition in Automated Specifications approach Security Extension aims to identify security requirements for software systems [8]. The methodology uses a goal-oriented framework and builds a model of the system, and then an anti-model which describes possible attacks on the system. Both models are incrementally developed: threat trees are derived from the anti-model and the system model adds security countermeasures to protect against the attacks described in the anti-model.

SecureUML enabled the design and analysis of secure systems by adding mechanisms to model role-based access control [11]. Authorization constraints are expressed in Object Constraint Language (OCL) for formal verification. Our security model focuses on protecting against an external attacker instead of access control. In contrast to formula-based constraints or queries, our approach to security analysis relies on graphically annotating the security properties to query within the model.

Another work [16] proposed modeling security in embedded systems with attack graphs to determine the probability that data assets could be compromised. While their approach is also UML-based, they focus on estimating probabilities of success for attacks, while ours focuses on verifying adequate placement of encryption.

UMLSec [5] is a UML profile for expressing security concepts, such as encryption mechanisms and attack scenarios. It provides a modeling framework to define security properties of software components and of their composition within a UML framework. It also features a rather complete framework addressing various stages of model-driven secure software engineering from the specification of security requirements to tests, including logic-based formal verification regarding the composition of software components. However, UMLSec does not take into account the HW/SW Partitioning phase necessary for the design of IoTs.

The Software Architecture Modeling (SAM) framework [1] aims to bridge the gap between informal security requirements and their formal representation and verification. SAM uses formal and informal security techniques to accomplish defined goals and mitigate flaws. SAM relies on a well established toolkit - SMV - and considers a threat model, but the "security properties to proof" process is not yet automated. In contrast, our work focuses on automatic formal verification from an abstract partitioning model.

In contrast to these approaches, our work involves a methodology for the modeling and analysis of security at all stages in the design process.

6   Conclusion

This paper presented how our enhanced SysML-Sec Methodology now considers security at all phases in the design process. We examined the security considerations in the design of a disaster relief drone, which must not be compromised or controlled by an attacker. First, the requirements and attacks phase helps us decide what data needs to be secure and which architectural locations are vulnerable, which then leads us to add abstract representations of security. Once an architecture and mapping are decided, then we can generate the base structure of the software models. The software model is then refined to include the algorithms and details of the software to be developed.

In future work, we plan to better connect the Analysis and Partitioning phases. Currently, the Analysis phase provides guidelines for the designer, but does not explicitly connect security requirements in the Requirements Diagram with the critical channels in the Mapping Models. We should add the capabilities to trace the fulfilment of each requirement. The attack paths in the Attack Trees could also provide more explicit information regarding the security of specific architectural elements, instead of needing to be deciphered by a designer. These additions will enhance our toolkit to better support the design of secure embedded systems.

Acknowledgment. This work was partly funded by the French Government (National Research Agency, ANR) through the Investments for the Future Program reference #ANR-11-LABX-0031-01 and Institut VEDECOM.

References

1. Ali, Y., El-Kassas, S., Mahmoud, M.: A rigorous methodology for security architecture modeling and verification. In: Proceedings of the 42nd Hawaii International Conference on System Sciences. IEEE (2009). 978-0-7695-3450-3/09
2. Apvrille, L., Roudier, Y.: SysML-Sec: a model driven approach for designing safe and secure systems. In: 3rd International Conference on Model-Driven Engineering and Software Development, Special session on Security and Privacy in Model Based Engineering. SCITEPRESS Digital Library, France, February 2015
3. Apvrille, L.: TTool, December 2003. ttool.telecom-paristech.fr
4. Hansson, J., Wrage, L., Feiler, P.H., Morley, J., Lewis, B., Hugues, J.: Architectural modeling to verify security and nonfunctional behavior. IEEE Secur. Priv. 8(1), 43–49 (2010)
5. Jürjens, J.: UMLsec: extending UML for secure systems development. In: Jézéquel, J.-M., Hussmann, H., Cook, S. (eds.) UML 2002. LNCS, vol. 2460, pp. 412–425. Springer, Heidelberg (2002). https://doi.org/10.1007/3-540-45800-X_32
6. Kamkar, S.: Skyjack: autonomous drone hacking (2003). http://www.samy.pl/skyjack/
7. Kordy, B., Kordy, P., Mauw, S., Schweitzer, P.: ADTool: security analysis with attack–defense trees. In: Joshi, K., Siegle, M., Stoelinga, M., D'Argenio, P.R. (eds.) QEST 2013. LNCS, vol. 8054, pp. 173–176. Springer, Heidelberg (2013). https://doi.org/10.1007/978-3-642-40196-1_15
8. van Lamsweerde, A.: Elaborating security requirements by construction of intentional anti-models. In: Proceedings of the 26th International Conference on Software Engineering, ICSE 2004, pp. 148–157 (2004)
9. Li, L.W., Lugou, F., Apvrille, L.: Security-aware modeling and analysis for HW/SW partitioning. In: Conferénce on Model-Driven Engineering and Software Development (Modelsward 2017), Porto, Portugal, February 2017
10. Lin, C.W., Zheng, B., Zhu, Q., Sangiovanni-Vincentelli, A.: Security-aware design methodology and optimization for automotive systems. ACM Trans. Des. Autom. Electroni. Syst. (TODAES) 21(1), 18 (2015)
11. Lodderstedt, T., Basin, D., Doser, J.: SecureUML: a UML-based modeling language for model-driven security. In: Jézéquel, J.-M., Hussmann, H., Cook, S. (eds.) UML 2002. LNCS, vol. 2460, pp. 426–441. Springer, Heidelberg (2002). https://doi.org/10.1007/3-540-45800-X_33
12. Lugou, F., Li, L.W., Apvrille, L., Ameur-Boulifa, R.: SysML models and model transformation for security. In: Conferénce on Model-Driven Engineering and Software Development (Modelsward 2016), Rome, Italy, February 2016
13. Rodday, N.: Hacking a Professional Drone, March 2016. Slides at www.blackhat.com/docs/asia-16/materials/asia-16-Rodday-Hacking-A-Professional-Drone.pdf
14. Roudier, Y., Idrees, M.S., Apvrille, L.: Towards the model-driven engineering of security requirements for embedded systems. In: Proceedings of MoDRE 2013, Rio de Janeiro, Brazil, July 2013
15. Tanzi, T.J., Sebastien, O., Rizza, C.: Designing autonomous crawling equipment to detect personal connected devices and support rescue operations: technical and societal concerns. Radio Sci. Bull. 355(355), 35–44 (2015)
16. Vasilevskaya, M., Nadjm-Tehrani, S.: Quantifying risks to data assets using formal metrics in embedded system design. In: Koornneef, F., van Gulijk, C. (eds.) SAFE-COMP 2015. LNCS, vol. 9337, pp. 347–361. Springer, Cham (2015). https://doi.org/10.1007/978-3-319-24255-2_25

Circle of Health Based Access Control for Personal Health Information Systems

Ryan Habibi[✉], Jens Weber, and Morgan Price

LEAD Lab, University of Victoria, 3800 Finnerty Rd, Victoria, Canada
rphabibi@uvic.ca
http://www.leadlab.ca

Abstract. Patients can track, manage, and share their personal health information (PHI). There are security concerns with the ownership and custodianship of PHI. Traditional provider-facing access control (AC) policies have been applied to many patient-facing applications without consideration as to whether these controls are comprehensible and sufficient. We have conducted a scoping literature review of on AC and patient privacy (n = 31) to identify the state of knowledge and to understand what is being done to address this gap. Synthesizing the results we propose Circle of Health Based AC, a graphical patient-centric AC model. The model has been validated with a panel of user experience, healthcare, and security experts. This work will discuss the scoping literature review and describe the proposed model and justification for it's applications for user-defined access policy.

Keywords: Attribute-based access control
Personal Health Information · Circle of Care · Graph transformations

1 Introduction

Personal health management technology is an emerging field raising questions about ownership of personal health information (PHI). Traditional privacy tools and strategies have been applied but consideration of how patients understand PHI, its sensitivity, or storage and retrieval have been sparsely reported; this leaves users vulnerable when the user's mental model of their privacy is not expressed clearly. According to Norman, the user's mental model is not based on facts but what the user believes about the system at hand [1]. We will examine access control paradigms and the user context surrounding patients engaged proactively or reactively in their healthcare. We conclude by proposing the Circle of Health Based Access Control (CoHBAC) as a user-centric, graph-based access control policy for health applications.

2 Background

Access control (AC) models are one facet of design required to develop secure systems. Other commonly required mechanisms include identification and authentication, data encryption, audit trails, etc. The focus of this work is on AC. The other mechanisms are assumed to be sufficient as prerequisites.

© Springer International Publishing AG 2018
P. Liu et al. (eds.): GraMSec 2017, LNCS 10744, pp. 107–114, 2018.
https://doi.org/10.1007/978-3-319-74860-3_8

Price describes a Circle of Care (CoC) as a system centered on a patient which contains providers, information, and activities related to the patient's care [2]. Relationships between patients and the actors in their CoC are complex and constantly evolving. CoC's can be quite extensive; Pham et al. found that patients managing multiple health concerns may see up to 16 physicians in a single year [3]. Furthermore, Price points out that providers in the CoC may not be limited to formal care givers.

We extend the CoC to encompass trusted laypeople who may assist a subject of care. We name this broader collection the Circle of Health (CoH). In addition to more comprehensively encompassing the actors in an individual's contextual healthcare process, this extension also considers that many patients engage in healthcare unrelated to ongoing treatment. We use the illustration of mobile fitness, which allows individuals to proactively manage their health when no health concern is present.

Users may have a disconnect between expectations of privacy and the potential consequences of using a service. Users must agree to terms of service in order to track and aggregate data. Few users possess the knowledge and skills to create meaningful metrics from the data independently. Several important questions emerge from the transfer of data. Users may not fully understand viewing/editing rights, ownership, or to what extent data can be erased. Companies may own data reported allowing them to sell the raw data or inferences which can be made from its analysis.

PHI (including clinical, fitness, location, and demographic data) is sensitive. Publication of some or all of a patients' data can have social or financial repercussions. Kahn et al. describe principles for an ideal personal health record system as one that will require "information to be protected and private; that ownership lie solely with the consumer; that storage and use of the data be approved by the patients;" [4]. These three principals form a basis for patient-centric policy. However, they are not sufficient to protect users from harm caused by misunderstanding and/or misuse of the system which adheres to these principles. Granting ownership is not enough. Patients must have a sufficient knowledge of the data, usable privacy and access controls, and understand the consequences of use.

User-centric AC design increases security by reducing human error when defining and reviewing AC policy. Having established the necessity for user-centric AC in healthcare the remainder of this work is as follows: In Sect. 3 we will discuss a scoping literature review and synthesis of AC models in healthcare. In Sect. 4 we will formalize the results of the literature review into our graph model. Section 5 will discuss strengths and limitations of our model. Finally, Sect. 6 will address future work.

3   Scoping Literature Review

We conducted a scoping literature review [5] on AC models for user-centric health information systems. This review was conducted to rapidly map key concepts underpinning the emerging research field, identify main sources, and types of evidence available. Our initial research was:

"What is known in the current literature about AC models for consumer health informatics applications, including their effectiveness, limitations, and comprehensibility."

The search was restricted to English online sources published between 2004 and 2015. We searched Compendex and INSPEC with controlled terms "access control", "health care", "health", and "social networks" for inclusion. Controlled terms such as "biometrics", "sensor nodes", and "quality of service" were selected for exclusions to focus results. Moreover, we added uncontrolled keywords "patient", "client", or "consumer". This resulted in 124 unique publications. Additionally, we searched MedLine utilizing MeSH controlled vocabulary terms "personal health records", "consumer health information", "social support", "confidentiality", and "computer security". This resulted in an additional 49 unique publications. The 173 collected abstracts were screened and excluded if:

- Meta-data (title/abstract/keywords) does not express any focus on consumer-facing health informatics application. This may be expressed by mentioning a consumer-facing technology (such as PHR), a representative of such a technology (such as Google Health), the reference to consumers/patients as direct users of a system, or the use of terms that indicate a patient-facing component of the IT solution (e.g., Telehealth).
- Meta-data does not express any focus on patient driven AC or security models.

The remaining publications (n = 31) made up the corpus for this review and were analyzed for key themes and grouped based on type of AC mechanism.

3.1   Themes

Three themes emerged from the literature: (1) Definition of privacy, (2) Measuring user trust and, (3) Temporal access constraints.

Definition of Privacy. In the included corpus, several authors characterize requirements to govern the design of AC mechanisms for patient-controlled PHI, referencing various legal and social frameworks. Hue et al. use Westin's definition of privacy as representing "the claim of individuals, groups, or institutions to determine for themselves when, how, and to what extent...informations about them is communicated to others" [6]. This definition has been used as the basis for the U.S. Health Insurance Portability and Accountability Act, the European Data Protection Direction, the Data Protection Act of Japan, and others. We will also use Westin's definition of privacy as a basis for our AC model.

Measuring User Trust. An empirical study on consumer requirements and factors influencing patient-centric AC model requirements was published by Trojer et al. [7]. Trust relationships were reported to be the most important factor for patient decision making. This was explored by Levy et al., in their work on trust-aware privacy controls they proposed a formal trust metric. [8] Margheri et al. states that many formalisms for defining AC policies are not user-friendly and impede human understanding [9].

Temporal Access Constraints. Access to PHI often has a temporal dimension. Sicuranza and Esposito [11] proposed a combination of role-based AC, mandatory AC, and a temporal aspect which allows patients to provide time-limited consent directives for patients who are aware of how long an actor will be in their CoH.

3.2 AC Models

Although several AC paradigms were discussed, few complete AC models were presented. Commonly, a specific aspect of AC was addressed. Examples of AC aspects discussed in the corpus not discussed above are: requirements gathering for AC in healthcare; work-flow based consent directives; emergency response; intended data usage and social networks; default policy, overrides, access revocation; and verification and validation of AC Policies.

3.3 Synthesis

The conducted review informed our research question and provided a basis for defining an AC model. It is clear from the literature review that patient ownership and custodianship of PHI is a relatively new concept and there are few proposed AC models. Based on the available literature we identified the following ten requirements:

Data Objects

- [R1] Differentiate data by sensitivity
- [R2] Differentiate data by type or treatment (episodic) context
- [R3] Maintain data provenance (origin, time of creation, time of last access)
- [R4] Provide data compositionality

Subjects (Actors in the CoH)

- [R5] Subjects may be individuals, groups, or entire organizations
- [R6] Subjects may contribute data to a patient, or may just be viewing data.

Circle of Care (Actors and Rights)

- [R7] Differentiate CoH by trust criteria. (Patients may have multiple CoHs)
- [R8] Allow for ephemeral CoHs as well as for persistent ones.
- [R9] Subjects may stay anonymous with respect to other subjects in the CoH

Usability

- [R10] The model should be easy to use and comprehend from a patients perspective

4 Circle of Health Based Access Control

We formalized the Circle of Health Based Access Control (CoHBAC) model
(Fig. 1) to meet the ten requirements identified from the literature review in the
Canadian healthcare context. This method is based on graphs and graph transformation systems [12]. Figure 1 shows a graph schema to represent CoHBAC
policies. CoHBAC is a generalizable patient-centric privacy control paradigm
and is intended to be extensible and flexible as needs evolve.

Users in CoHBAC are actors. Two principal types of actors exist: patient
or provider. The difference between providers and patients is that the latter
have a personal CoH and PHI. The provider role extends beyond primary care
providers. Organizations can be represented as providers. Organizations (care
facilities, support groups, and health authorities) can act as a single provider.

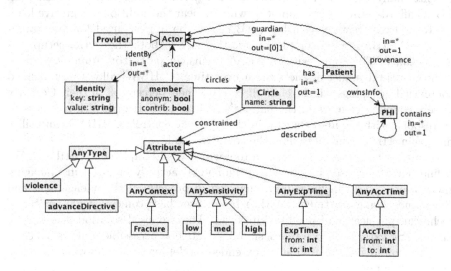

Fig. 1. Formalized CoH-based AC model

To better match the patient's privacy mental model, all privacy controls are
implemented on groups of actors, referred to as circles, to better map changes
in context to policy creation and maintenance.

4.1 Satisfying Requirements

PHI can be described and constrained by attributes. [R1], [R2], [R3] and [R8]
are satisfied by extending CoHBAC to include the attributes modeled in Fig. 1.
Any data object may be a collection of data by [R4] and allows inherited access
controls to be implemented on any level of the hierarchy. Actors may be identified
as a provider by [R5]. The patient may have any number circles by [R7]. In
others' circles actors can be granted editing rights, [R6], and choose anonymity
from other members in that circle, [R9].

[R10] is more challenging to prove due to its dependence on interface; however, in this section we will argue why CoHBAC is accessible and knowable by design.

CoHBAC is a combination of Role-Based AC (RBAC) and Attribute-Based AC (ABAC). It can implement either model or a combination of both based on user needs and limitations. While RBAC is the dominant model applied in provider facing systems it is commonly not considered to provide sufficient granularity for patient-controlled PHI [10]; most patient-centric AC models identified in the review provided some combination of role-based and identity-based policy statements.

An individual's relationship with members of their CoH exist on a continuum of trust and therefore must be addressed on a case by case basis; this further emphasizes the users' need to define AC policy with a high degree of granularity. Despite many users' mental model of their privacy being more detailed than RBAC affords, some users cannot or will not bear the additional cognitive load.

To address trust relationships, ABAC can be implemented for fine granularity AC. ABAC adds complexity for the user in both the initial setup and maintenance. The complexity of ABAC stems, in part, from difficulties managing a mental model of the system over time. CoHBAC allows user defined contextual groupings which relate directly to their perception of their CoH. By closely coupling changes in the patient's real world CoH or health concerns to correspond with required changes in their privacy controls CoHBAC can utilize fine grain ABAC while lessening the cognitive load.

Consider the potential users of a tool which would implement CoHBAC. We define our target user base as "Any individual actively engaged in managing their health". This includes users involved in proactive PHI management and those undergoing treatment. With a broad user base comes a wide variety of technical, physical, and mental skill levels. The proposed solution needs to be flexible and extensible such that a simplified model is accessible to users deficient in the required skills as well as an extended model for users who want to define very specific policy.

Individual CoHBAC actors are not granted data access. Instead, actors are members of a patient's circles. The context of each circle may be defined by involvement in care for an illness or injury, or it may relate to a dimension of health such as fitness, diet, or mental health. Patients are expected to know when to update their access policy as it reflects changes in their context.

Instances of the CoHBAC exists on a continuum from lowest granularity (RBAC) to highest granularity (ABAC) inclusively, dependant on the user's circles. It is possible to implement RBAC or ABAC using CoHBAC. Generally, as the number of circles increases and the average number of members per circle decreases the model tends towards ABAC. Instances with one member per circle and each actor included in a single circle most closely resembles traditional ABAC. As the number of circles decreases and the number of members per circle increases membership criteria becomes more abstract resembling traditional RBAC.

5   Limitations

In this work we have discussed the CoHBAC model and the evidence-based approach used to design a patient-centric AC model. Our investigation of literature was not exhaustive on account of our selection of primary publications databases and choice to limit the search to electronically available publications in English. While Inspec, Compendex, and Pubmed are comprehensive indexing databases covering a large portion of engineering and health IT venues, the consideration of additional databases or printed resources may yield further relevant studies. Emphasis was placed on the use of controlled vocabularies in searching these databases which may have caused us to overlook publications which were not explicitly associated with the controlled terms.

6   Future Work

The CoHBAC model was developed with a panel of experts including a physician, a safety engineer, and user experience experts. Further refinement requires user feedback. Several medium and high fidelity interactive prototypes were created to allow the interdisciplinary team to visualize and discuss difficult edge cases in healthcare. Further work testing CoHBAC user interfaces will uncover strengths and limitations from provider and patient viewpoints.

One way of specifying a secure AC model is to define a secure initial state and a set of secure transformations that are guaranteed to output a secure state given that their input is a secure state. We define the initial state of our AC graph as the empty graph, which, can be considered secure, as it provides no privileges. A graph rewriting language allows us to formally specify all actions on the AC model and to verify that insecure states cannot be reached. We leave out the formal set of secure graph transformations to describe CoHBAC due to space limitations. We plan to extend this work by comparing CoHBAC to other AC models implemented in healthcare.

7   Conclusion

The Circle of Health defines the context and actors that surround an individuals health management and recovery. Users expect connectivity and interoperability despite risks. Sharing of PHI has the potential to help care providers understand the context surrounding patients and empower those patients to take a more prominent role in their health management. CoHBAC seeks to move away from the assumptions made by provider-facing AC models. By focusing on extensibility and usability by design CoHBAC matches any user's need to describe the complex trust relationships associated with their health management bounded by their physical and cognitive skills. A graph based formalism including graph tests and secure transformations enable precise definition and verification of AC decisions. CoHBAC couples usability by design with formal graph models to create a new paradigm where users can own their data and understand the privacy and security surrounding it.

References

1. Norman, D.A.: The Design of Everyday Things: Revised and Expanded Edition. Basic Books, New York (2013)
2. Price, M.: Circle of Care Modeling: Seeking Improvements in Continuity of Care for end of life patients. PhD Dissertation, School of Health Information Science, University of Victoria (2009)
3. Pham, H., Schrag, D., O'Malley, A., Wu, B., Bach, P.: Care patterns in Medicare and their implications for pay for performance. New Engl. J. Med. **356**(11), 1130 (2007)
4. Kahn, J.S., Aulakh, V., Bosworth, A.: What it takes: characteristics of the ideal personal health record. Health Aff. **28**(2), 369–376 (2009)
5. Arksey, H., O'Malley, L.: Scoping studies: towards a methodological framework. Int. J. Soc. Res. Methodol. **8**(1), 19–32 (2005)
6. Hue, P.T.B., Wohlgemuth, S., Echizen, I., Thuc, N.D., Thuy, D.T.B.: An experimental evaluation for a new column-level access control mechanism for electronic health record systems. Int. J. U- E-Serv. Sci. Technol. **4**(3), 73–86 (2011). http://www.sersc.org/journals/IJUNESST/vol4_no4/1.pdf
7. Trojer, T., Katt, B., Ozata, T., Breu, R., Mangesius, P., Schabetsberger, T.: Factors of access control management in electronic healthcare: the patients perspective, pp. 2967–2976. IEEE (2014). https://doi.org/10.1109/HICSS.2014.369
8. Levy, K., Sargent, B., Bai, Y.: A trust-aware tag-based privacy control for eHealth 2.0. In: Proceedings of the 2011 Conference on Information Technology Education. ACM (2011)
9. Margheri, A., et al.: On a formal and user-friendly linguistic approach to access control of electronic health data, pp. 263–268 (2013)
10. Ssembatya, R.: An access control framework for protecting mobile health records: the case study of developing countries. In: Proceedings of the Ninth International Network Conference (INC 2012) (2012). Lulu.com
11. Sicuranza, M., Esposito, A.: An access control model for easy management of patient privacy in EHR systems. In: 2013 8th International Conference for Internet Technology and Secured Transactions (ICITST), pp. 463–470 (2013). https://doi.org/10.1109/ICITST.2013.6750243
12. Ehrig, H., Ehrig, K., Prange, U., Taentzer, G.: Graph transformation systems. In: Ehrig, H., Ehrig, K., Prange, U., Taentzer, G. (eds.) Fundamentals of Algebraic Graph Transformation. EATCS, pp. 37–71. Springer, Heidelberg (2006). https://doi.org/10.1007/3-540-31188-2_3

New Directions in Attack Tree Research: Catching up with Industrial Needs

Olga Gadyatskaya[(✉)] and Rolando Trujillo-Rasua

SnT, University of Luxembourg, Esch-sur-Alzette, Luxembourg
{olga.gadyatskaya,rolando.trujillo-rasua}@uni.lu

Abstract. Attack trees provide a systematic way of characterizing diverse system threats. Their strengths arise from the combination of an intuitive representation of possible attacks and availability of formal mathematical frameworks for analyzing them in a qualitative or a quantitative manner. Indeed, the mathematical frameworks have become a large focus of attack tree research. However, practical applications of attack trees in industry largely remain a tedious and error-prone exercise.

Recent research directions in attack trees, such as attack tree generation, attempt to close this gap and to improve the attack tree state-of-the-practice. In this position paper we outline the recurrent challenges in manual tree design within industry, and we overview the recent research results in attack trees that help the practitioners. For the challenges that have not yet been addressed by the community, we propose new promising research directions.

1 Introduction

Attack trees are one of the most popular graphical models for information security assessment. Proposed originally by Bruce Schneier in 1999 [57], they are intuitive and relatively easy to master, yet they enjoy well-studied formalizations and quantitative analysis means [4,5,31,39]. Security risk assessment at industry has long appreciated attack trees as a means to solve cognitive scalability issues related to securing large systems [46], and as a tool to enable communication among different stakeholders and facilitate brainstorming [15,59].

From the graphical perspective an attack tree resembles a mind map [11,59]: a powerful cognitive tool used often in Psychology and Education. It has a single root node, representing the main attacker's goal, which is subsequently **refined** in sub-goals captured by child nodes. But this is where the analogy ends, as attack trees have a precise mathematical interpretation based on well-defined refinement operators [39]. The most frequently used refinement operators are the conjunctive (AND) and disjunctive (OR) refinements. The AND-refinement sets that all child nodes need to be performed to achieve the parent node, while the OR-refinement states that if the attacker can achieve any of the child nodes, then the parent node will also be achieved [39]. The leaf nodes, i.e., the nodes that do not have any children, represent atomic or self-evident attack steps.

© Springer International Publishing AG 2018
P. Liu et al. (eds.): GraMSec 2017, LNCS 10744, pp. 115–126, 2018.
https://doi.org/10.1007/978-3-319-74860-3_9

Attack trees are traditionally regarded as both a formal framework and a tool to communicate security risks, but these two aspects are rarely considered together in the literature. For example, research in attack trees strongly focuses on improving expressiveness of the formalism through new refinement operators (e.g., sequential AND [3,26]), proposing new flavors of attack trees (e.g., attack-defense trees [31] or attack-countermeasure trees [55]), and developing various quantitative analysis methods with attack trees [7,8,19,28,39]. Quantitative analysis techniques give rise to optimization problems, such as cost-effective countermeasure selection [4,18,55] and ranking of attacks [19]. In parallel, new attack tree semantics are being developed that translate attack trees into other formalisms, such as timed automata [17,32], stochastic games [5] and Markov chains [25], which offer advanced computational capabilities.

Mostly separately from those efforts, researchers have looked into integration of attack trees with security risk management methodologies [18,47,49] and applying attack trees to model threat scenarios in a large variety of domains, e.g., SCADA systems [41,63], RFID systems [7], and ATM systems [15].

More recently, researchers have started to look into the questions emerging when applying attack trees in industry. Indeed, practical applications of attack trees pose many challenges, including noticeable time investment into the tree design, significant cognitive burden on the analyst when dealing with large trees, and multitude of possible interpretations for even the most basic refinement operators AND and OR that may lead to conceptual misalignments within a single tree created and read by a group of people. This is why attack trees are sometimes mentioned in security threat assessment guidelines as an "advanced" and "alternative" model [40,44,59]. In this position paper we overview the emerging research directions for practical applications of attack trees and identify the gaps that are still to be investigated by the research community interested in attack trees. We argue that there are many exciting research problems that can contribute to better acceptance of attack trees in practice and to a better synergy between the academic and industry worlds.

We start by reviewing some practical challenges with attack trees and lessons we learned while working with attack trees (Sect. 2). Then we overview the emerging research directions in attack trees that focus on improving the acceptance of the formalism in practice (Sect. 3). Subsequently, we propose additional research themes that are currently not so active, but will be appreciated by practitioners (Sect. 4).

2   Challenges with Attack Tree Design in Practice

Attack trees allow to structure quite diverse threat scenarios (e.g., attacks occurring at physical, digital or social levels, or a combination of those) and to reason about these scenarios at different levels of abstraction. Yet, this strength comes at the cost of **substantial time and effort investment** into the design of a comprehensive tree. Like any other security assessment methodology, a thorough attack tree model requires a diverse set of skills from its authors. Typically, an attack tree design exercise requires domain expertise (i.e., stakeholders providing in-depth knowledge of the system) and security expertise (persons providing security knowledge and experience in the methodology). For example, the attack-defense tree for the relatively small ATM case study reported in [15] required a team of two domain experts and two security analysts working jointly for 6 days. Furthermore, one of the stakeholders has spent 10 days before the case study meeting on preparing the documentation, reviewing ATM crime reports, outlining the scenario, and collecting statistical data for quantitative analysis. This amount of effort can be prohibitive for small organizations.

A delaying factor in designing attack trees is that, although they may seem to be quite simple and intuitive [57–59], there is still a **space for misconceptions and a multitude of interpretations** about the meaning of refinement operators or tree semantics. These discrepancies are often neglected in the literature, but they become apparent when a group of people with diverse backgrounds starts working together on an attack tree. For example, in case of attack-defense trees applied in [15], the meaning of defense nodes was problematic. For the stakeholders, the defense nodes represented anything that is a security control, irrespectively of its type (preventive, detective or reactive). However, the attack-defense tree formalism provides a uniform meaning to defense nodes through semantics and attribute domain specification [31], and it does not allow to specify explicitly different countermeasure types.

Attribute domains can introduce confusion even for pure attack trees without countermeasure nodes. For example, the traditional AND operator specifies that all children nodes need to be fulfilled to fulfil the parent node. Its interpretation in the minimal attack time attribute domain depends whether the children node actions can be done in parallel or they are sequential. The ADTool software, for example, includes both options, and so the practitioners have to choose which one to work with [30]. This means, they need to be aware of this choice, and they need to interpret it correctly and consistently for the whole tree.

In fact, attack tree guidelines existing today in the literature are quite vague, and they usually operate within the top-down approach. The team needs to start with the top node representing the attacker's main goal, that can be refined into subgoals and more concrete steps until very precise attack actions are found [1,39,57,59,62]. The guidelines do not specify what is the best way to structure the tree, how to deal with repeating nodes, how to label the nodes in the best way, or how to arrange the work on the attack tree so that everybody has the same understanding of the attack tree elements meaning. This means that, in the best case, these choices are strategically made by the most experienced team members, who, however, do not share them with the wider community, or they are made ad-hoc or even post-hoc. In the worst case, these aspects are not agreed upon at all, and, therefore, the resulting tree can be inconsistent. Furthermore, this tree will likely be less comprehensible, due to the **absence of empirically founded best practices** in tree structure and comprehensible tree design.

Absence of **errors** is another big concern for practitioners when designing attack trees [57,59]. These errors can be on both sides, and, therefore, optimally, the designed tree should be both complete (no attacks are omitted) and sound (does not contain attacks that do not exist in the actual system). Practitioners can apply some tree validation techniques to ensure this. For example, in the ATM case study semantics-based validation (checking that attack bundles in the multiset semantics [31] represented meaningful attacks), data-based validation (investigating any discrepancies between the expected attribute value and the value computed in the quantitative analysis), and catalogue-based validation (ensuring that all attacks collected by an industry specific catalogue are captured) were applied [15]. However, these validation techniques are limited when applied by human analysts, because it is impractical to check by hand all possible attack bundles or data value discrepancies.

Certainly the attack tree construction process is an excellent opportunity for brainstorming about potential security threats and cost-effective countermeasures. But its main value comes from post-analysis and subsequent communication with other stakeholders. We observe that in practice **analysis and comprehensibility of attack trees are in conflict**. On the one hand, fine-grained analysis benefits from large trees describing all attacks on a concrete system. But on the other hand, large models can strain analysts' cognitive capabilities, and the practitioners may find it difficult to comprehend all described attack scenarios, especially after a certain time.

Acquisition of input data is a challenge by itself in risk assessment methodologies [67], and attack trees magnify it due to a large number of leaf nodes [7,45]. The standard approach for attack trees, when only leaf nodes are annotated with values can be too restrictive, as often data for intermediate nodes can be more readily available than data for leaves. This observation is further reinforced if we consider the costs of data collection in an organization (in terms of effort, time, etc.). Sometimes, more generic data than expected is available, e.g. from historical databases, multiple surveys and empirical results [15]. In this case, correlation and normalization of data to fit the attack tree methodology can become a challenge.

We notice that there exists a **conceptual mismatch** between research on attack trees and practical applications of attack trees. As we mentioned, in practice, attack trees are constructed by following the top-down approach. Yet, academic papers on attack trees define semantics and quantitative analysis techniques for these models via the leaf nodes, i.e., the lowest-level events (bottom-up approach). This makes it hard to implement a consistent feedback loop between design and analysis.

3   Research Trends in Attack Tree Applications

Given the challenges summarized in Sect. 2, several promising research directions have emerged recently to address the needs of practitioners.

Attack tree generation. Manual design is the state-of-practice for attack trees [56,59]. However, this exercise is time-consuming and error-prone. Automated tree generation techniques have emerged very recently, and there are few approaches reported in the literature yet [16,20,24,50,66]. These works provide means to generate attack trees from some system model, under assumption that it is easier for the team to design a good system model than a good attack tree. However, there is still some way to go before generated attack trees can be used in the security risk assessment practice. First of all, the techniques reported in [24,66] generate refinement-unaware trees, i.e., trees that do not support the user in understanding the various levels of abstraction. In tradition with the propositional semantics of attack trees [39], but in contrast with the expectations of a security analyst, [66] interprets each intermediate node only as a combination of children nodes. The techniques [16,24] offer trees with meaningful intermediate nodes, yet still lacking a proper refinement structure, when more abstract subgoals are refined into more precise attack steps.

The earliest approach capable of generating refinement-aware trees is ATSyRA [50,51]. It extracts the refinement structure from a hierarchy of actions in the model defined by the expert. More recently, Gadyatskaya et al. [20] showed that both the semantical domain and refinement structure of a tree can be obtained from a system model; without the need of expert intervention. Although the approach is promising, as it allows for fully automatic attack tree generation, it still cannot produce proper labels for the refinement structure.

Other attack tree generation approaches work with established security catalogues and knowledge bases, and attempt to construct attack trees from them. Knowledge bases and catalogues that systematize information on attacks, vulnerabilities and countermeasures are a trusted source of information for security risk practitioners, and many security risk management techniques include one or more catalogues [2,9,42]. Suggestions to apply established catalogues of threats to facilitate manual tree design have been voiced in [15,59]. Furthermore, for some knowledge bases, it is straightforward to transform certain attack scenarios described in those into attack trees. Then an analyst can manually produce more complex threat scenarios from these attack trees [21,64]. Techniques to automate attack tree generation using security catalogues and libraries have been reported in [46,52]. The TREsPASS project [53,65] has applied a security knowledge base to attack trees generated from a system model in order to refine leaf nodes of particular types, mainly for precise attacks on human agents and processes, such as social engineering or hacking.

Attack tree generation allows to reason on formal properties of obtained models. Indeed, for manually designed trees, it is understood that these models are as complete as the knowledge and experience of experts who designed them [57,59]. When attack trees are produced from an underlying system model or a knowledge base, it is possible to define the notion of **completeness** with respect to the model, and one can investigate whether an approach generates complete trees. For example, completeness with respect to a knowledge base is established as a desired property in [46], and completeness of a generated tree with respect to a system model is established in [20,24]. Completeness is especially critical for risk managers and security consultants, as they want to be reassured that no important attacks are missed.

Another interesting property of generated attack trees is **soundness** with respect to a system model, i.e., whether all attack scenarios captured by a tree are valid attacks in the model. Audinot and Pinchinat defined the soundness property for generated attack trees [6]. Soundness is critical for generating refinement-aware trees. Indeed, refinement establishes how abstract actions can be represented as combinations of more precise ones. Yet, not all combinations of precise actions can result in a valid attack in the system model.

Attack tree visualization. The TREsPASS project has proposed means for visualizing large attack trees [22,37,48]. This visualisation portfolio strives to hide away complexity of the tree by removing the node labels, arranging the tree circularly, linearizing complex attack scenarios, and supporting zooming-in and out (at the visualization level). These methods lead to reduction of the cognitive effort needed to process a complex tree, yet they contrast with the traditional manually designed attack trees, where meaningful node labels are essential, trees are arranged vertically to allow label readability, and non-linearism of attack scenarios gives an opportunity to reason about complex attacks [58,59].

Empirical studies with attack trees. To the best of our knowledge, Opdahl and Sindre [43] and Karpati et al. [27] have been the only ones reporting on empirical studies with attack trees. These studies compared attack trees with misuse cases in the context of threat assessment, and they have reported that attack trees allowed the participants to find more threats.

4   Next Steps and Conclusions

Comparing the challenges enumerated in Sect. 2 and research results summarized in Sect. 3, we can see that some challenges are addressed by an ongoing or past research effort. Indeed, *generation techniques* strive to reduce the *time and effort required to produce attack trees*, and to provide a framework for guaranteeing *absence of errors* in the obtained model. *Visualization approaches* are helping the analysts to better *comprehend* attack trees and to improve the *cognitive scalability* of the method. Yet, these results can still be strengthened and extended towards more user-friendly models.

In particular, the generation techniques can be improved by working on the refinement-awareness for the produced models. To achieve this, we propose to establish a new refinement-aware semantics for attack trees that will allow to assign meaning to intermediate nodes independently of their children nodes. The generated trees will need to be correct with respect to this semantics. Refinement relationship can be either defined by an expert as in [50], or it can be extracted from the system model itself [20] or from an appropriate knowledge base. Furthermore, the generated trees can be transformed into semantically-equivalent forms that have less nodes [29,39], what could potentially improve the comprehensibility of these smaller trees.

Comprehensibility and readability of graphs and the limits of human cognitive capabilities while reading and analyzing graphical data have been explored in, e.g., [13,54]. Information visualization challenges related to usability and scalability were highlighted in [12]. It will be interesting to see the findings of these works applied in the attack tree domain.

In the security risk assessment area, comprehensibility studies of visual and textual security risk models were reported in, e.g., [23,35,38]. A classification of scenarios for empirical studies in information visualization was proposed by Lam et al. [36], and visualization evaluation for cyber security was discussed by Staheli et al. [61]. To the best of our knowledge, there have been yet no empirical studies of attack tree comprehensibility, and this could be a promising research direction. Indeed, outside the attack trees topic, there is a rich empirical research literature on security modeling and assessment [10,33,34], software engineering [68], and requirements engineering [60]. This literature can be used by the attack trees community to build upon.

The challenges *acquisition of input data, absence of empirically grounded best practices, the trade-off between analysis and comprehensibility*, and the *conceptual mismatch between the top-down manual tree design process and the bottom-up formal semantics* have not yet been addressed in the attack trees community.

The data issues for quantitative analysis is a complex problem, because the quality and quantity of available data strongly depend on the application domain. In the quantitative risk analysis domain data-related challenges are known, and there exist methodologies for validating the data [67]. The attack tree community may thus strive to devise new methodologies for data validation and data-based tree validation.

We observe that the tension between detailed analysis, which requires large-scale trees, and comprehensibility, which tends to drop with the size of the tree, can be mitigated by means of model transformation techniques. Model transformation is fundamental in Computer Science and key in Model-driven software development [14], as it provides models at different levels of abstraction in a synchronized way. In that regard, attack tree generation can be seen as a model transformation approach; from a system model to an attack tree model. It would be interesting to see other types of transformations, e.g., from an attack tree to an attack tree, that could yield more condensed yet human-readable trees.

We argue that the misconceptions and multitude of interpretations of attack trees can be addressed by establishing a more rigorous methodology for practical application of attack trees that will include an initial phase when interpretations of the tree semantics and refinement operators are agreed upon. This methodology needs to be grounded in empirical studies with attack tree practitioners, in which they could report on what are the most frequent communication pitfalls they face, and how do they interpret different attack tree-related aspects, such as operators, semantics, etc.

Overall, we can conclude that the attack tree research community has made a substantial progress in developing the formal framework underpinning the model. We as researchers have a huge choice of attack tree semantics, quantitative analysis techniques, software tools, and means to apply attack trees in security assessment case studies. It is also exciting to see that the research community has started to focus on the practical needs of security analysts working with manually designed attack trees in organizational threat modeling and security risk management. We believe that this synergy between research and industry can further enhance the attack tree formalism and it will open new horizons in the attack tree research.

Acknowledgements. The research leading to these results has received funding from the European Union Seventh Framework Programme under grant agreement number 318003 (TREsPASS) and from the Fonds National de la Recherche Luxembourg under grant C13/IS/5809105 (ADT2P).

References

1. Amenaza: Creating secure systems through attack tree modeling (2003). http://www.amenaza.com/
2. ANSSI: EBIOS – Expression des Besoins et Identification des Objectifs de Securite (2010)
3. Arnold, F., Guck, D., Kumar, R., Stoelinga, M.: Sequential and parallel attack tree modelling. In: Proceedings of SAFECOMP and Workshops, pp. 291–299 (2015)
4. Aslanyan, Z., Nielson, F.: Pareto efficient solutions of attack-defence trees. In: Focardi, R., Myers, A. (eds.) POST 2015. LNCS, vol. 9036, pp. 95–114. Springer, Heidelberg (2015). https://doi.org/10.1007/978-3-662-46666-7_6
5. Aslanyan, Z., Nielson, F., Parker, D.: Quantitative verification and synthesis of attack-defence scenarios. In: Proceedings of CSF. IEEE (2016)
6. Audinot, M., Pinchinat, S.: On the soundness of attack trees. In: Kordy, B., Ekstedt, M., Kim, D.S. (eds.) GraMSec 2016. LNCS, vol. 9987, pp. 25–38. Springer, Cham (2016). https://doi.org/10.1007/978-3-319-46263-9_2
7. Bagnato, A., Kordy, B., Meland, P.H., Schweitzer, P.: Attribute decoration of attack-defense trees. Int. J. Secure Softw. Eng. (IJSSE) **3**(2), 1–35 (2012)
8. Buldas, A., Laud, P., Priisalu, J., Saarepera, M., Willemson, J.: Rational choice of security measures via multi-parameter attack trees. In: Lopez, J. (ed.) CRITIS 2006. LNCS, vol. 4347, pp. 235–248. Springer, Heidelberg (2006). https://doi.org/10.1007/11962977_19
9. Bundesamt fur Sicherheit in der Informationstechnik: IT-Grundschutz-Catalogues, 13th version (2013)
10. Buyens, K., De Win, B., Joosen, W.: Empirical and statistical analysis of risk analysis-driven techniques for threat management. In: Proceedings of ARES. IEEE (2007)
11. Buzan, T., Buzan, B.: The mind map book: how to use radiant thinking to maximize your brain's untapped potential. Plume, reprint edn., Mar 1996. http://www.amazon.com/exec/obidos/redirect?tag=citeulike07-20&path=ASIN/0452273226
12. Chen, C.: Top 10 unsolved information visualization problems. IEEE Comput. Graph. Appl. **25**(4), 12–16 (2005)
13. Cleveland, W.: The elements of graphing data. AT&T Bell Laboratories (1994)
14. Czarnecki, K., Helsen, S.: Feature-based survey of model transformation approaches. IBM Syst. J. **45**(3), 621–645 (2006)

15. Fraile, M., Ford, M., Gadyatskaya, O., Kumar, R., Stoelinga, M., Trujillo-Rasua, R.: Using attack-defense trees to analyze threats and countermeasures in an ATM: a case study. In: Horkoff, J., Jeusfeld, M.A., Persson, A. (eds.) PoEM 2016. LNBIP, vol. 267, pp. 326–334. Springer, Cham (2016). https://doi.org/10.1007/978-3-319-48393-1_24

16. Gadyatskaya, O.: How to generate security cameras: towards defence generation for socio-technical systems. In: Mauw, S., Kordy, B., Jajodia, S. (eds.) GraMSec 2015. LNCS, vol. 9390, pp. 50–65. Springer, Cham (2016). https://doi.org/10.1007/978-3-319-29968-6_4

17. Gadyatskaya, O., Hansen, R.R., Larsen, K.G., Legay, A., Olesen, M.C., Poulsen, D.B.: Modelling attack-defense trees using timed automata. In: Fränzle, M., Markey, N. (eds.) FORMATS 2016. LNCS, vol. 9884, pp. 35–50. Springer, Cham (2016). https://doi.org/10.1007/978-3-319-44878-7_3

18. Gadyatskaya, O., Harpes, C., Mauw, S., Muller, C., Muller, S.: Bridging two worlds: reconciling practical risk assessment methodologies with theory of attack trees. In: Kordy, B., Ekstedt, M., Kim, D.S. (eds.) GraMSec 2016. LNCS, vol. 9987, pp. 80–93. Springer, Cham (2016). https://doi.org/10.1007/978-3-319-46263-9_5

19. Gadyatskaya, O., Jhawar, R., Kordy, P., Lounis, K., Mauw, S., Trujillo-Rasua, R.: Attack trees for practical security assessment: ranking of attack scenarios with ADTool 2.0. In: Agha, G., Van Houdt, B. (eds.) QEST 2016. LNCS, vol. 9826, pp. 159–162. Springer, Cham (2016). https://doi.org/10.1007/978-3-319-43425-4_10

20. Gadyatskaya, O., Jhawar, R., Mauw, S., Trujillo-Rasua, R., Willemse, T.A.C.: Refinement-aware generation of attack trees. In: Livraga, G., Mitchell, C. (eds.) STM 2017. LNCS, vol. 10547, pp. 164–179. Springer, Cham (2017). https://doi.org/10.1007/978-3-319-68063-7_11

21. Ghani, H., Luna Garcia, J., Petkov, I., Suri, N.: User-centric security assessment of software configurations: a case study. In: Jürjens, J., Piessens, F., Bielova, N. (eds.) ESSoS 2014. LNCS, vol. 8364, pp. 196–212. Springer, Cham (2014). https://doi.org/10.1007/978-3-319-04897-0_13

22. Hall, P., Heath, C., Coles-Kemp, L., Tanner, A.: Examining the contribution of critical visualisation to information security. In: Proceedings of NSPW. ACM (2015)

23. Hogganvik Grøndahl, I., Lund, M.S., Stølen, K.: Reducing the effort to comprehend risk models: text labels are often preferred over graphical means. Risk Anal. 31(11), 1813–1831 (2011)

24. Ivanova, M.G., Probst, C.W., Hansen, R.R., Kammüller, F.: Transforming graphical system models to graphical attack models. In: Mauw, S., Kordy, B., Jajodia, S. (eds.) GraMSec 2015. LNCS, vol. 9390, pp. 82–96. Springer, Cham (2016). https://doi.org/10.1007/978-3-319-29968-6_6

25. Jhawar, R., Lounis, K., Mauw, S.: A stochastic framework for quantitative analysis of attack-defense trees. In: Barthe, G., Markatos, E., Samarati, P. (eds.) STM 2016. LNCS, vol. 9871, pp. 138–153. Springer, Cham (2016). https://doi.org/10.1007/978-3-319-46598-2_10

26. Jhawar, R., Kordy, B., Mauw, S., Radomirović, S., Trujillo-Rasua, R.: Attack trees with sequential conjunction. In: Federrath, H., Gollmann, D. (eds.) SEC 2015. IAICT, vol. 455, pp. 339–353. Springer, Cham (2015). https://doi.org/10.1007/978-3-319-18467-8_23

27. Karpati, P., Redda, Y., Opdahl, A., Sindre, G.: Comparing attack trees and misuse cases in an industrial setting. Inf. Softw. Technol. 56(3), 294–308 (2014)

28. Kordy, B., Mauw, S., Schweitzer, P.: Quantitative questions on attack–defense trees. In: Kwon, T., Lee, M.-K., Kwon, D. (eds.) ICISC 2012. LNCS, vol. 7839, pp. 49–64. Springer, Heidelberg (2013). https://doi.org/10.1007/978-3-642-37682-5_5

29. Kordy, B., Kordy, P., van den Boom, Y.: SPTool – equivalence checker for SAND attack trees. In: Cuppens, F., Cuppens, N., Lanet, J.-L., Legay, A. (eds.) CRiSIS 2016. LNCS, vol. 10158, pp. 105–113. Springer, Cham (2017). https://doi.org/10.1007/978-3-319-54876-0_8

30. Kordy, B., Kordy, P., Mauw, S., Schweitzer, P.: ADTool: security analysis with attack–defense trees. In: Joshi, K., Siegle, M., Stoelinga, M., D'Argenio, P.R. (eds.) QEST 2013. LNCS, vol. 8054, pp. 173–176. Springer, Heidelberg (2013). https://doi.org/10.1007/978-3-642-40196-1_15

31. Kordy, B., Mauw, S., Radomirović, S., Schweitzer, P.: Attack-defense trees. J. Log. Comput. 24(1), 55–87 (2014). http://people.rennes.inria.fr/Barbara.Kordy/papers/ADT12.pdf

32. Kumar, R., Ruijters, E., Stoelinga, M.: Quantitative attack tree analysis via priced timed automata. In: Sankaranarayanan, S., Vicario, E. (eds.) FORMATS 2015. LNCS, vol. 9268, pp. 156–171. Springer, Cham (2015). https://doi.org/10.1007/978-3-319-22975-1_11

33. Labunets, K., Massacci, F., Paci, F.: On the equivalence between graphical and tabular representations for security risk assessment. In: Grünbacher, P., Perini, A. (eds.) REFSQ 2017. LNCS, vol. 10153, pp. 191–208. Springer, Cham (2017). https://doi.org/10.1007/978-3-319-54045-0_15

34. Labunets, K., Massacci, F., Paci, F.: An experimental comparison of two risk-based security methods. In: Proceedings of ESEM. pp. 163–172. IEEE (2013)

35. Labunets, K., Massacci, F., Paci, F., Marczak, S., de Oliveira, F.: Model comprehension for security risk assessment: an empirical comparison of tabular vs. graphical representations. Empir. Softw. Eng. 22(6), 3017–3056 (2017)

36. Lam, H., Bertini, E., Isenberg, P., Plaisant, C., Carpendale, S.: Empirical studies in information visualization: seven scenarios. IEEE Trans. Vis. Comput. Graph. 18(9), 1520–1536 (2012)

37. Li, E., Barendse, J., Brodbeck, F., Tanner, A.: From A to Z: developing a visual vocabulary for information security threat visualisation. In: Kordy, B., Ekstedt, M., Kim, D.S. (eds.) GraMSec 2016. LNCS, vol. 9987, pp. 102–118. Springer, Cham (2016). https://doi.org/10.1007/978-3-319-46263-9_7

38. Matulevičius, R.: Model comprehension and stakeholder appropriateness of security risk-oriented modelling languages. In: Bider, I., Gaaloul, K., Krogstie, J., Nurcan, S., Proper, H.A., Schmidt, R., Soffer, P. (eds.) BPMDS/EMMSAD -2014. LNBIP, vol. 175, pp. 332–347. Springer, Heidelberg (2014). https://doi.org/10.1007/978-3-662-43745-2_23

39. Mauw, S., Oostdijk, M.: Foundations of attack trees. In: Won, D.H., Kim, S. (eds.) ICISC 2005. LNCS, vol. 3935, pp. 186–198. Springer, Heidelberg (2006). https://doi.org/10.1007/11734727_17

40. Microsoft: Threat modeling (2003). https://msdn.microsoft.com/en-us/library/ff648644.aspx

41. Nielsen, J.: Evaluating information assurance control effectiveness on an air force supervisory control and data acquisition (SCADA) system. Technical report, DTIC Document (2011)

42. NIST: Special Publication 800-53 Revision 4. Security and privacy controls for federal information systems and organizations (2013). http://nvlpubs.nist.gov/nistpubs/SpecialPublications/NIST.SP.800-53r4.pdf

43. Opdahl, A.L., Sindre, G.: Experimental comparison of attack trees and misuse cases for security threat identification. Inf. Softw. Technol. 51(5), 916–932 (2009)

44. OWASP: CISO AppSec guide: criteria for managing application security risks (2013)

45. Schweitzer, P.: Attack–defense trees. Ph.D. thesis, University of Luxembourg (2013)
46. Paul, S.: Towards automating the construction & maintenance of attack trees: a feasibility study. In: Proceedings of GraMSec (2014)
47. Paul, S., Vignon-Davillier, R.: Unifying traditional risk assessment approaches with attack trees. J. Inf. Secur. Appl. **19**(3), 165–181 (2014)
48. Pieters, W., Barendse, J., Ford, M., Heath, C., Probst, C.W., Verbij, R.: The navigation metaphor in security economics. IEEE Secur. Priv. **14**(3), 14–21 (2016)
49. Pieters, W., Davarynejad, M.: Calculating adversarial risk from attack trees: control strength and probabilistic attackers. In: Garcia-Alfaro, J., Herrera-Joancomartí, J., Lupu, E., Posegga, J., Aldini, A., Martinelli, F., Suri, N. (eds.) DPM/QASA/SETOP -2014. LNCS, vol. 8872, pp. 201–215. Springer, Cham (2015). https://doi.org/10.1007/978-3-319-17016-9_13
50. Pinchinat, S., Acher, M., Vojtisek, D.: Towards synthesis of attack trees for supporting computer-aided risk analysis. In: Canal, C., Idani, A. (eds.) SEFM 2014. LNCS, vol. 8938, pp. 363–375. Springer, Cham (2015). https://doi.org/10.1007/978-3-319-15201-1_24
51. Pinchinat, S., Acher, M., Vojtisek, D.: ATSyRa: an integrated environment for synthesizing attack trees. In: Mauw, S., Kordy, B., Jajodia, S. (eds.) GraMSec 2015. LNCS, vol. 9390, pp. 97–101. Springer, Cham (2016). https://doi.org/10.1007/978-3-319-29968-6_7
52. Fredslund, M.P.: Automated synthesis of attack-defense trees using a library of component attacks. Master thesis, University of Luxembourg (2015)
53. Probst, C.W., Willemson, J., Pieters, W.: The attack navigator. In: Mauw, S., Kordy, B., Jajodia, S. (eds.) GraMSec 2015. LNCS, vol. 9390, pp. 1–17. Springer, Cham (2016). https://doi.org/10.1007/978-3-319-29968-6_1
54. Purchase, H.C., Cohen, R.F., James, M.I.: An experimental study of the basis for graph drawing algorithms. J. Exp. Algorithmics (JEA) **2**, 4 (1997)
55. Roy, A., Kim, D.S., Trivedi, K.: Scalable optimal countermeasure selection using implicit enumeration on attack countermeasure trees. In: Proceedings of DSN. IEEE (2012)
56. Saini, V., Duan, Q., Paruchuri, V.: Threat modeling using attack trees. J. Comput. Sci. Coll. **23**(4), 124–131 (2008)
57. Schneier, B.: Attack trees. Dr. Dobb's J. Softw. Tools **24**(12), 21–29 (1999). http://www.ddj.com/security/184414879
58. Schneier, B.: Secrets and Lies: Digital Security in a Networked World. Wiley, New York (2011)
59. Shostack, A.: Threat Modeling: Designing for Security. Wiley, Hoboken (2014)
60. Sommerville, I., Ransom, J.: An empirical study of industrial requirements engineering process assessment and improvement. ACM Trans. Softw. Eng. Methodol. **14**(1), 85–117 (2005)
61. Staheli, D., Yu, T., Crouser, R.J., Damodaran, S., Nam, K., O'Gwynn, D., McKenna, S., Harrison, L.: Visualization evaluation for cyber security: trends and future directions. In: Proceedings of VizSec. ACM (2014)
62. Synopsis: How mapping the Ocean's Eleven heist can make you better at application security testing (2015). https://www.synopsys.com/blogs/software-security/oceans-eleven-make-you-better-at-application-security-testing/
63. Ten, C.W., Liu, C.C., Govindarasu, M.: Vulnerability assessment of cybersecurity for scada systems using attack trees. In: Power Engineering Society General Meeting. IEEE (2007)

64. Tøndel, I.A., Jensen, J., Røstad, L.: Combining misuse cases with attack trees and security activity models. In: Proceedings of ARES. pp. 438–445. IEEE (2010)
65. TREsPASS: Technology-supported Risk Estimation by Predictive Assessment of Socio-technical Security, FP7 project, grant agreement 318003 (2012–2016). http://www.trespass-project.eu/
66. Vigo, R., Nielson, F., Nielson., H.R.: Automated generation of attack trees. In: Proceedings of CSF. IEEE (2014)
67. Vose, D.: Risk Analysis: A Quantitative Guide. Wiley, New York (2008)
68. Wohlin, C., Runeson, P., Höst, M., Ohlsson, M., Regnell, B., Wesslén, A.: Experimentation in Software Engineering. Springer, Heidelberg (2012). https://doi.org/10.1007/978-3-642-29044-2

Employing Graphical Risk Models to Facilitate Cyber-Risk Monitoring - the WISER Approach

Aleš Černivec[1], Gencer Erdogan[2(✉)], Alejandra Gonzalez[3], Atle Refsdal[2],
and Antonio Alvarez Romero[4]

[1] XLAB Research, Ljubljana, Slovenia
ales.cernivec@xlab.si
[2] SINTEF Digital, Oslo, Norway
{gencer.erdogan,atle.refsdal}@sintef.no
[3] AON, Milan, Italy
alejandra-gonzalez@alice.it
[4] ATOS, Sevilla, Spain
antonio.alvarez@atos.net

Abstract. We present a method for developing machine-readable cyber-risk assessment algorithms based on graphical risk models, along with a framework that can automatically collect the input, execute the algorithms, and present the assessment results to a decision maker. This facilitates continuous monitoring of cyber-risk. The intended users of the method are professionals and practitioners interested in developing new algorithms for a specific organization, system or attack type, such as consultants or dedicated cyber-risk experts in larger organizations. For the assessment results, the intended users are decision makers in charge of countermeasure selection from an overall business perspective.

Keywords: Cyber risk · Security · Risk modelling · Risk assessment
Risk monitoring

1 Introduction

Cybersecurity is of critical importance for small businesses, large companies, public administrations and everyone involved in the digital economy. Millions of euros are lost to cyber-crime each year. Online security is a growing concern for businesses, with attacks increasing against large corporate business and critical infrastructures, but also against small enterprises that lack the time, money and human resources to dedicate to consolidating their cyber-risk management.

There are currently a number of tools available to support cyber-risk management. Most such tools focus on the technical aspects of detecting vulnerabilities and attacks, without relating these to the wider business context of the organization. This may provide useful support for IT administrators. However, managers and decision makers need to understand the impact of cyber-risks on their business objectives in order to determine how to deal with them from a

© Springer International Publishing AG 2018
P. Liu et al. (eds.): GraMSec 2017, LNCS 10744, pp. 127–146, 2018.
https://doi.org/10.1007/978-3-319-74860-3_10

more strategic perspective. This impact can be expressed either quantitatively or qualitatively. Quantitative estimates of the likelihood of incidents and the consequence in terms of money allow risks to be weighed against the cost of available countermeasures. Unfortunately, providing trustworthy numbers can be very difficult, as this requires access to good empirical data and statistics to serve as a foundation for quantified estimates. Such data is often unavailable. Even if we can obtain the data, analyzing it to understand its impact on the assessment is a major challenge [32]. This means that providing good quantitative assessments is not always feasible. In such cases, a qualitative approach can be a good alternative. By qualitative, we mean that we use ordinal scales, for which the standard arithmetic operators are not defined, to provide assessments. Each step is usually described by text, such as {Very low; Low; Medium; High; Very high}. More informative descriptions of each step can of course be given. Ordinal scales imply that values are ordered, thereby making it possible to monitor trends.

Cyber-risks depend on many different factors, many of which are highly technical. Moreover, the risks are continuously changing due to updates in the target ICT infrastructure or the way it supports the business, discovery of new vulnerabilities, and a rapidly evolving threat landscape. Therefore, rather than providing a snapshot representing one point in time, we want to facilitate monitoring by providing automated updates of risk level assessments based on dynamic input that captures vulnerabilities, events observed in the target ICT infrastructure, as well as the business configuration. To achieve this, we need executable algorithms that define how the risk level assessments change as a result of changes in the dynamic input, as well as an assessment infrastructure that can automatically collect the input, execute the algorithms, and present the results.

Developing risk level assessment algorithms requires a good understanding of the relevant threats, threat scenarios, vulnerabilities, incidents and assets. The CORAS risk modelling approach has proved to be well suited for establishing such an understanding and supporting risk level assessments [21,35]. However, the CORAS approach was created to perform manual assessments representing a single point in time, rather than establishing algorithms for automated assessments.

In this paper, we present a method for developing quantitative and qualitative cyber-risk assessment algorithms by exploiting the structure of CORAS risk models, together with a cyber-risk monitoring framework that automatically collects the dynamic input, executes the algorithms, and presents the results. The method and framework were developed in the WISER project [39].

In the following, we start by presenting the cyber-risk monitoring framework in Sect. 2. We then give an overview of the method for risk modelling, which includes the algorithm development, in Sect. 3. The method consists of two main steps. Sections 4 and 5 presents each step in more detail. In Sect. 6 we present related work, before discussing and concluding in Sect. 7.

2   Cyber-Risk Monitoring Framework

In this section, we present the framework developed in the WISER project to assess and monitor cyber-risk for companies from the business perspective. Figure 1 shows an overview of the essential components in the framework.

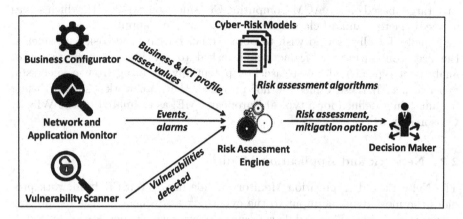

Fig. 1. Overview of the WISER framework.

The brain of the WISER framework is the Risk Assessment Engine. It produces an assessment of the risk the company faces, based on a cyber-risk model with an associated risk assessment algorithm. As illustrated by the left-hand side of Fig. 1, there are three different types of dynamic input to this algorithm. By "dynamic" we mean that the input values may change between each execution of the algorithm. The first input type is provided by the user configuring the framework for the company via a business configuration interface. The second input type is events and alarms obtained from monitoring the network and application layers of the ICT infrastructure, while the third input type is information about detected vulnerabilities provided by vulnerability scanners. We use the term *indicator* to denote the inputs to the algorithm. The output of the Risk Assessment Engine is an assessment of quantitative and/or qualitative risk levels. In addition, a proposal for mitigation options will also be triggered if risk levels exceeds a set threshold. However, mitigation options are beyond the scope of this paper. The reader is referred to [31] for further details on this.

In the remainder of this section, we explain how the input to the assessment algorithms, i.e. the indicator values, are obtained.

2.1   Business Configurator

As already noted, the first input type in Fig. 1 is provided by the user configuring the framework for a client/organization. This is done through a Business Configuration interface by answering general questions about the business, ICT profile and security management of the organization. Furthermore, the user is asked to provide information about the machines and applications to be protected, which we refer to as the targets of analysis.

For each target of analysis, the user assigns a level of importance with respect to confidentiality, integrity, and availability, which will depend on the way in which this target supports the business processes. The user also characterizes each target based on the ACM Computing Classification System [1], which serves as the de facto standard classification system for the computing field.

Finally, for clients who wish to obtain quantitative cyber-risk assessments, the user configuring the framework is asked to provide, for each target of analysis, a typical and worst-case loss potentially resulting from a successful cyber-attack. If these values are not provided, the framework resorts to using default values defined for a typical European SME, as estimated by the WISER Consortium [31].

2.2   Network and Application Monitor

The Network and Application Monitor module in the WISER framework provides the most dynamic input to the cyber-risk assessment, as the monitoring occurs in real time. The module consists of sensors which generate events (messages announcing unusual activity or values of observed metrics) and a Monitoring Engine, which generates alarms by correlating and combining several events. Various sensors, installed on the client's infrastructure, continuously observe numerous network and application-level parameters to provide input values for risk assessment indicators. Both events and alarms are fed into the Risk Assessment Engine. Alarms can also be used independently from the Risk Assessment Engine to notify the responsible users about ongoing attacks or emerging security threats.

The monitoring architecture incorporates two layers: the Resource Layer and the Provider Layer. The Resource Layer consists of WISER Agents and sensors installed on the client's infrastructure, providing data about the infrastructure to the Provider Layer. The Provider Layer supports the monitoring capabilities with back-end core services for event aggregation and correlation and a central data storage facility, serving monitoring data to the Risk Assessment Engine.

Monitoring sensors are able to detect several types of attacks and anomalies in the network infrastructure as well as in applications installed on the client's premises. The following sensors, which are further described in [36], are employed by WISER:

- DNS Traffic Sensor: monitors DNS requests to detect patterns of traffic that potentially belong to botnets.
- Snort: a network-based intrusion detection system, detecting network reconnaissance attempts, malware signatures and denial of service attacks.
- OSSEC: a host-based intrusion detection system, monitoring application-level activity and detecting anomalies in operation of core operating system services and user applications, recognizing viruses and attackers.

– Cowrie: an SSH-based honeypot used to attract attackers and detect their presence while averting attacks from other machines on the network.

The WISER Agents are responsible for the collection, normalization and transfer of data of the events to the provider layer. The Agents gather the data from sensors installed on the same network through encrypted syslog channels, adds common information about the organization, and forwards the messages in a common format to the provider layer communication bus, supported by the AMQP-based RabbitMQ server. RabbitMQ is responsible for message queuing and distribution to other components on the monitoring provider layer.

The Monitoring Engine, part of the Provider layer, is composed of a SIEM (Security Information and Event Management) solution and a correlation engine that provides continuous analysis of security-related events, aggregating data from the sensors and generating reports and alarms, taking a predefined set of correlation rules and security directives into consideration.

For each generated alarm, the Monitoring Engine computes a risk score, which combines measures of potential attack damage, likelihood of the attack and the value of assets compromised. If the risk score is high enough, the WISER Framework can automatically notify a responsible person. Notice that these risk scores should not be confused with the risk level assessments provided by the Risk Assessment Engine when executing the algorithms addressed in Sects. 3–5. The former provides low-level assessments according to fixed rules to facilitate a quick response by an ICT administrator. The latter provides more high-level assessments, where several events and alarms from the Monitoring Engine can be considered in conjunction with other types of indicators to provide more ICT and business context, and where the algorithms can be tailored to a specific organization or system.

2.3 Vulnerability Scanner

The Vulnerability Scanner module automatically identifies security vulnerabilities in the client's web applications. The Vulnerability Scanner acts similarly as a monitoring sensor, installed at the clients premises. It scans specified target websites periodically (in a configured time interval) and reports the results to the Risk Assessment Engine, like monitoring sensors. The vulnerabilities found by each scan can also be seen in the WISER Dashboard along with their mitigation suggestions. The vulnerability scanner in this mode of operation can scan public websites as well as web applications that are only accessible from inside the organization's network. This means that it can be used to test specialized web applications and also websites during their development process.

The Vulnerability Scanner is based on combining results from several tools for vulnerability scanning, such as W3af [38] and OWASP ZAP [29]. These tools automatically gather responses from the targeted website and compare them to their databases of known vulnerabilities to find which vulnerabilities might be present in the web application. The vulnerability databases contain explanations of the vulnerabilities and their mitigation proposals, which are included in the reports.

3   Method for Cyber-Risk Modelling

In this section, we explain the overall method for risk modelling. The risk modelling described here will typically be a part of a wider risk management process, such as ISO 31000 [17], and can be "plugged into" any such process. We focus on the methodological aspects that are special in our context, which are the following:

- For risk level assessment, the goal is not to perform an assessment representing a snapshot of one particular point or period in time, but rather to develop algorithms for automated assessment. The algorithms can be either qualitative or quantitative.
- Identification of threats, vulnerabilities, threat scenarios, incidents and risks is done using CORAS diagrams (models).
- For the elements of a risk model described above, we also identify the dynamic factors that can be provided by the framework, i.e. the indicators, as explained in Sect. 2. The indicators serve as input for the assessment algorithms.

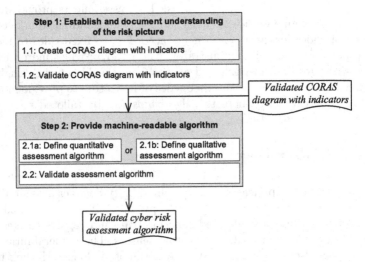

Fig. 2. Method for cyber-risk modelling.

Figure 2 shows the overall method used for cyber-risk modelling, considering these aspects. The outcome of the first step is a validated CORAS diagram with indicators. This diagram captures the relevant assets, risks, the ways in which these risks may materialize, and the relation between these elements and the available business configuration indicators, vulnerability scan indicators, network monitoring indicators and application monitoring indicators that can be employed to assess the risk and the involved threats, vulnerabilities and threat scenarios.

The outcome of the second step is a machine-readable algorithm for risk level assessment (and mitigation proposals) that can be automatically executed by the Risk Assessment Engine. The dynamic input for this assessment algorithm consists of the indicators identified in the first step. In the next two sections, we explain the steps in further detail.

4   Step 1: Establish and Document Understanding of the Risk Picture

4.1   Step 1.1: Create CORAS Diagram with Indicators

As illustrated by Fig. 2, this step is the same irrespective of whether the aim is to develop a qualitative or a quantitative assessment algorithm. The reason is that the purpose of this particular step is not to assess risk levels or define an assessment algorithm, but to identify the potential chains of events that may lead to risks materializing. This includes identifying all the threats, vulnerabilities, threat scenarios and incidents involved in such chains. Moreover, we identify the indicators that can provide information about all risk elements that can serve as useful input for the assessment algorithm to be developed in Step 2.

For creating security risk models, we use CORAS [21], which is a graphical risk modeling language that has been empirically shown to be intuitively simple for stakeholders with very different backgrounds [35]. Moreover, CORAS comes with a method that builds on established approaches (in particular ISO 31000 [17]), and includes detailed guidelines for creating CORAS models, which can be applied to carry out Step 1.

Figure 3 gives an overview of the CORAS notation. Threats, threat scenarios, unwanted incidents, assets, relations and vulnerabilities are collectively used to create CORAS risk models, which document risks as well as events and circumstances that can cause risks. Notice that the different relations are used to connect different nodes: the *initiates* relation goes from a threat to a threat scenario or an unwanted incident. The *leads-to* relation goes from a threat scenario or an unwanted incident to a threat scenario or an unwanted incident. The *impacts* relation goes from an unwanted incident to an asset. The indicator construct, which is not part of the standard CORAS notation, is introduced to capture dynamic factors that are obtained by the framework, as explained in Sect. 2.

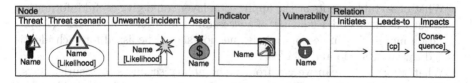

Fig. 3. CORAS notation. cp = conditional probability.

To support risk estimation, CORAS uses likelihood values, conditional probabilities, and consequence values (enclosed in brackets) on certain nodes and relations, as illustrated in Fig. 3. These will be represented by variables in the risk assessment algorithms. It is therefore useful to establish a naming convention for the variables, as well as for the nodes and indicators in the diagram. Table 1 shows our naming convention.

Table 1. Naming conventions for defining likelihood and consequence variables. The letters x and y represent integers.

Name	Meaning
Ax	Asset x
Sx	Scenario x ("S" means threat scenario)
Ux	Incident x ("U" means unwanted incident)
IN-x	Indicator x
l_Ux	Likelihood of Ux
l_Sx	Likelihood of Sx
c_Ux_Ay	Consequence of Ux for Ay
cp_Sx_to_Sy	Conditional probability of Sx leading to Sy
cp_Sx_to_Uy	Conditional probability of Sx leading to Uy

Figure 4 shows a CORAS risk model for a session hijacking in the context of web-applications. This risk model is (a slightly simplified version of) one of 10 risk models we developed in the WISER project [39]. These risk models were not developed for a particular target of analysis, but primarily intended for an arbitrary European SME. Notice that some of the indicators appear more than once, as they are attached to more than one element.

Indicators are normally identified after the assets, threats, threat scenarios, unwanted incidents and vulnerabilities. Indicator identification is not covered by the standard CORAS method [21]. We therefore present here the guiding questions used for this purpose:

- What observable events at the network layer could give useful information about the likelihood/frequency of attacks? (Network monitoring indicators.) This question should be asked for each identified threat scenario and incident.
- What observable events at the application layer could give useful information about the likelihood/frequency of successful or unsuccessful attacks? (Application monitoring indicators.) This question should be asked for each identified threat scenario and incident.
- What information can we get from vulnerability scanners or security tests? (Test result indicators). This question should be asked for each identified vulnerability.

– What do we otherwise know about the threats, vulnerabilities, threat scenarios, incidents or assets that could help us assess the level of cyber-risk? (Business configuration indicators.) These questions should be asked for each element of the risk model.

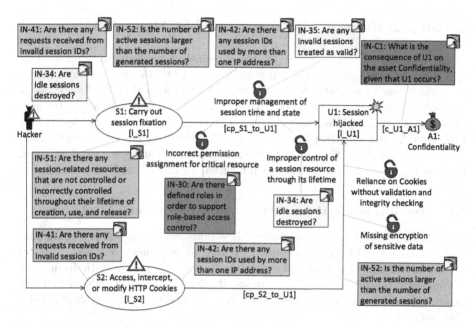

Fig. 4. CORAS risk model for *Session hijacking*. *IN-34* and *IN-35* are vulnerability scan indicators. *IN-30* and *IN-C1* are business configuration indicators. *IN-41*, *IN-42*, *IN-51*, and *IN-52* are application monitoring indicators.

4.2 Step 1.2: Validate CORAS Diagram with Indicators

The CORAS diagram provided in Step 1.1 serves as the basis for developing the machine-readable algorithm in Step 2. Therefore, before moving on, it is essential to ensure that the CORAS diagram reflects, as far as possible, the actual reality with respect to potential threats, vulnerabilities, threat scenarios and risks. Of course, as risk assessments concern what might happen in the future, there is no way we could ensure that a CORAS diagram (or any other form of risk model) is objectively correct and complete with respect to reality. Instead, what we aim for here is a convincing argument that the diagram reflects available knowledge and beliefs among qualified cybersecurity experts. Such an argument can be established, for example, by showing that the CORAS diagram faithfully captures information available from well-reputed standards, repositories, text books, research papers or similar sources; some examples include ISO 27001 [15], ISO 27005 [18], ISO 27032 [16], CAPEC [23] and OWASP [28]. If possible, the validation of the CORAS diagram should be carried out by a group of cybersecurity experts who, after relevant information sources have been identified and obtained, go through each part of the diagram in a systematic manner to identify elements that need to be added, removed, or otherwise improved. The validation terminates when no such elements are found.

5   Step 2: Provide Machine-Readable Algorithm

In the following, we explain how to define quantitative (Sect. 5.1) and qualitative (Sect. 5.2) assessment algorithms based on a CORAS model, before briefly discussing how to validate the results (Sect. 5.3). Notice that the two types of algorithms are independent alternatives, and readers who are only interested in one type can skip the other section. For both alternatives, our focus here is on establishing the algorithm structure. Therefore, we do not go into details regarding estimations that must be done in order to complete the algorithms, but provide references where further information can be found where relevant.

5.1   Step 2.1, alt. a: Define Quantitative Assessment Algorithm

For defining quantitative assessment algorithms we follow an actuarial approach, where the likelihood (frequency) and consequence (economic loss) of unwanted incidents are modelled separately through the probabilistic framework of *Bayesian Networks* (BN) [25]. More specifically, we use hybrid BNs [24], which means that the random variables are not bound to be discrete or (conditionally) Gaussian.

The algorithm is implemented using the **R** programming language [34] for statistical computing. The underlying calculations are performed by Markov-Chain-Monte-Carlo simulation. However, in this paper we focus on the exploitation of CORAS diagrams to establish the BN structure. Understanding this does not require prior knowledge about the **R** programming language, hence we do not show any **R** code. Detailed guidelines on how to create an **R** script from a CORAS model are provided in [31].

BN Skeleton. The first step is to define a BN skeleton based on the structure of the CORAS model. Figure 5 shows the BN skeleton reflecting the CORAS model in Fig. 4. A risk captured in a CORAS diagram (by an *impacts* relation from an unwanted incident to an asset) is represented by a childless node in the BN (*R1* in Fig. 5). The overall goal is to compute a risk level for risk nodes, as a function of indicators. Any risk node has two parent nodes: one representing the frequency of the unwanted incident and another representing the consequence for the asset. In our example, the risk node *R1* has the parent nodes *L_U1* and *c_U1_A1*, representing the frequency of the incident *U1* and its consequence for the asset *A1*, respectively.

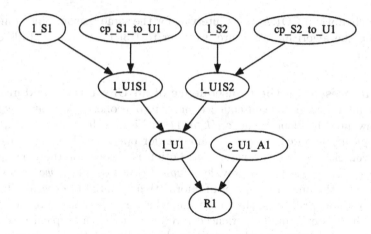

Fig. 5. BN skeleton for CORAS model in Fig. 4.

Nodes Representing the Frequency of an Unwanted Incident. The frequency of unwanted incidents is calculated following the underlying logic of the CORAS model. The frequency node of an unwanted incident has a parent node for each incoming *leads-to* relation to the incident in the CORAS diagram, representing the likelihood contribution from each incoming relation. For example, node l_U1 in Fig. 5 has two parent nodes: l_U1S1 and l_U1S2.

The likelihood contribution from each *leads-to* relation depends on the likelihood of its threat scenario (the source node) and the conditional probability that an occurrence of this threat scenario will lead to the unwanted incident. Therefore, the node l_U1S1 depends on the parentless nodes l_S1 (likelihood of scenario $S1$) and $cp\_S1\_to\_U1$ (the conditional probability that an occurrence of $S1$ will lead to $U1$). Similarly, l_U1S2 depends on l_S2 and $cp\_S2\_to\_U1$. In our example, the probability distribution of the frequency node l_U1 is defined as follows[1]:

$$l\_U1 = l\_U1S1 + l\_U1S2$$
$$= l\_S1 \cdot cp\_S1\_to\_U1 + l\_S2 \cdot cp\_S2\_to\_U1$$

Notice that node l_U1 is deterministic, since its value at each step of the simulation is calculated by a formula from the values of its parent nodes.

The indicators, which represent the input to the final algorithm, are not included in the BN structure. They will be used to compute the values for the parentless ancestor nodes of l_U1 (l_S1, l_S2, $cp\_S1\_to\_U1$ and $cp\_S2\_to\_U1$ in Fig. 5). These nodes are represented by uniform distributions whose extremes depend on the indicators affecting the nodes. The functions from indicator values to the extremes of the distributions are defined based on expert estimates and available empirical data. We chose uniform distributions in order to ease the

---

[1] This formula assumes that the scenarios for the incoming *leads-to* relation are separate, as further explained in [21, p. 224].

estimate elicitation. CORAS uses intervals for the same reason. Since our focus here is on the algorithm structure, we refer to [13] for further details on the estimation.

Nodes Representing the Consequence of an Unwanted Incident. Consequence nodes model the consequence, in terms of economic loss per occurrence of an unwanted incident (node *c_U1_to_A1* in Fig. 5). Here we follow an approach typically adopted in scenario analysis for operational risk management. For a given risk, a two-parameter distribution is chosen for the consequence, and experts are requested to provide a *typical case* loss and a *worst case* loss. This provides the minimal amount of information required to describe the main features of the distribution, that is a value which is experienced frequently and a value which is extreme (experienced rarely). Usually, the typical case loss is identified with a location index, such as the median of the distribution. The worst case loss is identified with a suitably large quantile of the distribution. This gives a nonlinear system of two equations in two variables (the parameters of the distribution), which can be solved by a Newton-like numerical approximation method [2,10,26]. We adopted the lognormal distribution for modeling consequence nodes. In modelling loss data, the lognormal distribution is observed to provide good fits in many cases; for this reason it is often used for modelling consequence in operational risk and particularly for the scenario analysis component, see e.g. [11,19].

Nodes Representing Risk Level. Risk level nodes model the yearly aggregate loss distribution, which depend on the frequency and consequence of the unwanted incident. In our example, the risk level is represented by node *R1* in the BN. The probability distribution assigned to *R1* is defined as follows:

$$R1 = l\_U1 \cdot c\_U1\_to\_A1$$

5.2 Step 2.1, alt. b: Define Qualitative Assessment Algorithm

For defining qualitative assessment algorithms we use DEXi [12], which is a computer program for development of multi-criteria decision models and the evaluation of options. We briefly present DEXi before explaining how to create a DEXi model from a CORAS diagram. For a detailed description, we refer to the DEXi User Manual [6].

A multi-attribute model decomposes a decision problem into a tree (or graph) structure where each node in the tree represents an attribute. The overall problem is represented by the top attribute, also called the root. All other attributes represent sub-problems, which are smaller and less complex than the overall problem. Each attribute is assigned a value. The set of values that an attribute can take is called the *scale* of the attribute. DEXi supports definition of ordinal scales; typically, each step consists of a textual description.

Every attribute is either a basic attribute or an aggregate attribute. *Basic attributes* have no child attributes. This means that a basic attribute represents an input to the DEXi model, as its value is assigned directly, rather than being computed from child attributes.

Aggregate attributes are characterized by having child attributes. The value of an aggregate attribute is a function of the values of its child attributes. This function is called the *utility function* of the attribute. The utility function of each aggregate attribute is defined by stating, for each possible combination of its child attribute values, what is the corresponding value of the aggregate attribute. The DEXi tool automatically computes the value of all aggregate attributes as soon as values have been assigned to the basic attributes. Hence, a DEXi model can be viewed as an algorithm where the basic attribute values constitute the input and the values of the aggregate attributes constitute the output. A java library and a command-line utility program for DEXi model execution is available [12], meaning that functionality for executing DEXi algorithms can be easily integrated in software systems. This, combined with the fact that DEXi has been designed to produce models that are comprehensible to end users [9], was our reason for choosing DEXi. Its comprehensibility seems to be confirmed by its application in several different domains, involving a wide range of stakeholders [7–9].

Figure 6 shows an example of a DEXi model which consists of three aggregate attributes and three basic attributes; the latter are shown as triangles. The top attribute, which is an aggregate attribute, is named *Risk* and has two child attributes (*Likelihood* and *Consequence*) that are also aggregate attributes. The *Likelihood* attribute has in turn two basic attributes as child attributes (*Likelihood indicator 1* and *Likelihood indicator 2*), while the *Consequence* attribute has one basic attribute as child attribute (*Consequence indicator 1*).

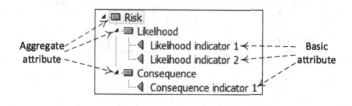

Fig. 6. DEXi model.

We now show how to build a security risk assessment algorithm, in the form of a DEXi model, based on a CORAS model. We use the model in Fig. 4 as an example. This means that the decision problem represented by the top attribute in the DEXi model concerns deciding the risk level. We start by explaining how each fragment of the CORAS model can be schematically translated to a corresponding fragment of the DEXi model. Since our focus here is on the algorithm structure, we do not address the definition of scales and utility functions, but refer to [14] for further discussion on this.

Risk. In the CORAS model, a risk corresponds to an *impacts* relation from an unwanted incident to an asset. The risk level depends on the likelihood of the incident and its consequence for the asset, as represented by l_U1 and c_U1_A1 in Fig. 4. In the DEXi model, a risk is therefore represented as a top (i.e. orphan) attribute that has two child attributes, one representing the likelihood of the incident and one representing its consequence for the asset. Figure 7(a) shows the DEXi-representation of the (only) risk shown in Fig. 4. The value of the top attribute *R1* represents the risk level. Notice that *R1* does not occur as a separate name in the CORAS diagram, as a risk is represented by the combination of the incident, the asset, and the relation between them, rather than by a separate node.

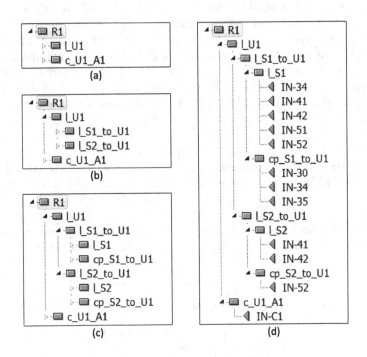

Fig. 7. Screenshots from the DEXi tool.

Node with Incoming leads-to Relations. In a CORAS model, the likelihood of a node with incoming *leads-to* relations[2] depends on the likelihood contributions from each relation. In the DEXi model, such a node is therefore represented by an attribute with one child attribute for every incoming *leads-to* relation. The attribute *l_U1* in Fig. 7(b), which represents the likelihood of *U1*, therefore has two child attributes, *l_S1_to_U1* and *l_S2_to_U1*, representing the likelihood contributions from *S1* and *S2* via their outgoing *leads-to* relations.

---

[2] Recall from Sect. 4 that threat scenarios and unwanted incidents are the only node types that may have incoming *leads-to* relations.

Node with Outgoing leads-to Relation. The contribution from a *leads-to* relation to its target node depends on the likelihood of the source node and the conditional probability that an occurrence of the source node will lead to an occurrence of the target node. The latter is assigned to the *leads-to* relation in a CORAS model. In the DEXi model, a source node with an outgoing *leads-to* relation is therefore represented by an attribute with two child attributes, one representing the likelihood of the source node and one representing the conditional probability that an occurrence of the source node will lead to the target node. As illustrated in Fig. 7(c), the attribute *LS1_to_U1* representing the likelihood contribution from *S1* to *U1* therefore has two child attributes, *LS1* representing the likelihood of *S1* and *cp_S1_to_U1* representing the conditional probability of *S1* leading to *U1* (and similarly for *LS2_to_U1*).

Node with Attached Indicators. In a CORAS model, indicators can be attached to a node to show that the indicators are used as input for assessing the likelihood of the node. In the DEXi model, indicators attached to a node are therefore represented as basic attributes under the attribute representing the node. Figure 7(d) shows the complete DEXi tree structure derived from the CORAS risk model in Fig. 4. The basic attributes in Fig. 7(d) correspond to the indicators in Fig. 4. Here we see that *LS1* has a child attribute for each of the indicators *IN-34*, *IN-41*, *IN-42*, *IN-51* and *IN-52* attached to *S1* in Fig. 4, while *LS2* has child attributes representing the indicators *IN-41* and *IN-42*, which are attached to *S2* in Fig. 4.

Notice that we may have cases where a node has incoming *leads-to* relations in addition to attached indicators, although this is not the case in the example. In such cases, the attribute representing the node can have child attributes representing the incoming branches in addition to the child attributes representing indicators.

***Leads-to* Relation with Attached Indicators.** In a CORAS model, indicators can be attached to a *leads-to* relation from one node to another, or on a vulnerability attached to such a relation, to show that the indicators are used as input for assessing the conditional probability of an occurrence of the source node leading to the target node. In the DEXi model, indicators attached to a *leads-to* relation (or vulnerability) are therefore represented by basic attributes under the attribute representing the conditional probability assigned to the relation. Therefore, in Fig. 7(d) we see that *cp_S1_to_U1* has a child attribute for each of the indicators *IN-30*, *IN-34* and *IN-35*, while *cp_S2_to_U1* has one child attribute representing *IN-52*.

Other CORAS Model Fragments. We have not provided separate guidelines for threats, *initiates* relations, and indicators attached to *impacts* relations. For the latter, the reason is that a CORAS model does not provide any support for consequence assessment beyond the assignment of a consequence value to the *impacts* relation from an unwanted incident to an asset. All indicators relevant for consequence assessments are therefore represented as basic attributes directly under the attribute representing the consequence, as illustrated by *c_U1_A1* in

Fig. 7(d). In our example, the single indicator *IN-C1* attached to the *impacts* relation from *U1* actually provides the consequence value directly, which means that the *IN-C1* attribute could have been attached directly under *R1*, without the intermediate *c_U1_A1* attribute. We chose to include *c_U1_A1* to illustrate the general structure.

Concerning threats and *initiates* relations, we rarely assign likelihoods to these CORAS elements in practice, as estimating threat behavior is very difficult. Instead, we assign a likelihood directly to the target node of the *initiates* relation. An indicator assigned to a threat or to an *initiates* relation can therefore be handled as if it was assigned directly to the target node.

5.3   Step 2.2: Validate Assessment Algorithm

Before putting the algorithm in operation, it should be validated to verify that its output can reasonably be expected to reflect reality. When dealing with the kind of cyber-risk assessment addressed in this paper, we typically need to rely on expert judgment for this. We first select a set of validation scenarios and then validate the output from the algorithm for each scenario with a team of experts. As the CORAS model does not provide any support for consequence assessment beyond annotation on *impacts* relations, we focus here primarily on the likelihood assessment.

A validation scenario is a set of indicator values representing one possible snapshot of the dynamic factors that influence the likelihood assessment (and hence also the risk level). Thus, the number of possible scenarios is the product of the number of possible values for each such indicator. This often results in many possible scenarios, which may be infeasible to validate. Our example in Fig. 4 includes 7 different Boolean indicators affecting the likelihood assessment (as well as one affecting the consequence). This gives 128 possible scenarios.

We therefore need to select a reasonable number of scenarios depending on the available effort. As a minimum, we suggest selecting validation scenarios based on the following two criteria: (1) cover the extreme scenarios where none or all of the indicators are triggered (yielding the minimum and maximum frequency values), and (2) cover each path in the CORAS risk model, meaning that for each path p (from the threat to the unwanted incident) in the risk model, there must be a scenario where one or more indicators along the path is triggered and the indicators for all other paths are not triggered unless these indicators also affect path p. By triggered, we mean that the indicator value contributes to the increase of likelihood. For example, for *IN-34* (Are idle sessions destroyed?), the value False (=No) would imply a higher likelihood than True (=Yes), since idle sessions can be exploited by an attacker.

For validating the output of the algorithm with the experts, we recommend using a well-established approach, such as the Wide-band Delphi method [4]. This is a forecasting technique used to collect expert opinion in an objective way, and arrive at consensus conclusion based on that. Another similar estimation approach is the Constructive Cost Model (COCOMO) [5].

6 Related Work

Most security risk approaches aim to provide either quantitative or qualitative assessments capturing the risk level at a single point in time, rather than continuous monitoring. However, there are also approaches that address dynamic aspects and offer support for updating assessments based on new information.

Poolsappasit et al. [30] propose an approach for dynamic security risk management using Bayesian Attack Graphs (BAGs). This approach is dynamic in the sense that it allows system administrators to tweak the probability of events captured by a BAG in order to see how this propagates in the complete risk picture. While their approach facilitates manual update of probability of events, our method facilitates both manual and automatic update of the likelihood of events indirectly through the different types of indicators. The manual update in our method is based on input provided by representatives of the target under analysis (business configuration indicators), while the automatic update is based on input collected from vulnerability scanning, application-layer monitoring, and network-layer monitoring.

The first use of measurable indicators as dynamic input to provide risk level assessments based on CORAS was presented in [33]. This is a quantitative approach where indicators are represented by variables in arithmetic formulas for computing risk levels, without using distributions or BNs. As argued by Neil et al. [25] BNs provide a flexible and attractive solution to the problem of modeling (operational) risk. In particular, BNs enable an analyst to combine quantitative information (e.g. available historical data) with qualitative information (e.g. subjective judgments) regarding the loss-generating processes. In the context of cyber-risk, BNs have been used for a variety of purposes, such as to model attack graphs or loss event frequencies [20,30].

The consequence assessment for the quantitative version of our approach is based on the Loss Distribution Approach (LDA), which is typically used to model operational risk and its insurability [22], provided that a sufficient amount of data is available. In the LDA, the temporal occurrence of the losses is frequently modeled by a Poisson process, while various families of distributions (Gamma, Generalized Pareto, Lognormal, etc.) might be used to model the severity of the losses. Biener et al. [3] study whether models which prove to be useful for operational risk can also be applied to an analysis of cyber-risk. They conclude that the LDA approach is suitable to model cyber-risk and that it provides useful insights regarding, e.g., the distinct characteristics of cyber-risk with respect to operational risk in general.

For the qualitative version of our method, we chose DEXi due to its simplicity and ease of integration in the WISER framework. DEXi is one of many approaches within the field of multi-criteria decision making (on which there is a huge literature [37]), and has been tried out in a wide range of domains, such as health care, finance, construction, cropping systems, waste treatment systems, medicine, tourism, banking, manufacturing of electric motors, and energy [9,12]. To the best of our knowledge, DEXi has not been used for security risk assessment. However, it has been applied to assess safety risks within highway traffic [27] and ski resorts [8].

Although they focus on safety risks, the approaches provided by Omerčević et al. [27] and Bohanec et al. [8] are similar to our approach in the sense that they use DEXi models as the underlying algorithm to compute an advice based on relevant indicators. Unlike our approach, they do not employ any dedicated risk modeling language to provide a basis for developing the DEXi models.

7   Discussion and Conclusion

The framework presented in Sect. 2 has been successfully demonstrated in three different pilot organizations, using quantitative and qualitative algorithms based on 10 different CORAS models, all developed following the method outlined in Sect. 3. Due to the structure of a CORAS model and the simple relationship to the algorithm structure, we believe that most cyber-risk practitioners who are familiar with CORAS and the chosen algorithm language (**R** or DEXi) will have little problems establishing the algorithm structure from a CORAS model.

Having established the structure of an algorithm, the remaining challenge is to fill in the details, in particular deciding the impact of the indicators. This amounts to defining the functions from indicators to the parentless nodes in the BN skeleton (in the quantitative approach) or defining the scales and utility functions for the attributes (in the qualitative approach). We provide further guidelines for this in [13,14], respectively.

An inherent limitation of the approach is that new and unforeseen threats, vulnerabilities and attack types can only be addressed by updating the relevant risk models and algorithms (or creating new ones) manually. The only dynamic changes automatically covered by the monitoring are those captured by changing indicator values. Periodic evaluations are therefore needed to decide whether new or updated models and algorithms are required. Of course, this limitation applies to all methods that rely on human experts for risk identification.

Although our own experiences from applying the method and framework are promising, further empirical studies are needed to evaluate them in a wider context. In particular, we hope to investigate to what degree cyber-risk practitioners outside the WISER consortium are able to establish algorithms that are sufficiently correct to provide useful decision support for those in charge of dealing with cyber-risk for an organization.

Acknowledgments. This work has been conducted as part of the WISER project (653321) funded by the European Commission within the Horizon 2020 research and innovation programme.

References

1. The ACM Computing Classification System (CCS). https://dl.acm.org/ccs/ccs. cfm. Accessed 3 Nov 2017
2. Atkinson, K.A.: An Introduction to Numerical Analysis. Wiley, New York (1989)
3. Biener, C., Eling, M., Wirfs, J.H.: Insurability of cyber risk an empirical analysis. Geneva Pap. Risk Insurance Issues Pract. **40**(1), 131–158 (2015)

4. Boehm, B.W.: Software Engineering Economics. Prentice Hall, Upper Saddle River (1981)
5. Boehm, B.W., Abts, C., Brown, A.W., Chulani, S., Clark, B.K., Horowitz, E., Madachy, R., Reifer, D.J., Steece, B.: Software Cost Estimation with COCOMO II. Prentice Hall, Upper Saddle River (2000)
6. Bohanec, M.: DEXi: program for multi-attribute decision making. User's Manual v 5.00 IJS DP-11897, DEXi (2015)
7. Bohanec, M., Aprile, G., Costante, M., Foti, M., Trdin, N.: A hierarchical multi-attribute model for bank reputational risk assessment. In: DSS 2.0 - Supporting Decision Making with New Technologies, pp. 92–103. IOS Press (2014)
8. Bohanec, M., Delibašić, B.: Data-mining and expert models for predicting injury risk in ski resorts. In: Delibašić, B., et al. (eds.) ICDSST 2015. LNBIP, vol. 216, pp. 46–60. Springer, Cham (2015). https://doi.org/10.1007/978-3-319-18533-0_5
9. Bohanec, M., Žnidaršič, M., Rajkovič, V., Bratko, I., Zupan, B.: DEX methodology: three decades of qualitative multi-attribute modeling. Informatica (Slovenia) 37(1), 49–54 (2013)
10. Bus, J.C.P.: Convergence of Newton-like methods for solving systems of nonlinear equations. Numerische Mathematik 27(3), 271–281 (1976)
11. Chernobai, A.S., Rachev, S.T., Fabozzi, F.J.: Operational Risk: A Guide to Basel II Capital Requirements, Models, and Analysis. Wiley, Hoboken (2007)
12. DEXi: A program for multi-attribute decision making. http://kt.ijs.si/MarkoBohanec/dexi.html. Accessed 19 Oct 2017
13. Erdogan, G., Gonzalez, A., Refsdal, A., Seehusen, F.: A method for developing algorithms for assessing cyber-risk cost. In: Proceedings of the 2017 IEEE International Conference on Software Quality, Reliability, & Security (QRS 2017), pp. 192–199. IEEE (2017)
14. Erdogan, G., Refsdal, A.: A method for developing qualitative security risk assessment algorithms. In: Proceedings of 12th International Conference on Risks and Security of Internet and Systems (CRiSIS 2017). Springer (2017, to appear)
15. International Organization for Standardization: ISO/IEC 27001 - Information technology - Security techniques - Information security management systems - Requirements (2005)
16. International Organization for Standardization: ISO/IEC 27032 - Information technology - Security techniques - Guidelines for cybersecurity (2005)
17. International Organization for Standardization: ISO 31000:2009(E), Risk management - Principles and guidelines (2009)
18. International Organization for Standardization: ISO/IEC 27005:2011(E), Information technology - Security techniques - Information security risk management (2011)
19. Klugman, S.A., Panjer, H.H., Willmot, G.E.: Loss Models: From Data to Decisions. Wiley, New York (2012)
20. Le, A., Chen, Y., Chai, K.K., Vasenev, A., Montoya, L.: Assessing loss event frequencies of smart grid cyber threats: encoding flexibility into FAIR using Bayesian network approach. In: Hu, J., Leung, V.C.M., Yang, K., Zhang, Y., Gao, J., Yang, S. (eds.) Smart Grid Inspired Future Technologies. LNICST, vol. 175, pp. 43–51. Springer, Cham (2017). https://doi.org/10.1007/978-3-319-47729-9_5
21. Lund, M.S., Solhaug, B., Stølen, K.: Model-Driven Risk Analysis: The CORAS Approach. Springer, Heidelberg (2011). https://doi.org/10.1007/978-3-642-12323-8
22. McNeil, A.J., Frey, R., Embrechts, P.: Quantitative Risk Management: Concepts, Techniques and Tools. Princeton University Press, Princeton (2015)

23. Common Attack Pattern Enumeration and Classification (CAPEC). https://capec.mitre.org/. Accessed 18 Oct 2017
24. Mittnik, S., Starobinskaya, I.: Modeling dependencies in operational risk with hybrid Bayesian networks. Methodol. Comput. Appl. Probab. **12**(3), 379–390 (2010)
25. Neil, M., Fenton, N., Tailor, M.: Using Bayesian networks to model expected and unexpected operational losses. Risk Anal. **25**(4), 963–972 (2005)
26. Solve Systems of Nonlinear Equations. https://cran.r-project.org/web/packages/nleqslv/nleqslv.pdf. Accessed 19 Oct 2017
27. Omerčević, D., Zupančič, M., Bohanec, M., Kastelic, T.: Intelligent response to highway traffic situations and road incidents. In: Proceedings of the Transport Research Arena Europe 2008 (TRA 2008), pp. 21–24 (2008)
28. The Open Web Application Security Project. www.owasp.org. Accessed 18 Oct 2017
29. OWASP Zed Attack Proxy Project. https://www.owasp.org/index.php/OWASP_Zed_Attack_Proxy_Project. Accessed 2 Nov 2017
30. Poolsappasit, N., Dewri, R., Ray, I.: Dynamic security risk management using Bayesian attack graphs. IEEE Trans. Dependable Secure Comput. **9**(1), 61–74 (2012)
31. Refsdal, A., Erdogan, G., Aprile, G., Poidomani, S., Colgiago, R., Gonzalez, A., Alvarez, A., González, S., Arce, C.H., Lombardi, P., Mannella, R.: D3.4 - cyber risk modelling language and guidelines, final version. Technical report D3.4, WISER (2017)
32. Refsdal, A., Solhaug, B., Stølen, K.: Cyber-Risk Management. Springer, Cham (2015). https://doi.org/10.1007/978-3-319-23570-7
33. Refsdal, A., Stølen, K.: Employing key indicators to provide a dynamic risk picture with a notion of confidence. In: Ferrari, E., Li, N., Bertino, E., Karabulut, Y. (eds.) IFIPTM 2009. IAICT, vol. 300, pp. 215–233. Springer, Heidelberg (2009). https://doi.org/10.1007/978-3-642-02056-8_14
34. The R Project for Statistical Computing. https://www.r-project.org. Accessed 19 Oct 2017
35. Solhaug, B., Stølen, K.: The CORAS language - why it is designed the way it is. In: Proceedings of the 11th International Conference on Structural Safety & Reliability (ICOSSAR 2013), pp. 3155–3162. Taylor and Francis (2013)
36. Černivec, A., Alvarez, A., González, S., Arce, C.H., Žitnik, A., Plestenjak, R., Biasibetti, A.L.: D4.2 - WISER Monitoring Infrastructure. Technical report D4.2, WISER (2016)
37. Velasquez, M., Hester, P.T.: An analysis of multi-criteria decision making methods. Int. J. Oper. Res. **10**(2), 56–66 (2013)
38. Web Application Attack and Audit Framework. http://w3af.org/. Accessed 2 Nov 2017
39. Wide-Impact cyber SEcurity Risk framework (WISER). https://www.cyberwiser.eu/. Accessed 16 Oct 2017

Author Index

Printed in the United States
By Bookmasters